# INDEX

ON CENSORSHIP

Cuba 1994

Cover photo: Erma/Camera Press

INDEX ON CENSORSHIP 6 1994

*Index on Censorship* (ISSN 0306-4220) is published bimonthly by a non-profit-making company: Writers & Scholars International Ltd, Lancaster House, 33 Islington High Street, London N1 9LH
Tel: 071-278 2313  Fax: 071-278 1878
E-mail: indexoncenso@gn.apc.org
Internet Gopher site: mary.iia.org 70

*Index on Censorship* is associated with Writers & Scholars Educational Trust, registered charity number 325003

Second class postage (US subscribers only) paid at Irvington, New Jersey. Postmaster: send US address changes to Index on Censorship c/o Virgin Mailing & Distribution, 10 Camptown Road, Irvington, NJ 07111

Subscriptions 1994 (6 issues p.a.): £30 (overseas £36 or US$48). Students £23/US$35

# EDITORIAL

## New worlds for old

Memories are short, and getting shorter, in the world of the commu-nications revolution. Not only are people already forgetting what ended the Communist imperium, but even the complex reality of that period itself. With the crumbling of an empire have come extraordinary shifts in the balance of world power. One consequence has been a huge increase in nationalist conflicts, many of them little understood by the outside world. Now a burning issue — not only in the former Soviet Union — is the question of how nations, each with their own language, culture and, above all, set of national loyalties and priorities, manage to relate to each other.

But there is another sign that the era of superpower confrontations is over — the response to some of the internecine wars being waged around the world. Once such internal conflicts would have been an excuse for the superpowers to extend their sphere of influence. No longer. Intervention, formerly such a bogey word, has arrived on the civil and human rights agenda. 'Human rights give rise to a new legal permeability,' said Boutros Boutros Ghali, secretary general of the UN. 'The international community must take over from the states that fail to fulfil their obligations.'

Questions which were in effect muzzled by the Cold War polarities are now a matter of urgency. How are the rights of nation states recon-ciled with the individual human rights of their people? At what stage and against what scale of abuse of human rights is intervention justified? How does the agenda of the intervenors compare with the needs and desires of the people on whose behalf they say they are intervening? Should we be questioning more carefully, as Alex de Waal does in his important and provocative essay, the entirely new phenomenon, unthinkable five years ago, of humanitarian organisations calling for military intervention — in Somalia, Bosnia, Rwanda?

This issue of *Index* addresses these and other questions. It reveals a world in many ways no less disturbing than the one whose ending was celebrated with such hope and wild rejoicing five years ago. ❏

*Ursula Owen*

# CONTENTS

## VOLUME 23

(NEW SERIES) NUMBER 6 NOVEMBER/DECEMBER 1994 (161)

# LETTERS

## In need of truth and principles

**From Peter Wilkin**
*Lecturer in Politics and International Relations, Lancaster University, UK*

The interview with Umberto Eco in *Index* May/June 1994 was provocative and important in its urgent consideration of the resurgent xenophobia and fascism throughout Europe and beyond, but it was most significant in the way that it revealed the limitations of post-modernist accounts of democracy and freedom as guiding aims — clearly not principles — for political practice. Eco made a number of comments that seemed to be irreconcilable without recourse to the kind of modernist language he seeks consciously to distance himself from: namely, the ideas of truth and principle in political judgement.

In seeking to set the boundaries of 'tolerance and the intolerable' we appear to move from the realm of liberal pluralism, which is central to post-modernism, to the realm of universal liberal principles, which is antithetical to it. Eco, however, resists this and claims that we need not be concerned with the truth as 'there are only opinions, some of which are preferable to others.' At the same time, though, not all preferences are equally valid. As Eco says: 'If we think all ideas have the same value, that one must never, under any circumstances, reject anything, we end up seriously confused.'

Agreed: so where does this leave us? Clearly, we still have to choose between these competing values, but on what basis can we make this choice? Since Eco does not want to fall back into bad old Enlightenment habits of raising questions of truth or principle, we might consider his 'respect for the body and its functions' as a universal basis for distinguishing the tolerable from the intolerable. It is unclear, though, how Eco could evade the gravity of political principles and truth by pursuing this line: outlining what is tolerable and intolerable on this basis must equally involve fundamental issues of political philosophy concerning justice, equality, liberty and the good life. And we cannot resolve these issues by retreating into a realm of preference because, at best, such a manoeuvre merely avoids these matters rather than acknowledging their continued importance.

I cannot see, then, that Eco's ethics of the body adds anything to human rights discourse. Indeed, his avoidance, or fear, of being caught in possession of a true statement or a principle might well diminish the strength of the defence of human rights. Surely Eco wishes to say that that defence is central to respect for the body in the same way that a democratic society is. Is he saying that there are no truths about democracy and fascism to which we can turn? To say that there is merely preference, or opinion, or liberal pluralism, overlooks the historical reality that certain principles are central to the possibility of achieving substantive democracy, among them the classical liberal principles which *Index* was founded to help protect.

But there are, indeed, both principles to be defended in a democratic society and truths about fascism and democracy to which we can refer. We do not have to assume the absolutisms of past political doctrines that Eco and post-modernists are keen to denounce to recognise that, even in the liberal pluralist society they champion, certain principles are needed if that society is to remain democratic and free. As Ronald Dworkin noted in the same issue of *Index* [A New Map of Censorship], the question of freedoms of speech, thought, and so on, are synonymous with the possibility of democracy. They are not just means to other truths, but are part of the truth about what democracy must entail.

This does not mean that the principles and freedoms in democratic society are either fully realised or incontestable. Nevertheless, there are distinctions between democracy and fascism that are as profound and true as they are irreconcilable. These truths are so familiar to us that we need only read Eco's interview to stir our memories: fascism reduces all questions of truth to questions of

power, denies individual freedom, and defends violence and war as overt principles for the 'good society'. Whatever the weaknesses, limitations and horrendous failings that democratic societies have in practice brought us, it would be a huge error to believe that democratic societies were not significantly different to fascist states.

I am still unsure, then, what Eco is saying about free speech itself: is it a principle to be defended or a preference to be granted to some and not others? We might agree that fascism is abhorrent and must be opposed, but how? One way is to curb the political freedoms that have been established through struggle over the decades: we might ban political parties, restrict freedom of speech, movement and association, and invite the state to prevent these groups establishing themselves. Dworkin's article outlined some of the dangers involved in this method.

Alternatively, we might resurrect some of those failed principles of modernist political discourse: we can focus on the causes of fascism, which lie at least in part in the fundamental inequalities of democratic societies; and we can use education to establish organisations opposed to fascism to defend ourselves. Freedom is best defended by recognising the strength of the principles that we know to represent it, not by reducing them to preferences. While Eco's opposition to fascism is clear, he leaves us with important questions which his avoidance of the ideas of truth and principle does nothing to resolve. ❑

# US pride

**From Robert H Haines**, *New York*

*Tu Quoque* is never an adequate response to justifiable criticism; but criticism which suggests that the faults are unique, and which deals exclusively with faults, indicates bias. Your editorial and Noam Chomsky's article in the July/August issue indicate such bias.

Your editorial compares (unfavourably to the West) the treatment of Kuwait with Bosnia and Rwanda. You don't mention Somalia (which is not richly endowed). You ignore the real problems of effective military intervention in the former Yugoslavia, the French effort in Rwanda and the massive effort to alleviate refugee suffering in that country resulting, as you know, from what is clearly a civil war.

Professor Chomsky, as usual, bashes the United States while also indulging in his preferred activity of Israel-bashing. Many of Chomsky's criticisms of America are valid, but he feels he must support his America-bashing by harking back to the treatment of Indians, slavery and the Vietnam War. I deny chauvinism, but I am proud of America's progress. We have learned from the past. We did abolish slavery.

Although we have not abolished racism, we have achieved more than any country in the world in making racism illegal and unacceptable. The same is true of our religious tolerance. Name one other county with a comparable mix and a comparable achievement.

You know that the rest of the world, those who can, takes its direction from our decisions on free speech and freedom of publication. Sure, a nation's reach can exceed its grasp, but why not acknowledge the effort? ❏

# So simple

**From Judith Moses**
*Committee to Protect Journalists, New York*

The article written by Abdullahi An-Na'im in the *Index* of September-October 1994 leads your readers to believe that the director of one of our country's most prestigious human rights organisations — Human Rights Watch/Africa — condones the *fatwa* against Salman Rushdie. There can be no equivocation about Salman Rushdie's status. Rushdie is under a life-long threat of death issued by a sovereign state because he expressed views with which that state disagrees. Mr Rushdie, therefore, enjoys neither freedom of expression, freedom of movement, freedom of association, freedom of religion nor freedom from arbitrary assassination, all of which human rights Human Rights Watch/Africa purports to protect. Mr An-Na'im's call for 'dialogue' to resolve the Rushdie affair is an unacceptable bureaucratic response to an act of state terrorism against an individual. Human rights are that simple. ❏

# MARK BONHAM CARTER

*Mark Bonham Carter,* Index *chairman 1978-1989, died 4 September 1994, aged 72*

IVAN KYNCL

Mark Bonham Carter was in no respect pompous and stuffy, but always warm and sincere. He had great likes and dislikes, of which he made his friends fully conscious. He was serious and also extremely amusing. He gave generously of his time and work. He always said what he thought and the effects of this could be gratifying — or devastating.

During the years when he was chairman of *Index on Censorship* he gave unstintingly of his time and energy, accepting heavy responsibilities of policy and — the heaviest burden on our directors — fund-raising. All here who worked for and with him were conscious of the time, energy and initiative he put into this work.

He had very good friends, but he was not in the least afraid of making enemies. He always said exactly what he thought, though this might on occasions be the opposite of what a particular friend with whom he was talking thought. I am always rather pleased when someone I know seems exactly to illustrate some word describing human conduct. There were times when Mark seemed the living embodiment of the word 'abrasive'.

One sometimes had the impression that here was a man gifted to be a great public figure — prime minister, perhaps. In a time when public life is dominated by politicians who seem mere ciphers, it was lamentable that a man with as real a personality as Mark was not in the Cabinet. That his great public gifts were only partly used was part of the tragedy of the decline of political Liberalism.

It was perhaps partly because being a peer gave him public recognition and, to some extent, a public platform, that he was glad to be elevated to the peerage. He enjoyed immensely being in the House of Lords. The last years of his life were probably happier than those immediately preceding them.

He could express his opinions and he had acquired a role. It is sad for his family and friends that he did not have more time in which to play it.❑

*Stephen Spender*

# YOU MUST BE JOKING...

'Here I am wholly available', 'Let me have my way among you' or 'I can come no other way, Take me deeper into you' — no, not what they seem, but modern hymn lyrics, and the erotic connotations are upsetting some leading experts on Church music. Others, however, see this as part of a long and honourable tradition going back to the Song of Songs. 'Call me naive and innocent' said a representative of the Evangelical Association, 'but I have never thought of associations like these before. What about "The Lord is my shepherd"? Doesn't "he make me down to lie"?'

There's a reader in Long Buckby library who may soon turn his attention to hymn-books. A local activist has been deleting the four-letter words from dozens of books in the village library. One borrower commented: 'The prude obviously reads the books right to the end.'

The spread of satellite television is having some curious consequences. In India, competition from satellite has caused a transformation in the traditionally coy film industry. Chart-topping film songs now have refrains such as 'Drag your cot next to mine'. The 'Sexy, Sexy' song, which repeats the word 'sexy' more than 100 times, has become a playground favourite. And government film censorship is being undermined by local cinemas, who routinely splice banned footage back into films. The government is threatening tougher censorship, but music shops are making a killing.

The fight against Western decadence is being pursued with similar vigour further East. In Singapore an advertisement featuring a toddler wearing a baseball cap and demanding of all things a nutritional supplement was criticised by the prime minister for 'promoting American-style youth insolence'.

Pretentious menus are all too common, but this is an especially tasty example. The waitress-service restaurant at the BBC no longer lists steamed currant pudding as 'Spotted Dick'

— it appears on the menu as 'Spotted Richard'. An official explained: 'We've been told we can't use the d★★★ word any more.' The policy carries over into music too. The Lemonheads were persuaded by the BBC to change the lyrics of their song 'Big Gay Heart' so that the phrase 'suck my dick' was changed to 'duck my sick'. Well, at least it avoids the d★★★ word.

MILEN RADEV

Newspaper proprietors faced with the problem of disposing of journalists who don't quite fit in may wish to study management practices at *Slobodna Dalmacija*, a daily newspaper in the Croatian town of Split. After it came under government control last year, a number of staff were identified as 'temporary technological surplus manpower' and placed on a waiting list for redeployment. Posts later offered included assigning an economics specialist, the author of an internal policy column, as a junior accounts clerk, and instructing their former correspondent in Korcula to sell newspapers in a kiosk. Because there are no newspaper kiosks in Korcula, this involves a boat trip to a kiosk in Orebic. Several other journalists are still awaiting re-assignment.

And finally — perhaps one can sympathise with the International Federation of Tour Operators, who are not at all amused by travellers who make jokes about bombs or hijacking. As well as displaying signs at security desks reading 'Please don't make jokes — we don't find them funny,' they have threatened that jokers will be refused carriage, given no refunds and be liable to prosecution. You have been warned. ❏

**ET**

Operation Restore Hope, Somalia 1992: paras to the rescue

# Intervention unbound

Humanitarian aid and military intervention make disturbing bedfellows, argues Alex de Waal, co-director of African Rights. Can NGOs really call for the military occupation of a country with complete impunity?

# ALEX DE WAAL

# African encounters

## The context of the call for military intervention in Africa

The last three years have seen humanitarian organisations calling for military intervention in Bosnia, Somalia, Rwanda and elsewhere. Both relief agencies and human rights organisations have vocally implored the United Nations, or individual Western countries, to despatch troops to strife-torn nations facing humanitarian disaster. What is commonplace today would have been unthinkable even five years ago.

This paper examines the reasons for this extraordinary shift in the capacity of humanitarian organisations to make these dramatic statements, and asks whether the analysis, capacity and accountability of these organisations matches their power. It focuses on central and north-east Africa, a region that has the dubious distinction of leading the world in the depth and complexity of its politically-caused humanitarian emergencies.

## The Cold War: humanitarianism in a strait-jacket

Until very recently, relief agencies were operating within well-defined limits imposed by the political order established in the wake of World War II. Sovereign governments ruled. Charitable relief agencies — or, as they prefer to call themselves, non-governmental organisations (NGOs) — were required to conform to their rules, which prohibited taking a political stand. Those who broke the rules faced expulsion from the countries where they worked.

One consequence of the depoliticisation of relief was that a 'natural disaster' model of human suffering prevailed. Repeatedly, when a government reduced its own citizens to a state of acute hunger and desperation, through corruption, ineptitude or brutal counterinsurgency warfare, the blame was put on the weather. The famine in Ethiopia during 1983-85 was perhaps the most spectacularly successful example of this — a famine caused in large part by a combination of military strategy and Stalinist social engineering was attributed to drought and ecological crisis. Even the rainfall statistics were first suppressed and then fiddled. Most NGOs swallowed this line. Others went along with this deception, believing that to dispute it in public would prevent them feeding the hungry.

Throughout Africa, relief operations mounted under such politically-constrained circumstances were less than successful. The literature on the last decade of relief operations in Africa contains little true analysis and much hagiography. The standards of assessment would have made any district officer in the British Raj in India blush with shame. For example, the number of studies of famine mortality in village populations can be counted on the fingers of one hand — students of famine demographics are advised to consult nineteenth century Indian statistics if they want to test their hypotheses. But, gradually, a shocking picture of ineptitude and massive diversion is emerging. There have been some successes, particularly in emergency care in refugee camps, but the sad truth is that the huge pouring of relief aid into Africa for over a decade has contributed to the institutionalisation of violence.

Ethiopia is a case in point. It is now no longer seriously disputed that the massive inflow of aid following BandAid contributed more to the survival of the Ethiopian government — whose army was the main reason for the famine — than the famine-stricken peasantry. Large amounts of international food aid were diverted to the government militias. The flow of aid allowed the army to maintain garrisons that would otherwise have surrendered, and kept open roads that enabled the military to resupply its front line. Food aid distributions enticed young men forward who were forcibly conscripted. Perhaps most insidiously, the aid programmes gave the government spurious humanitarian credentials — while its soldiers were busy destroying farmers' livelihoods and hence forcing them into relief shelters, the government could claim the credit for allowing international agencies to feed these captive peoples.

The government of Mengistu Haile Mariam became a master at

managing humanitarian propaganda. It recognised that the international press is more concerned with the marginal contribution made to rural people's survival — overall no more than 10 per cent of the average daily ration — provided by international food aid, than the 90 per cent provided by the people's own efforts. The latter could be destroyed without international protest, neatly providing a captive population for the military, and a needy population for the relief agencies. Humanitarianism became a component of counterinsurgency.

The alternative option for NGOs was to work in the areas controlled by the liberation movements. This entailed several sacrifices. One was being labelled as a 'solidarity' organisation, and hence somehow less professional than those who maintained an operational presence. Perhaps more important, it involved foregoing the chance for publicity, as until the last two years of the war, no television journalists travelled in the rebel-held areas. This was certainly the deciding factor for at least one major US NGO. None of the larger relief organisations trod this path until the final days of the war.

The more perceptive relief workers came to recognise this travesty for what it was. In the late 1980s there was the beginning of a vigorous debate about the abuse of aid for military ends. Unfortunately, this debate became sidetracked by a single issue, namely the ability of the sovereign government to control the great majority of the aid flows, thereby enabling it to deny relief to civilians in areas held by rebel forces. The questions were: which side should receive the aid; how can relief be transported across battle lines? The central issue of the marginality of relief aid itself was never fully acknowledged. Perhaps this is not surprising given the institutional commitments of all those involved in the debate. The idea of proposing *less* relief aid was taboo, and lip-service only was paid to the imperative of pressuring governments for substantial changes in military strategies.

## Violating sovereignty

A pseudo-solution to the problem of strait-jacketed humanitarianism came with Operation Lifeline Sudan. Launched in April 1989, this was a path-breaking exercise in the violation of national sovereignty in the name of providing humanitarian aid to civilians on all sides of a conflict — in this case, southern Sudan. The Sudan government, then engaged in peace talks with the rebel Sudan People's Liberation Army (SPLA), agreed to the plan. The aid flowed; famine was stemmed. The relief operation was given the credit, and for much of the succeeding five years, Operation Lifeline Sudan has been held up as a model for a relief operation that reaches all sides of a conflict.

The reality is somewhat different. On the ground, the main contribution to ending hunger was a simultaneous ceasefire that enabled farmers to plant crops and pastoralists to travel more freely and begin to market their animals. When the ceasefire broke down at the end of 1989, Operation Lifeline Sudan acquired a very different dynamic.

As in the case of Ethiopia, food aid has been used to sustain armies, maintain garrison towns, keep open supply routes, and allow generals to don the humanitarian mantle. The difference is that it has done this for both sides at the same time. Hundreds of millions of dollars have been spent by the international community on a 'humanitarian' operation that is in fact feeding soldiers more than it is feeding their victims. The SPLA's quartermaster is the World Food Programme, USAID and an array of NGOs. Government garrisons live on international food aid. But no-one knows the true figures for the impact of the programmes, or the rates of diversion, because no proper studies have been done. Meanwhile, the war is in a stalemate.

**BandAid contributed more to the survival of the Ethiopian government than the famine-stricken peasantry**

In southern Sudan, humanitarianism has found itself a new strait-jacket. The relief agencies could pull out, but in doing so they would certainly unleash acute suffering on the people of the war-affected areas. Some civilians are dependent on the airdrops. Soldiers would turn to looting and pillaging to feed themselves. It is a dilemma without a solution. Only recently has it become more widely accepted among NGOs that Operation Lifeline Sudan is not the success that has been claimed. Moreover, this opinion is still almost entirely a private one. Policy is still being made in an empirical and analytical vacuum, by agency staff who have donned, not only in public, an impenetrable armour of moral righteousness.

Operation Lifeline, Sudan 1989: fed armies not their victims

## Beyond sovereignty

The next step in the relief agencies' evolution can be seen in Somalia, where the central government collapsed completely at the beginning of 1991. Sovereignty in the conventional sense, as exercised by a government, became irrelevant. Instead, relief agencies found themselves in a wholly new situation — the state had collapsed altogether. Somalia was in fact only the most marked manifestation of a trend that had been evident for some time, notably in Mozambique, but it stands out as a defining case.

The United Nations agencies and bilateral institutions such as USAID had a straightforward response to the 1991 crisis in Somalia — they withdrew and did nothing. A handful of international NGOs stayed. In Mogadishu, these agencies were not only the providers of emergency medical supplies and child nutrition, but the sole links with the international community. In the absence of a police force, they had to provide their own security. Without a ministry of health, they could formulate their own medical policies. It was both a formidable challenge and a boon. Aid workers in the field had to take on the jobs of diplomats, security experts, news agencies, policy advisors, as well as administering their own programmes. It was frightening, but also exhilarating.

The power of the few aid NGOs that remained was magnified by their treatment by the international media. Foreign journalists who visited Somalia stayed with the aid agencies, were given guided tours by them, accepted their analyses and prognoses, and in turn quoted them at length and gave them enormous publicity. The symbiotic relationship between the Western media and its favourite aid agencies has long been noted; in Somalia this reached new heights. Some journalists even admitted that they deliberately selected their pictures so as to exaggerate the human degradation in the feeding shelters, and all of them skimmed over the shortcomings of the relief agencies' programmes.

Somalia was a guinea-pig for post-Cold War humanitarianism. It was the first time that the International Committee of the Red Cross hired armed guards. It was the first time that relief agencies such as the Save the Children Fund took such publicly outspoken positions criticising the absence of the United Nations. And finally, it was the first time that international agencies successfully called for Western military intervention.

The agency most responsible for the call for intervention was CARE-US. The CARE-International programme in Somalia was adrift. Designed along conventional lines, with staff recruited for logistical experience rather than diplomatic finesse and local understanding, it faced enormous difficulties. The ICRC, with a more flexible and creative approach, and above all by its close working relationship with its local partner, the Somali Red Crescent Society, moved far more food far more quickly. But CARE, partnered with the extremely inept World Food Programme, became mired down.

The president of CARE-US, Philip Johnston, led the calls for international military intervention. His long-term motives may have included creating a niche for CARE as the lead agency in future programmes under international military protection. The stated rationale was not that the intervention would save Somalia, but that it would save the CARE-WFP relief programme — subject to inordinate diversion and delay. Such was the automatic equation of a successful relief programme with the conquest of famine that few stopped to consider that the famine might be healing itself although the CARE-WFP programme had yet to become properly functional. Hence the US marines landed in the week that saw death rates in Baidoa, the epicentre of the famine, fall to one tenth of their famine peak, and just as farmers in the Shebelle valley, breadbasket of Somalia, prepared to gather in their harvest.

The UN, the Pentagon and other relief agencies joined the calls for intervention because they saw institutional advantages: new, expanded roles at a time when budgets were being cut. US citizens were also caught up in the moral panic that gripped the country in that political no-man's land between a lost presidential election and the inauguration of the new president. It was also the time of Thanksgiving and Christmas, a period when the conscience politic is particularly vulnerable, and when charities raise most of their funds. Once the momentum in favour of intervention had gathered force, no agency dared speak up against it — though many field staff had serious doubts.

**Somalia was the guinea-pig for post-Cold War humanitarianism... The guinea-pig, of course, bit back**

Above all, however, the call for intervention was a call of desperation. In common with many of his colleagues, Philip Johnston was simply lost in the Somalia of 1992. Violence he could not understand he characterised as 'random', authority structures he did not have the patience to deal with he called 'anarchic'. With an inchoate urge to 'do something', he called on the US marines to save the day.

Most accounts of 'Operation Restore Hope' in Somalia argue that the intervention was sound in its early, US-led and 'purely humanitarian' phase, and went wrong later on when the UN (at US bidding) sought to confront General Mohamed Farah Aidid. This is not correct. Operation Restore Hope was flawed in its conception; it was aimed at supplying massive food aid to a region that no longer needed massive food aid. Meanwhile it neglected the most pressing relief needs: a programme against malaria and effective measles vaccination. There is in fact no evidence that the intervention had any impact on mortality rates at all.

It is quite possible that Operation Restore Hope did save hundreds of thousands of lives. But no one can be sure. Such is the absence of systematic accountability in the famine relief business that no proper investigations have been done. What has been researched and written are internal analyses that look at the logistics of food movement, inter-agency co-ordination and the provision of security. None of the reports investigate whether lives were saved, rehabilitation facilitated, or a sense of hope restored. They simply claim that it was so. Humanitarianism, it seems, is its own justification.

The guinea-pig, of course, bit back, discrediting military humanitarian intervention for some time to come. But rather than examining the shameful indifference to Somalia in the prolonged gestation of the crisis, when both the UN and the USA turned their backs on the country, the lesson learned seems to be one of further disengagement. Did the NGOs learn anything? That remains to be seen.

## The search for new humanitarian principles

The end of the capacity of the governments of poor countries to exercise total control over the activities of humanitarian agencies operating within their borders opens up new and exciting possibilities. In theory, no longer should aid agencies be compelled to remain silent when they witness grave abuses of human rights. They should be able to develop integrated analyses of the situations in the countries, and lobby in an unconstrained manner for integrated solutions. Subject only to the attentions of the Charity Commissioners — whose interest in and expertise on most African countries is not great — relief agencies should be able to become much more political. And, as the emergencies in question are essentially political emergencies, this should free the agencies to make real progress.

But it has not happened like that. Some aid agency staff are pressing in this direction. But another powerful set of constraints is at work: the donors.

Non-governmental relief agencies have grown enormously in size in the last 15 years. They have become the preferred conduits for emergency aid from Western governments. This is for a variety of reasons. One is that donor governments have become tired of the inefficiency of host government bureaucracies. A second is that donations to Western NGOs gain them favourable publicity and can obscure the reality of declining aid budgets. A third is that grants through NGOs are much more discretionary than to governments, and subject to much less formality. This gives more room for flexibility and rapid response, but it also removes a central component of accountability — there is no obligation for the donor to provide the resources. If an NGO is present in a certain country, that country is privileged — NGOs have no duty to be present.

In turn, NGOs become more closely tied to donor governments. Some try to put a ceiling on the proportion of income they will take from governments, but this ceiling rarely applies in the case of emergency grants. Hence, emergency officers in NGOs are continually forced into the donors' mindset simply in order to receive funds. An agency that undertakes radical development projects may be exceptionally conservative when it comes to relief. There are, in fact, no radical relief agencies.

Equally important is the role of public appeals. The majority of the large agencies believe, along with most journalists, that only a certain kind of humanitarian story will elicit public sympathy and public funds. The story is stripped down to its barest essentials: helpless victim, evil bandit or warlord, and saviour — the latter invariably white. At least this is an improvement on earlier days when the villain was the weather.

While maintaining the charitable imperative at the core of their activities, NGOs have also sought to expand their mandates for humanitarian intervention. Two concepts have crept in: peacemaking and human rights. These are strictly ancillary to responding to immediate human need. When Oxfam ran its campaign, 'H stands for hunger, Oxfam stands for justice,' it never meant that it proposed establishing human rights principles for its programmes, nor campaigning on human rights issues. But, Oxfam staff assure one, human rights are at the centre of the organisation's mandate. Similarly, peacemaking has become a vogue term — but while many NGOs are implicitly pacifist in conviction, none has developed a set of clearly defined principles for operation in a war zone. The exception to this is the ICRC.

The pressure for expanded mandates has also come from outside the agencies. With the Western disengagement from poor countries in Africa, donor governments have sought to use NGOs more and more as an instrument of policy. The analyses and opinions of NGO staff — often young and inexperienced — are sought after and listened to. Now that African countries lack commercial or strategic importance, Western interest is often confined to maintaining good publicity at home, which

Somalia 1992. Italian paratroops: 'out of their depth'

means supporting international NGOs and keeping human suffering to acceptable, or at least invisible levels. The NGOs are thus pushed by their donor governments into taking on political concerns.

Meanwhile, with the humanitarian space no longer defined by the diktat of the host government, the agencies have to demarcate it for themselves. They do this using two notions in particular. One is 'fieldcraft' — ie making compromises with the governing authorities (frequently abusive authorities) for the greater good. This principle allows the field officer to tolerate a certain level of diversion. The level is never defined, and what is unacceptable in one situation is tolerable in another. 'Fieldcraft' also makes a mockery of any avowal of human rights. A field officer will be required to turn a blind eye to human rights abuses in order to protect the agency's programme, becoming a silent witness. In human rights, consistency is all: once an organisation has publicly affirmed that it is committed to human rights, it cannot compromise in this way.

The second concept is 'neutrality'. The ICRC has a highly developed doctrine of neutrality, which involves slow, convoluted and expensive procedures. It also involves discretion: the ICRC is the most publicity-shy relief organisation. The ICRC's neutrality involves a readiness to withdraw if its principles are flouted, no matter how desperate the immediate human need. It also involves a recognition that any relief involvement in a conflict brings material or moral benefit to the combatants — hence the elaborate procedures to try to minimise the imbalance of this, and hence also the secrecy of many operations.

Other NGOs have, however, assumed that simply putting a flag on a landrover and proclaiming neutrality is enough to establish neutral status. This is nonsense. As publicity-seeking institutions, most NGOs have neither the patience nor money for the kind of procedures followed by the ICRC, and would not accept the constraints imposed by discretion under any circumstances. Hence NGO programmes run the risk of becoming inadvertently partisan. This is a dangerous state of affairs, not only for the staff on the ground who often believe their own humanitarian propaganda, but for the principles of humanitarianism themselves.

**The UN stand (on Rwanda) was the antithesis of moral leadership**

It is important to distinguish *operational* neutrality from *objectivity* or neutrality of principle. Operational neutrality means refusing to take sides in a conflict, or to take any action or make any public pronouncement that could be interpreted as being partisan. The ICRC once again manifests this: it refuses to take a position on the waging of war, refuses to condemn violators (except when the violations are committed against the ICRC itself), and is thoroughly discreet.

Some other NGOs espouse a watered-down version of this. For example, they refuse to condemn one side to a conflict without also condemning the other, and call for the investigation and punishment of human rights abuses without naming the perpetrators. They regard operational neutrality as incompatible with naming names. In certain circumstances this is undoubtedly true, and hence it cannot be aspired to by any human rights organisation that works through public campaigning.

Neutrality of principle, or objectivity, means assessing the parties to a conflict according to the same standards. This is what human rights organisations aspire to do. This often means that one party is criticised far more than the other, reflecting the reality that some governments and armies are far more abusive than others. In extremis, one side may be guilty of a horrendous crime, such as genocide, of which the other is innocent — a state of affairs that obliges selective action against one party to the conflict. A human rights organisation that failed to follow this principle, and instead preferred to 'balance' its criticism, would be applying double standards, and hence would, in fact, be partisan towards the more abusive party.

The cost of objectivity can be the inability to operate in a certain country or region. A human rights organisation must always be prepared to run the risk of being declared persona non grata.

One of the problems faced by operational relief agencies that have tried to take on human rights concerns is that they run the risk of confusing the two kinds of neutrality, and ending up achieving neither. One way out of this dilemma is to panic and call for international military intervention.

## Rwanda: mandates at odds

The mass murder of the political opposition and the genocide in Rwanda presented exceptional challenges to relief agencies. The traditional approach of providing relief, no questions asked, would certainly have made agencies complicit in mass murder, because there can be no doubt that the majority of relief aid would have been taken directly by the army and *interahamwe* militia, which were responsible for most of the killing. In the event, this problem did not arise inside Rwanda as significant relief operations did not get under way in government-controlled areas while the massacres were going on. It has, however, occurred in the refugee camps, where effective authority is often in the hands of the men who supervised the genocide.

Rwanda presents a stark conflict between operational neutrality and human rights objectivity. The government was guilty of genocide, and the rebel Rwandan Patriotic Front (RPF) was not. The genocide was meticulously planned and all the institutions of government were dedicated to a policy of massacres. The Genocide Convention, and any form of moral argument, led to the conclusion that the Rwandan government needed to be ostracised and defeated and the architects of genocide brought to trial for crimes against humanity.

One NGO that took a prominent public stand on Rwanda rapidly found itself impaled on the horns of this dilemma. This was Oxfam. Other NGOs took a range of similar positions; this discussion will focus solely on Oxfam, to illuminate the nature of the dilemma.

In late April, three weeks after the killing was unleashed, Oxfam publicly called it 'genocide'. For an organisation with human rights near the centre of its mandate, the implications were clear: those guilty of the crime should be named and every effort should be made to bring them to court. But Oxfam is also an operational agency, with expertise in the provision of safe water supplies to refugee camps, and funds from a public appeal to spend on humanitarian work. The refugee camps contained many of the men responsible for the slaughter. Oxfam believed it could not simultaneously name certain people as international criminals and then try to carry out its humanitarian work alongside them, or even with their co-operation.

Oxfam had widened its mandate without fully considering the implications, and now had to choose between its priorities. Its solution was to fudge the issue of genocide. It did this in two ways. One was by calling for a UN investigation into the genocide, and refusing to name names itself. Given Oxfam's knowledge of the situation on the ground and its moral authority, this came as a severe disappointment to many Rwandans who were looking for international moral leadership.

The second element of the fudge was to call for international military intervention to stop the genocide. This position was deeply flawed.

The call for UN military intervention presupposed, first, that there was no effective alternative and, second, that it would work. Some Oxfam staff certainly recognised that neither of these assumptions was true, and the agency even conceded publicly that UN troops alone could not stop the killing. But the impact of their public advocacy was to present the Rwandan disaster as one soluble only by international forces.

The greatest failing of military intervention is that, the moment it is canvassed, it dominates the debate like a huge dark cloud, and obscures the need and opportunity for other forms of international action. In Somalia and Bosnia there were vital opportunities for civil initiatives that were not taken because of the blinkered obsession with troops. In the event, the presence of the troops did not solve problems, it merely

Emergency aid, Rwanda 1994: Oxfam disoriented

HOWARD DAVIES/PANOS PICTURES

changed them. But, even after these debacles, military intervention is still heralded as a trump card.

In Rwanda too, there were alternatives. The genocide was planned and implemented by a group of well-known political extremists. These men, having put the genocidal machine into action, had the power to apply the brakes. This could have been done by severe moral and diplomatic sanctions: for example, by expelling Rwandan ambassadors, expelling Rwanda from the UN Security Council, publicly naming the genocidal maniacs in the interim government, and threatening them with prosecution for genocide unless the killing were halted at once. In the name of diplomatic operational neutrality, neither the UN nor its member countries tried any of these options. Rwanda even continued to sit on the UN Security Council throughout, and the interim foreign minister was permitted to deliver a racist diatribe at the Security Council in person. The UN stand was the antithesis of moral leadership.

The option of UN military intervention under established principles also presumed that authority had broken down. This was precisely what

French troops, Rwanda 1994: a very ambiguous intervention

the architects of genocide were anxious to tell the world, to cover their crime, and present the killing as an outbreak of 'spontaneous ethnic violence'. By murdering 10 Belgian UN soldiers on 7 April, the extremists had shown their willingness for military confrontation, so that a dedicated UN force would have had to be prepared to take casualties. Moreover, given the poor record of UN peacekeeping, it is difficult to see how UN intervention could have been a 'solution'.

The second option was to seek an indigenous military solution — that is, to advocate the defeat of the genocidal government by its internal opponents. This would have forsaken operational neutrality for practical human rights objectivity.

The genocide was brought to an end by the military advance of the RPF. The RPF was not implicated in the genocide, and its advance had the effect of halting the killing. It did this more swiftly and effectively than any UN intervention force could have done. Yet throughout, the UN and most international agencies were calling for a ceasefire. This was done for reasons of operational neutrality. But a ceasefire was precisely what the killers wanted — a chance to complete their genocide undisturbed. When the RPF declared a 96-hour ceasefire in May, the killings did not stop.

**At the hint of public debate, the moral armour is donned, and the shutters of self-censorship come down**

While there was no connection between a ceasefire and an end to the killing, a ceasefire could have helped to prevent the mass exodus of refugees to Zaire. The refugee crisis was, in some respects, a straightforward humanitarian emergency requiring food relief, clean water and medical care. NGOs were accustomed to responding to this sort of disaster, and had a perceived obligation to deal with it. Oxfam's position gave the priority to preventing a crisis of hungry refugees over stopping genocidal killing.

The RPF advance was a form of humanitarian intervention. But it was not recognised as such, because the RPF, as a party to the conflict, was not operationally neutral. But, as the only force capable of halting the genocide, it was morally bound to intervene. Arguably, as a component of the government under the peace agreement signed in 1993, it was also legally bound to do so under the provisions of the

Genocide Convention, to which Rwanda is a party.

The option of supporting the RPF advance, on the grounds that it was the quickest and most effective way of halting the killing, does not imply indemnifying the RPF for human rights abuses, nor refusing to criticise components of its past and present military, political and human rights policies. It merely means recognising that the RPF advance was the only effective way that the international community could have fulfilled its obligation to halt and punish the crime of genocide.

A UN military intervention could only have been achieved with a concomitant ceasefire. It is highly unlikely that the UN force would have been effective at halting the genocide. It would not have been prepared to take casualties, nor jeopardise its operational neutrality, by confronting the Rwandan army. Hence such an arrangement would have continued the killing, and also given impunity to the killers — because one cannot prosecute politicians with whom one is negotiating an agreement.

Oxfam did not advocate these alternatives, in order to preserve its operational neutrality. Probably, had a UN force been despatched and behaved in the manner suggested, Oxfam would also have been among its critics. When the French government — Rwanda's leading arms supplier and diplomatic ally — proposed a unilateral intervention in June, Oxfam opposed it. This was the correct line, but the French army could have legitimately complained, as the US marines did in Somalia, that agencies that called for a military presence had little right to criticise the soldiers for behaving in a military fashion after they arrived.

The redeeming feature of Oxfam's advocacy is that it failed in its specific goals, while it succeeded in gaining greater international attention for Rwanda. But this should give pause for thought to the senior staff of Oxfam and other NGOs that take public policy positions on issues of similar import. These are not commitments that can simply be taken up and cast off at will.

## Humanitarianism unbound

The case of the Oxfam lobby on Rwanda is striking because the dilemmas are so clear. But, like Somalia beforehand, it reflects the disorientation of the humanitarian agencies in the post-Cold War world. The NGOs have shaken off one straight-jacket, and they have broadened their mandate and seized immense new opportunities for political influence. International policies towards entire African countries can now be dominated by the NGOs' humanitarian agenda.

The powers of analysis and the rigours of accountability have not increased in step with the NGOs' influence. There are internal discussions within the agencies on these questions, to be sure, but the moment that there is a hint of public debate, the moral armour is donned, and the shutters of self-censorship come down. On several occasions, NGOs have reacted with outrage to the arguments presented here, but then refused to join the debate.

It is in this context that the call for military intervention has emerged: ungrounded in a sober and professional appraisal of the situation, unencumbered by demands for accountability, and subject only to the hasty demand to 'do something' by an array of organisations that have monopolised the moral high ground. Can the NGOs really call for the military occupation of a country with complete impunity? Are they really accountable only to a fawning and forgetful press? ❑

Zaire 1994: Rwandan refugee camps in Goma

**JANE REGAN**

# Won and lost

**Behind the dancing crowds, the drums and bamboo-pipe-trombones, the beautiful murals, smiling soldiers, new schools and cleaned-up sewers, there is another side to the US occupation of Haiti**

President Jean-Bertrand Aristide and his advisors cut a deal: they bargained they could come back to develop this tiny and proud nation as before. But in the process they bargained away most of Haiti's rights and even reneged on the promises made to Haiti's people when they went to the polls for him four years ago.

The US and its allies inside Haiti — the Haitian army, paramilitary forces and the elite — have been fighting an 'enemy' since before Aristide was born. The 19 September invasion was only the most recent phase in the war. The 'enemy' is the democratic and popular movement, made up of hundreds of peasant, neighbourhood, human rights, student, church and professional organisations fighting for democracy and justice.

It is rooted in the peasant struggles of last century, winds its way through the 'caco' guerrilla war against the US occupation forces earlier this century when 5,000 lost their lives, and was repeatedly and brutally repressed by Duvalier *père et fils*. Despite the 'dirty war' of killings, beatings and exiles, the movement continued and grew so strong that in 1986 the US made an end run around the floundering Jean-Claude Duvalier. 'In terms of maintaining the military as an institution, Duvalier had to be eased out,' explained US Colonel Steven Butler, part of the team that organised his flight.

The military, however, could not contain the movement and in 1990, after several puppet regimes, the US threw its weight behind the electoral process, advising and funding a favoured candidate. Embassy and Washington planners saw former World Bank employee Marc L Bazin as their ticket to a stable, open economy where US companies could get their brassières sewn and baskets woven. But a popular priest from the *ti legliz* (little church) liberation theology movement had other ideas. Three days before the registries closed, Father Jean-Bertrand Aristide joined the race. Hundreds of thousands registered to vote and, in December 1990, he won in a massive landslide.

The army, the elite and the US embassy were horrified and immediately began working to undermine the fledgling democracy. The Central Intelligence Agency perfected its local secret police unit, despite the new government's protests; the Agency for International Development (USAID) allied itself with elite business groups to work against Aristide's planned minimum wage hike (from US\$2.14 to US\$2.85 a day); and the Pentagon maintained its close ties with the army. The elite and traditional politicians schemed and made alliances, seducing the freeloaders who had ridden into office on Aristide's coat-tails. Seven months later, with CIA foreknowledge and with intelligence personnel actually present in the army headquarters as it happened, Aristide was overthrown in a bloody putsch.

To the surprise of the putschists and the world, however, Aristide did not go away. The army continued its war with a systematic and widespread repression and USAID also continued its work: they were still funding 'civic education' and 'human rights' long after the Europeans quit collaborating with the illegal regime. The CIA kept tabs on the new death squad/paramilitary group FRAPH (the *Front pour l'Avancement et le Progrès Haïtien*, founded by a CIA asset) and also embarked on a vicious anti-Aristide disinformation campaign. Through it all, Haitians resisted: a non-stop flow of terrified refugees kept Haiti on the six o'clock news, while politicians, movie stars, solidarity groups and people around the world rallied to the cause.

The 'international community' — dominated by the US through its strong-arming of the UN Security Council — realised they would have to bring Aristide back, but under tightly controlled conditions. The US wanted the democratic and popular movement under control once and for all and decided to go at it from all sides: a full-fledged military occupation to prevent popular uprisings; a nauseating barrage from propagandists as well as the president promoting 'reconciliation' with the human rights abusers and those Aristide once called the '*patripoche*' (patriots of the pocket) bourgeoisie — most of whom supported the coup; and an all-encompassing, invisible invasion of 'development aid'.

In neatly typed papers, consultants and planners have outlined a precedent-setting dose of US 'democracy enhancement': massive amounts of US-controlled aid, specifically targetted to counter nationalist, populist or revolutionary movements so that elections yield the desired results. These kinds of programmes, instrumental in creating the UNO coalition in Nicaragua, are characterised by massive meddling and outright bribery, where local leaders and officials are 'taught' democracy and are tempted with new sewage systems or highways. Over 2,000 elected offices expire in January, giving the US a shot at sweeping the field. 'Elections are the insurance policy for our aid,' said one USAID consultant. The reverse is also true.

The US also insisted Aristide fully embrace the neo-liberal economic model being pushed by USAID, the World Bank and the International Monetary Fund. Haiti will institute a strict 'structural adjustment' programme, 'democratise its asset ownership' (a new euphemism for 'privatise'), remove tariffs protecting its hundreds of thousands of peasants, and try to woo assembly plants where workers will earn little more than their busfare. The minimum wage now stands at US$1 a day. USAID has recommended it not be raised.

All of these programmes are being carried out in the presence of 15,000, mostly US, troops whose goal is to 'ensure a stable environment'. But contrary to US promises and despite UN pressure, the US forces do not intend to disarm the army and paramilitary apparatus which President Clinton had reviled as 'the most brutal, the most violent regime in our hemisphere' only four days before the 'permissive entry'.

Today, Haitian and US forces are 'cohabiting'. The US says the Haitians need their sidearms and rifles since they are responsible for 'law and order'. The US troops also turn over their arrests to the Haitian forces, who promptly release them. FRAPH, the brutal death squad, says it wants 'reconciliation' and is preparing a slate of candidates for the coming elections. FRAPH members — tens of thousands across the country — still have their arms. Reports of repression from the countryside and poor neighbourhoods continue daily.

ROGER HUTCHINGS/CAMERA PRESS

Haiti 1994: return of their leader

Behind the scenes, Aristide and the US government are struggling for control of the new security forces. Although the US promised that Aristide could decide which soldiers to expel and which to keep, a US-appointed board of Haitian officers (including several coup participants) now has the final say. The US also wants to run the new police academy, as it does in El Salvador, Guatemala and Panama. One Haitian parliamentarian explained: 'The US wants total exclusivity in the training because they say they are the best in the world; but I know Aristide will fight to the end to make sure there is a multinational presence.'

Not everyone is convinced Aristide will fight to the end. The Aristide who bargained with Washington is a new Aristide, and his bargain benefits new friends. The occupation is bringing major contracts to the 'five families', the wealthiest, monopolist stratum of Haiti's tiny but powerful elite that supported the coup with money, lawyers and lobbyists. They are selling and renting everything they can get their hands on and the privatisation schemes promise to yield millions through joint ventures.

Clinton's 'brutal thugs' and 'criminals' also appear to have fared well. Lt Gen Raoul Cédras made it out of the country with a rumoured US$100 million and a guaranteed income from the US government — the new tenant of his three luxurious homes. Other soldiers and de facto administrators will keep their jobs or receive new ones through USAID-funded 'demobilisation' programmes. President Aristide is insisting on 'reconciliation' but, to the outrage of many organisations and individuals, has not as yet announced plans to investigate, try and judge those responsible for the many brutal and heinous crimes of the past three years.

Aristide's closest supporters — the reformist branch of the democratic movement — are defending the president's bargain as 'inevitable' and blindly embracing neo-liberal capitalism. Father Antoine Adrien, a close friend, said: 'You have to understand the world has changed in these three years.' Aristide has also changed — he was a vehement opponent of neo-liberalism in the 1980s.

Predictably, Aristide and his government have lost the sympathy of the leaders of the democratic and popular movements and organisations who fought so hard to see him back in office. They say the invasion and occupation will bring little to Haiti's masses. The structural adjustment programme will have the same results as elsewhere in the developing world — higher prices, lower salaries, fewer services, greater poverty. The same repressive forces still have their guns and now the right-wing and 'moderate' politicians will be getting a shot of income and advice from US funders. The population is still euphoric at the return of their president, but students and professors, agronomists and popular leaders are agitating against the occupation with leaflets and bulletins, press conferences and sit-ins.

One mass organisation summed it up: 'We are stunned seeing how President Aristide is thanking Bill Clinton... The Yankees occupied Haiti for 20 years under the same pretext of re-establishing democracy in Haiti. Have we ever gotten that democracy? We think the response is "no". Instead, after the many massacres committed during the occupation, this same criminal army was left behind to crush the people from 1934 until today. Do the US imperialists have any interest in breaking down this army *san maman* (without mothers)? We think the response is "no".' ❏

## ZORAN FILIPOVIC

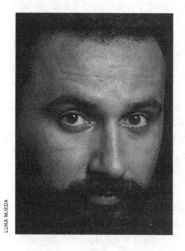

LUKA MJEDA

# With friends like these

During a break in the shelling Mujo runs into Fata in the *Bascarsija* quarter of Sarajevo. Fata is holding a PEKINESE in her arms. Mujo looks at her and can't get over it. 'Fata, poor Fata', he says, 'where on earth did you get a Pekinese in the middle of besieged Sarajevo?' Now it's Fata's turn to be amazed: 'What do you mean "where"? Why, from an UNPROFOR bloke.' Now Mujo is even more shocked. 'Fata, Fata, for God's sake, why didn't you get an abortion?'

Just a joke. As cruel and brutal as the life of Sarajevans themselves. Now into their third year of existence in a human reserve, they have become used and inured to everything. Even before all this they nurtured a sense of humour all their own, one for which they were well known and admired. This war has honed it to a still sharper point. Humour is becoming an important tool of self-defence. It is becoming life itself because often that's all there is. And life is becoming humour, mostly of the black variety, sparing no one, least of all itself.

The world-famous Sarajevo reserve has everything necessary to such places. Of course, the only protected game are the Sarajevans themselves. The living conditions in their reserve are worthy of any animal. Before it became a reserve, a UN protected zone, Sarajevo was already a hunting ground. Hunters came to hunt. Admittedly they were somewhat strange — human heads were their game — but these are strange times.

These hunters — in Sarajevo they called them CHETNIKS, which the latter approvingly encouraged — eventually became poachers, and

Sarajevans, their prey, became a PROTECTED species. But nothing really changed for either side. The hunters-poachers-Chetniks fired their guns whenever they felt like it and for as long as they could keep it up. Those down below — the Sarajevans, the 'protected' — did their best to keep out of the way but, alas, as in every hunt not everyone was that lucky and... The Sarajevo reserve wouldn't be the real thing without the third party — the guards. And this brings us back to the anecdote (?) with which we set out.

UNPROFOR, as its name indicates — the United Nations Protection Force — is in Sarajevo not as the butt of jokes but to bring some order to the reserve. Being constant targets seems to have made Sarajevans interesting to the rest of the world. Rule one of the law of economics: more supply, less demand, lower price. And vice versa: less supply, more demand, higher price.

As the stock of Sarajevans declines as a result of the remorseless hunt day and night, the price of a specimen has sky-rocketed. One need only leaf through the world press, or turn on the TV or radio. There they are, bristling with the latest, the freshest news from Sarajevo. Everyone cares about Sarajevo?!

Which is why the world community dispatched its 'protection forces' to Sarajevo: some order has to be restored to this hunt. Things can't go on like this anymore. There has to be a plan and a programme. Hunting may continue — but according to plan. And everybody — 'protected' and Chetniks alike — must abide by the plan. Anyone who fails to do so shall be punished.

And this is the plan: the Chetniks will continue to hunt and shoot and shell, but according to plan; the Sarajevans will continue to be 'protected' according to plan — until the end of time. Should they want to protect themselves, well, that's not allowed. They'll be punished for that, because it's not part of the plan. UNPROFOR is there to do the protecting, the Sarajevans to be 'protected'. End of the matter.

Should one of the 'protected' occasionally be felled by a bullet, that, certainly, is part of the plan. All you have to do, my dear Sarajevans, is lose your lives, the rest is UNPROFOR's concern. Don't worry!

So that the world might appreciate the difference between before and after (a whiff of civilisation: it is inhumane to kill), UNPROFOR introduced the 'FOTO-SAFARI', based on the 'Fly In' system. Come, see, film and then leave. Because the trip is so easy, the safari has caught on world-wide. Everyone wants to come and hunt in Sarajevo.

The Sarajevo safari is not solely the brainchild of UNPROFOR. The Serbs before them organised this sort of entertainment. Anyone who wanted to shoot at Sarajevo, but had not dared to do so earlier, could now make up for lost time without too many questions being asked. And, as with their UNPROFOR colleagues, they got a good response. They came in search of amusement from around the world. Even a poet, EDUARD LIMONOV by name, came from faraway, friendly Russia. The fun he had spraying Sarajevo with machine-gun fire was filmed on camera.

People have to kill time somewhere, even if it means killing somebody in the process. But it mustn't be boring. And in Sarajevo — the 'protected city' — death is a very, very frequent occurrence. The causes of death can vary. Most often it is from shells — tank or artillery, it's all the same — mortar or sniper fire, even hunger and cold. There are lots of causes but only one result: you are dead, you are no more, you are no longer to be found anywhere, not on the food ration lists, not in the water queues, not anywhere. Just a shallow grave dug in a park or in the practice ground of a sports stadium and — end of story. At least for you. You are done with all your problems, philosophically speaking. For Sarajevans this is a personal matter. As it is for those up there in the hills, for the Chetniks. They have a personal interest in improving the efficiency of their criminal labour.

For UNPROFOR, however, it's simply a matter of statistics; nothing personal. It's a game of letters and numbers, the latter mostly because the letters repeat themselves and that eventually becomes boring. Then some new game is invented, although not too often, adding some life to the deadly boring routine of war, and then everyone in the world writes about it at length,

LUBOMIR MIHAILOV

brimming with excitement.

Like last summer when they launched a retaliatory air attack on alleged Serbian positions and hit a Bosnian trophy tank left over from the last (second world) war. Later, UNPROFOR commander Sir Michael Rose, warned that they would fire at Serbian snipers as well, but that they couldn't do so yet because they were waiting for permission from the self-same Serbs they were supposed to shoot at. The man, bursting with determination, made his statement in front of the TV cameras, which televised it world-wide. He said it without blushing. I haven't heard such nonsense in a long time, believe me. But, it was worth the wait. Something similar happened not long ago. UNPROFOR's mighty forces, backed by NATO air support, again cosmetically attacked the unarmed weak and frail Serbs who have been besieging 'naughty' Sarajevo for the past two-and-a-half years. The attack, on the outskirts of Sarajevo, in the heavy weapons exclusion zone (?), was aimed at a Serbian tank (?) which, contrary to plan, had overdone its barrage on protected Sarajevo (?). This little unarmed (this time actually Serbian) tank, had two cluster bombs dropped on it (when the Serbs dropped them on us, we affectionately named them 'sows'), each of which carries 400 kilogrammes of explosives and creates a big BOOOOM, which can be heard miles away. The sound rather than the destruction seems to have been more important to those who ordered the attack. Tanks are demolished quickly and effectively using a quite different weapon. Obviously, UNPROFOR was more concerned that people should talk about its 'decisive' operation, than that it should actually achieve its purpose.

And while everyone is talking about them and doing their 'utmost' for them, Sarajevans are entering their third winter of war. While the entire world ponders how to help them, Sarajevans are wondering how to survive. While the world's best and brightest are trying to figure out what would be best for them, Sarajevans are preparing for the worst. They are fed up with everything: there is electricity and there isn't; there is gas and there isn't; there is food and there isn't; there is war and there isn't; there is life and there isn't; there is justice and there isn't; there is Bosnia and there isn't; there is Sarajevo and there isn't.

And fed up with it all, they scream to themselves: PLEASE... for God's sake...DON'T HELP US ANYMORE! ❏

*Zagreb: October 1994*                               *Translated by Christina Pribichevich-Zoric*

## JULIE FLINT

# Quit knocking sanctions

**It is not sanctions but Saddam's relentless war against his own people that is killing Iraqis**

On 21 July this year, Muhammad Taqi al-Khoei, a tenacious defender of Iraq's persecuted Shi'ites, sent a coded message to relatives in London warning that the regime was closing in on him. Twenty-four hours later he was dead, killed by an unlit articulated lorry that blocked his path as he drove back from weekly prayers in the city of Kerbala. His driver and six-year-old nephew died instantly; he and his brother-in-law were left by the roadside to bleed to death. It was almost two years to the day since the United Nations' Special Rapporteur for Human Rights in Iraq, Max van der Stoel, had alerted the Security Council to his 'particular concern' for the young cleric, son of the late spiritual leader of the world's Shi'ites.

In the wake of Muhammad Taqi's murder, his family called on the UN to establish an independent investigation into his death; protect relatives of more than 100 senior clerics imprisoned without trial; implement van der Stoel's recommendation for human rights monitors in Iraq; and oblige Saddam to cease his internal oppression in line with Security Council Resolution 688. In response, senior officials sent condolences and assurances of their commitment to 688. And that was it: more words to be appended to the last; more ammunition for those in the Arab and Islamic worlds who have always believed that the US-led intervention in Iraq was, and is, entirely self-serving.

As pressure grows for the lifting of the oil embargo imposed after the invasion of Kuwait, Saddam is increasing his defiance of the UN in the one area where he believes he can violate its resolutions with impunity

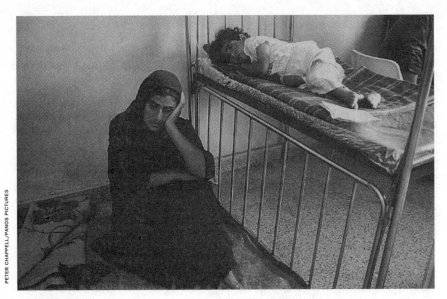

PETER CHAPPELL/PANOS PICTURES

Iraqi Kurdistan: victims of Saddam's indifference

— human rights. For while the world body has invested enormous effort in ensuring compliance with Resolution 687 demanding the destruction of weapons of mass destruction, it has failed to back 688 with anything more than words. Clandestine nuclear, chemical and biological arsenals have been tracked down thanks to a regime of absolute intrusiveness, but the 100 clerics, and thousands more like them, have been left to rot in jail. Allied planes have bombed missile sites when Iraq has misjudged the patience of weapons inspectors, but have been passive observers of the destruction of the marshes, and the murder of the Marsh Arabs, in the no–fly zone they enforce in southern Iraq. The Kurds, abandoned to their fate in the 1980s, have been allowed to suffer under a three-year-old blockade in the 1990s.

In defence of its inaction, the UN argues that 688 is not a mandatory resolution. But even if this is accepted as reason enough for tolerating Saddam's atrocities — and some experts say both the language and context of the resolution make it mandatory; what is missing is the political will for it to be so — it does not explain why human rights observers have not been sent to the one part of Iraq to which they cannot be denied access: the liberated Kurdish region from where the opposition

Iraqi National Congress monitors the regime and its abuses. Suspicions that old, economic interests are once again driving the international agenda strengthen as the same companies that initially armed Iraq line up to sign lucrative contracts for implementation, it is said, once sanctions are lifted. Collective amnesia threatens future disaster.

If the blind eye turned to human rights abuses has prolonged the old sufferings of the Iraqi people, failure to enforce UN sanctions equitably has broken the back of a nation devastated by a UN war that systematically destroyed its civilian infrastructure. With the Iraqi dinar now worth only a fraction of its pre-war value, most Iraqis can barely afford to buy food on the open market. Thousands of civilians die every month due to shortages of basic medicines. Corruption, crime and prostitution are increasing at an alarming rate, giving the regime a pretext for fresh arrests and executions in the name of law and order.

Sanctions need not have left Iraq in the cataclysmic state in which it finds itself today. Not only are food and medicine excluded from the embargo, but the Security Council has authorised, through Resolution 706, limited sales of oil to finance the distribution of food and medicine under UN supervision. Saddam, however, stockpiles medicines and refuses oil-for-food, arguing that 706 infringes Iraqi sovereignty — something he has never hesitated to compromise when his own survival has been at stake.

The UN, which sent scores of inspection teams to Baghdad to track down weapons of mass destruction in accordance with 687, has done nothing to stop Saddam starving his people by repudiating 706. Opposition leaders believe he would capitulate if the sanctions committee threatened to rescind approval for the sale to Jordan of petroleum products worth US$700 million a year, his largest remaining source of foreign currency. But rather than put pressure on him by turning the economic screws, the UN appears to reward Saddam for his intransigence by permitting a flood of contraband from Jordan, his main accomplice in sanctions-busting, and, more recently, Turkey — both of whom are pressing for the removal of sanctions in their own interests.

With the complicity — by default — of the UN, sanctions are hurting ordinary Iraqis far more than the regime. Four years after the invasion of Kuwait, Saddam has rebuilt his military to approximately 90 per cent of its pre-war strength. UN inspectors believe they have destroyed his long-range missiles, nuclear and chemical weapons, but acknowledge that the most rigorous verification regime cannot be foolproof if Saddam is determined to thwart it. And no one who knows him doubts that he is. The long-standing links between the Iraqi and Russian military establishments are already causing concern about the possible diversion of fissile material for a nuclear programme that has always been several steps ahead of Western intelligence.

Despite these concerns, and despite all the evidence that Iraq's compliance with sanctions is a myth, the oil embargo may well be lifted next spring. If it is, Saddam will use the revenue not to feed the impoverished people he now holds as propaganda weapons, but to rebuild the republic of fear on which his survival depends. International intervention will have done little but set back, for the moment, his ability to threaten Israel, Kuwait or Saudi Arabia (which are being re-armed even as Iraq is disarmed). Regional peace and democracy will not have been advanced.

**... the UN will ultimately be guilty of the same crime as Saddam himself — indifference to the needs of the Iraqi people**

The lifting of the embargo should have been linked, from the very start, to the implementation of all UN resolutions — not just those pertaining to weapons control. But this was not the case. The belated invocation of human rights not only adds insult to injury for Iraqis suffering the one-two punch of Saddam and sanctions, but further alienates those who believe the West puts no value on Arab lives and who accuse the USA of leading the UN into Kuwait to achieve regional objectives of its own.

Iraq cannot be kept in indefinite vassalage. Nor can the Iraqi people continue to bear the brunt of sanctions. In the months remaining before Saddam gets access to cash — the one thing he needs to restore his tyranny to its pre-war dimensions — human rights must be paid more than lip-service, sense made from the nonsense of the current sanctions regime, and a war crimes tribunal convened to condemn Saddam as a man with whom no-one can do business. Tons of documents seized in the Kurdish region provide ample evidence of crimes against humanity. If the current confusion is permitted to continue, with Washington demanding sanctions but tolerating sanctions-busting, the UN will ultimately be guilty of the same crime as Saddam himself — indifference to the needs of the Iraqi people. ❏

ACIL TABBARA

# Books for food

On the pavements of Rue Al-Moutanabbi, in the centre of Baghdad, writers, critics and former civil servants sell their books, spread out on the ground. Culture is not thriving in Iraq these days; a victim of sanctions.

Ahmad Saleh, a journalist and playwrite of 37, is not ashamed of what he is doing: 'My salary in the government office for theatre and cinema is 250 dinars, 50 cents on the blackmarket, plus a bonus of 500 dinars. That won't even feed my wife and two daughters for two days.'

So, one fine day he got up, took down the books from his library and installed himself at a street corner. 'Then I realised I could make a better living as a book dealer.' Not that he's given up his old job as a TV presenter of cultural programmes.

Ahmad Saleh specialises in scholarly and academic books; the state has imported no textbooks since sanctions were imposed four years ago. Students are reduced to searching for medical textbooks or dictionaries on secondhand bookstalls, jumbled with piles of ancient copies of magazines like *The National Geographic* from the 1970s, Egyptian romances and poetry collections.

The collapse of the Iraqi dinar means that an entire library can be bought for something like 10,000 dinars, US$20 at black market rates. A four-volume collection of the works of Al-Moutanabbi, one of the greatest poets of the Abbassid period (750-1250AD) in a 1950s edition goes for 2,500 dinars. A pair of Korean trainers costs double on today's market.

Hussein Hassan, a 40-year-old translator and poet, sits in the shade of an arcade in a narrow alley with his collection of English literature, hoping to do better at this than he now does at his former profession. He agrees that more and more distinguished Iraqi intellectuals are coming and asking him to buy their libraries. On Fridays, a holiday, well-known writers come themselves to join the pavement bookstalls. 'People have already sold their family jewels, furniture and electrical appliances. Now they're being forced to part with what they value most — their books,' Hassan says.

Naim Al-Chatri has been holding antiquarian book auctions in Rue Al-Moutanabbi since 1958. Now he says 'highly-placed people, scholars' are so desperate they are bringing him priceless volumes. 'The other day, a woman came to me saying she had nothing, her children would not eat, if I didn't buy her books. What could I do?' says the old man, bursting into tears before taking refuge in his shop. ❑

*Translated from* Libération, *Morocco by Judith Vidal-Hall*

# ANTHONY HYMAN

# A suitable case for intervention

**The rivalries of the Cold War found their ultimate battle ground in Afghanistan, the last old-style intervention fought out on foreign soil. The Cold War is consigned to history, but the war goes on and many Afghans want to know when they can expect the humanitarian intervention promised by the new era**

The last units of the Soviet army left Afghanistan in February 1989. After seven years of fruitless UN sponsored talks, aimed at linking a political settlement to the Soviet withdrawal, the UN congratulated itself on providing a fig leaf for Gorbachev's realism in ending what had become an impossible burden.

It was one of the longest and costliest interventions of the Cold War and the last battleground on which the superpowers fought out their rivalries. Crippled by the prevailing deadlock in the Security Council throughout its duration, the UN was powerless to intervene effectively; Kabulis can be forgiven for feeling abandoned by the UN now that it is reaping the benefits of superpower co-operation enabling it to intervene in other parts of the post-Communist world. Particularly since the hasty withdrawal of UN officials from the capital in the summer of 1992.

While the conflict in Afghanistan began as a civil war, the responsibility of the superpowers for escalating it into a far more deadly struggle are inescapable: in the one case by sustaining a minority government in power with all the might of its army and, in the other, by arming, financing and supporting politically the rival factions among the Afghan *mujahedin*.

Located at the boundaries of competing spheres of political influence, Afghanistan has repeatedly been the victim of the interests of its

Afghanistan 1988, departing Soviet army: goodbye to all that

bigger neighbours. In the nineteenth century, it was the board on which Britain and Russia played out the Great Game, the one seeking to protect its Indian Empire, the other coveting control of this borderland in its own imperial push south.

The Cold War period once more placed it on a fault line: the meeting point of Soviet and US spheres of influence. The change of regime in Kabul in December 1979, the beleaguered new government's invitation to Moscow to come to its aid and US efforts to 'roll back the tide of Communism', plunged it into deeper chaos, the effects of which are still felt by its population.

Between 1979 and the retreat of the Soviet army in 1989, both the USA and the USSR invested vast resources in their proxy war. What Moscow intended as a 'police action' of limited duration became a costly military adventure, with serious international and domestic side-effects. Moscow's assistance to the Kabul regime was estimated at between US$2 billion and US$3 billion in 1989.

In backing a guerrilla resistance to a puppet regime, the USA claimed to be supporting a national war against armed aggression: intervention in the cause of liberty. Without US aid — which by 1985 amounted to US$280 million in arms and funds, channelled through the military regime of General Zia-ul-Haq in Pakistan — the Afghan *mujahedin* could not have sustained their resistance. From 1986 the USA added more sophisticated hardware; by 1988, total aid from the USA, Saudi Arabia and smaller backers had reportedly reached around US$1 billion.

When the superpowers quit Afghanistan they left behind a devastated country, its agricultural infrastructure destroyed, fields sown with landmines, a landscape littered with razed villages and battered towns (*see p191*). It was denuded of over half its population — 5 million refugees in Pakistan and Iran, 1.5 million dead — hundreds of thousands of men, women and children maimed and wounded and many, many orphans.

Apart from a hiatus in 1992, when the Soviet-backed regime finally collapsed, the war has continued ever since. The Afghan *mujahedin*, awash in sophisticated US weaponry, turned it first on the regime in Kabul — and then on each other, completing the destruction they inherited. Kabul, relatively untouched by the war until 1992, has been reduced in parts to vast acres of rubble. The city is without most basic services; those citizens still living in the half-ruined capital run serious health risks.

The effects of the war are also evident in the continuing political instability. The government in Kabul rules only nominally; warlords or semi-independent commanders are in control of many areas where they continue to contest power with each other, with little regard for the centre. The poppy crop for opium and heroin exports is spreading as farmers turn to what is now the most lucrative cash crop, largely unhindered by any organised control. The disintegration of the country — a fragile state even before civil war broke out in 1978 — into mini-states formed along ethnic and tribal lines — seems a real possibility.

And the population — inside the country and outside in refugee camps — pin what hope is left on humanitarian intervention by the UN.

The UN explains its neglect of Afghanistan on the grounds that it is 'overstretched' from Somalia to Bosnia. More simply, Afghanistan is a low priority, an unending, unglamorous and unrewarding involvement. A peace mission under Mahmoud Mesteri, former foreign minister of Tunisia, did start work this year, but Afghan critics see it as little more than a token gesture. Even UN secretary-general Boutros Boutros Ghali's visit to Islamabad and New Delhi in September 1994 was more concerned with the Kashmir dispute than with Afghanistan.

Reconstruction aid for Afghanistan in the aftermath of the Soviet withdrawal was conceived on a grand scale, hundreds of millions of dollars annually. Now, with other calls on their money closer to home, pledges by big donors are hard to find.

An Afghan-originated peace plan, launched by a guerrilla commander, Maulvi Jalaluddin Haqqani, at the end of April, emphasised the need to find funding for peace: to pay Afghans not to fight, rather than leaving them dependent on warring rival leaders. The plan had little to tempt some of the key players, notably Gulbuddin Hekmatyar or General Dostum, and was still-born. Professor Rasul Amin, former head of the political science department of Kabul University and director of the Writers Union of Free Afghanistan (WUFA) based in Peshawar, states what many Afghans believe. Acknowledging the destructive personal ambition of the warlords, he nevertheless insists: 'The Russians and Westerners have a moral responsibility to clean up the mess they created in Afghanistan,' rather than shrug it off as an 'internal matter' for which the Afghans alone are responsible. What, he asks, is preventing the international community from mounting a humanitarian intervention?

**Afghanistan is a low priority, an unending, unglamorous and unrewarding involvement**

Many Afghans, including leaders among the warring factions, share his view; they are equally cynical about UN efforts to date and sceptical of any real help from that quarter. A stinging attack on the UN's record in Afghanistan appeared in *AFGHANews*, the organ of Jamiat Islami, in July this year. 'The UN officials responsible for Afghanistan have avoided the hardships of war, leading lives of relative luxury in Pakistan while receiving high salaries for duties they are unwilling to carry out,' claimed its editorial. 'The UN decision to open its main office in a provincial capital (not Kabul) plays into the hands of meddlers, by endangering central authority and national unity.' ❏

● *But the UN lately re-entered the arena: in November, President Rabbani and five of the guerrilla factions have accepted, in principle, its latest peace plan which, for the first time, could bring all the warring factions to the table*

# NEWS & MEDIA REVIEW

DAVID MILLER

# Auntie gets a whiff of glasnost

*A dismal retrospective of 25 years of television coverage of Northern Ireland had a happy ending: the IRA renounced violence and the government lifted the broadcasting ban*

*I think this was one of the BBC's darkest hours — what happened in August 1969. It was the case then that Catholics were being driven out of their homes in certain areas of West Belfast. There's no doubt about it. They were burned out, all one night. The next day we had all the pictures of them having been burned out. We had pictures of them fleeing. The Controller, Northern Ireland at the time, who had great power in these things, ordered me — because I was the reporter on the ground — that I was not allowed to identify the refugees as Catholics. He said that would be inflammatory and provoke more trouble. I was too green, too inexperienced and just probably didn't know enough at the time to stand my ground.*
Martin Bell, BBC reporter, 16 August 1994

*The sectarian riots [in 1969] led to the biggest movement of population western*

*Europe had seen since the Second World War. Catholics were put out of their homes by Protestants. Protestants were forced out by Catholics and, in some rare cases, people were even ordered to leave by their own side.*
BBC reporter, 9 O'clock News, BBC 19 August 1994

In 1969 Martin Bell had to be instructed by the Unionist-inclined Controller of BBC Northern Ireland, Waldo Maguire, to omit the sectarian character of the Protestant assault on Catholic homes. In 1994 no such pressure was required for a BBC journalist to indulge in rewriting history.

Bell was speaking on a *Late Show* special, part of the BBC's series *25 Bloody Years*. Billed as a season of programmes marking 25 years of the Troubles, it was, as *Fortnight* magazine's Paul Nolan observed, 'a history of British television in the troubles'. The series included three of the most controversial programmes of the Troubles: Kenneth Griffith's *Hang Out Your Brightest Colours*, about the life and death of IRA commander Michael Collins; Paul Hamman's *Real Lives* programme 'At the Edge of the Union', which aroused controversy over the appearance of Sinn Féin's Martin McGuinness; and Thames Television's 'Death on the Rock', which challenged the British government's version of the SAS killings of IRA operatives in Gibraltar. This was the first British television screening of *Hang Out Your Brightest Colours*, which had spent most of the previous 20 years locked in a safe after being banned in 1973.

At the time of 'Death on the Rock', BBC Northern Ireland also made a programme on the Gibraltar killings, but cautious senior BBC managers denied it a network showing. Throughout the 1980s, mounting government intimidation created an atmosphere of extreme caution in broadcasting, and particularly in the BBC. The screening of these three films alone, therefore, is suggestive of the thaw within the Corporation.

The series also included people from all sides — nationalist, unionist and British army — talking of their experiences in the troubles. There were moving accounts of the death of a relative in 'The Dead', and not only those killed by the 'terrorists' were featured. Peter Taylor presented 'A Soldier's Tale', in which British army personnel talked candidly of the suffering they had faced, but also the suffering they had inflicted, including beating up and torturing suspects. One more or less admitted to murder. Taylor also presented a personal compilation of the history of the troubles, which included many archive interviews with key players on the republican and loyalist side, such as Sean MacStiofain, a former IRA chief of staff.

Their appearance (their words spoken by actors to comply with the broadcasting ban) was a reminder that, if there is *glasnost* inside the BBC, it does not mean that journalists are as free to report as they were in the early 1970s. As Taylor pointed out, interviews with active current members of the IRA could not have been filmed for the series. Taylor also acknowledged, in a closing comment after Griffiths' film, that the likelihood of programmes such as *Hang Out Your Brightest Colours* 'being made and transmitted in 1994 is — to say the least — slim'.

In fact, there were also potential problems in screening the three controversial programmes in the series. The whole series had to be referred up to director-general John Birt and the inclusion of the three programmes did, according to BBC sources, 'raise the temperature'. Another problem was that Lord Howe, the former Foreign Secretary who had tried to have 'Death on the Rock' banned, wrote to the director-general complaining about the Corporation organising a 'fiesta of terrorism'. Birt, however, apparently wrote back dismissing his complaint.

The relatively more liberal atmosphere in the BBC might in part be due to broadcasters who take a long-term interest in covering Northern Ireland now occupying fairly senior positions in the Corporation, such as reporter Peter Taylor, head of documentaries Paul Hamman and executive producer of the *25 Bloody Years* series Steve Hewlett. The new atmosphere also seems to be related to the departure of Margaret Thatcher as prime minister, the more benign approach to the BBC of the post-Thatcher Conservative Party and the current weakness of the Major government.

The changing relationship between the government and the BBC has been described by John Naughton, the *Observer*'s television critic, using the example of *Panorama*, the BBC's flagship current affairs programme: '*Panorama* functions as a weathervane indicating how the wind blows in the BBC. Under Alasdair Milne it was a cheeky, nose-thumbing, fuck you kind of outfit. Under the early Birt regime it was a spavined hack kept under a tight leash lest it offend Mrs Hacksaw. It is significant that virtually the only seriously embarrassing *Panorama* investigation to reach the screen in that period was [a] report on [Robert] Maxwell — a well-known Labour supporter who funded Neil Kinnock's private office. Anything which might have been embarrassing to the Tories... was held back until the moment of maximum impact had passed. But now the wind has changed. The Charter is in the bag and the government is in disarray. After years of relentless sucking up to the Tories, John Birt is suddenly seen dancing the night away at Mrs Tony Blair's birthday party. Labour front-benchers can henceforth look forward to an endless round of BBC boxes at Ascot and Wimbledon.'

> The lifting of the ban does not mean the media will take on the role of fourth estate watchdog... other methods of control remain

The climate for covering Northern Ireland has also been shifted by the emergence of the peace process (although *25 Bloody Years* was commissioned before the peace process became even a whisper). The *25 Bloody Years* series was quickly followed by the IRA ceasefire on 31 August; and then, two weeks later, by the lifting of the broadcasting ban. The ban had been made untenable by the emergence of the peace process in which Sinn Féin had a central role. Sinn Féin's *de facto* exclusion from the news under the ban was ended and Gerry Adams and other Sinn Féin representatives appeared extensively. For the first time the ban began to look unsustainable.

It also began to be counterproductive for the government. John Major acknowledged as much when he lifted the ban: 'I believe the restrictions are *no longer* serving the purpose for which they were intended' (emphasis added). Major went on to state the other major reason for the lifting of the ban, which is the changed relationship between Sinn Féin and the government. 'Most importantly', he said, 'we are now in very different circumstances from those of 1988 when the restrictions originally came in.'

However, the lifting of the ban does not mean that the media will suddenly take on the role of fourth estate watchdog. Direct censorship may be gone but other methods of control — public relations, intimidation, the use of the law and self-censorship — remain. As the BBC news history of the 1969 riots quoted above shows, selective memory continues to afflict television news coverage of Northern Ireland. ❑

BASSEM EÏD

# Open letter to Yasser Arafat

*A Palestinian journalist warns the PLO leader against setting a dangerous precedent*

'Without the freedom to express our opinions there can be no human dignity. If this freedom is not respected, then the very foundations of human dignity are flouted. The recent decision by the president of the Palestine Liberation Organisation, Yasser Arafat, to halt the circulation of the paper *An-Nahar* in the Palestinian trust territories represents a serious attack on human rights and a heavy blow to the prospects of democracy in the future Palestinian state. This decision is all the more worrying because, in our modern society, the press plays an essential part in the struggle for human rights.

The reasons for the banning of *An-Nahar* are still to be fully explained. From high up on the balcony of his home, President Arafat looks down on the town of Gaza. It is, he explains, an administrative problem which will be cured once *An-Nahar* has a licence to circulate. On the other side of the mountains, in the town of Jericho, Jibril Rajoub, Palestinian security chief, claims that *An-Nahar* will never be allowed to print again. Yasser 'Abd Rabbo, communications minister for the Palestine National Authority, has tried to pacify critics of the ban with a series of nonsensical claims that he wasn't consulted about it. The other key characters in this drama are Nabil

LUBOMIR MIHAILOV

Sha'ath, who half-heartedly criticises his boss's decision, and Nabil Abu Radeina, Arafat's adviser on the media, who argues that *An-Nahar* is not a 'real' paper anyway. What on earth does he mean by that?

I would like to ask, sir, the following question: can you envisage a time when, the various problems of the self-governing Palestinian territories being solved, it would be a simple administrative matter to grant *An-Nahar* a licence?

A few days ago I was severely criticised following an interview I gave on the radio during which I had said that international aid granted to the Palestinian authorities should be stopped until such time as the ban on *An-Nahar* was lifted. In response to my demand my critics argued that thousands of starving Gazans would suffer if international aid were halted. If the well-being of the Palestinian people is indeed your first concern, Mr President, would that not be best served by lifting the ban on *An-Nahar*? Dozens of families who depend on the paper for their livelihoods.

I also have a second question: why does *An-Nahar* need a licence to be printed in Jerusalem when no other paper, Palestinian or Israeli, needs one?

Between you and me, Mr President, this ban came as no great surprise to me. What did surprise me is

**'I put my faith in the power wielded by journalists, free to report the truth as it happens'**

how quickly you acted. The banning of the paper came into effect within two weeks of your arrival in Gaza. Quick work. And I'm quite sure no-one could have convinced you to reverse your decision.

Our country is still young: I do not know if the people of Palestine realise how important a free and independent press really is. I can't quite understand why the daily *Al-Quds* has said nothing about the ban on *An-Nahar*. Could it be that *Al-Quds* has not managed to overcome the rivalry between the two papers which has existed ever since *An-Nahar* appeared in 1987? *Al-Quds* should have spoken out against the ban in the interests of a free and independent Palestinian press. I am also shocked by the fact that Palestinian human rights organisations have said nothing about it. I would like to ask them how long they intend to keep up this complicitous silence. The Association of Journalists has also kept quiet. When I rang them up to find out why they had not spoken out, I was told that the Association no longer existed and had not done so for a year.

The banning of *An-Nahar* foreshadows other attacks on our rights. It will clearly be difficult, if not impossible, to catalogue violations of human rights and protest against them if we no longer have independent media in which people are free to express themselves without the fear of a sword of Damocles hanging over them.

Editorials in the European press roundly condemned the banning of *An-Nahar*. These editorial writers have commented, rather naively, that this could be the way of things in our much-discussed 'new era'. But I put little store by public declarations: I put my faith in the power yielded by journalists, free to report the truth as it happens. Neither do I think that European editorial writers will have much influence on our leaders.

If this really is the 'new era' that we have been promised, I want it known that I count myself among those Palestinians who are entering it reluctantly, and with a heavy heart.

Yours sincerely...'

*Translated from* La Lettre *of Reporters Sans Frontières number 61 by Carmen Gibson*

● JVH adds: *An-Nahar* returned to the newsstands on 5 September. A front-page announcement in the Monday edition said the paper's former managing editor, Osman al-Anani, had departed. Al-Anani had been notably pro-Jordanian; the banning occurred only days after Israel had signed the peace deal with Jordan that angered the PLO. *An-Nahar*'s first issue after the banning praised Arafat as 'The Brother, The Leader, The Symbol', and made no reference to the matter of the licence. ❏

HERVÉ DEGUINE AND ROBERT MÉNARD

# Are there any journalists left in Rwanda?

*The long list of journalists killed since the massacres began on 6 April, puts a question mark over the future of the Rwandan media*

Journalists have never before been murdered in such numbers; even the macabre inventory of names as it stands today could yet be incomplete. The chaos inside and outside the country with millions displaced or in refugee camps makes a definitive list impossible.

While it may be true that certain journalists were killed because of their ethnic background — out of a total of 37, two thirds are Tutsi and one third Hutu — most of them were long-standing names on hit lists because of their professional activities and political involvement.

This is certainly true of André Kameya, editor of *Rwanda Rushya* and a member of the liberal party. In return for publishing a list of 200 massacred in Baggwe in January 1991, and an article denouncing the fact that Palipehutu militants were being trained by the Rwandan army, he had received death threats and been in and out of prison. His wife and one of his children were killed with him.

Vincent Rwabukwizi, a native of Gitarama, and director of the bi-monthly *Kanguka*, met the same fate. He was assassinated by soldiers around 12 April outside his home in the Nyamenango area of Kigali. Rwabukwizi, who was sympathetic to the Rwandan Patriotic Front (RPF), had been in the government's sights for four years. He was arrested on 3 July 1990 for publishing an interview with the last Tutsi king and sentenced to 15 years on 22 October 1990 for 'collaboration with the enemy'. Released on 7 May 1991 and confined to Kigali, he was incarcerated again on 29 May, on a charge of 'sapping the morale of the armed forces fighting the aggressors'. After being freed once again in September 1991, he lived in hiding.

Emmanuel-Damien Rukundo worked for *Rubyiruko-Rubanda* and was president of the newspaper publishers' association of journalistic standards. He was murdered on 24 April in the St Paul Centre, by a group of frenzied soldiers, after they had stripped him, lashed him to a truck and driven him through the streets. His executioners chopped his corpse into pieces.

★ ★ ★

There are few witnesses to such murders who lived to tell the tale. Charles Karinganire of *Le Flambeau* (The Flame), however, was killed in front of his young brother Théogène. 'I was with my brother at Kiyovu's house in Kigali on 24 April when soldiers and *interahamwe* — the party youth organisations turned death squads in the course of the fighting — came to the door. They caught Charles and hacked him to pieces right in front of me with machetes and knives.' Théogène escaped by leaping over a barrier. The attackers opened fire but failed to hit him and he hid in a church until his evacuation on 13 June.

Alfonse Rutsindura was attacked with machetes as he returned home on his motorbike; his wife, children and parents were murdered in their home. Rutsindura, the editor of *Amakuruki i Butare*, was first arrested on 5 October 1990 and held in prison for six months because of a report on the massacre of Butare students carried out by Rwandan army soldiers in May 1990.

**For most of the dead journalists there are no histories, no obituaries: they are just names on a long list**

For most of the dead journalists, there are no such histories, no obituaries: they are just names on a long list. But there were others who escaped to bear witness to the government's determination to wipe out any voices of opposition or admonition.

From the moment the killing began until the RPF's victory in July, André Sibomana, editor-in-chief of the Catholic weekly *Kinyamateka*, was a hunted man.

A Hutu turned Tutsi 'accomplice' for 'thought crimes', Sibomana was a prime target for the *interahamwe*.

Abbot Sibomana now does the work of a bishop in the cathedral at Kabgayi, the centre of Rwandan Christianity: his predecessor was murdered by the RPF along with about 15 other priests.

Despite frequent battles with the Catholic hierarchy, Sibomana had made *Kinyamateka* the country's most

Rwanda 1994: the RPF arrive in Kigali

serious newspaper and, in the process, become the 'father of journalism' for a whole new generation of journalists in the independent press that came into being along with political pluralism in the early 1990s.

Now he wants to get back to journalism: 'I prefer it to my mitre.'

The day before they came to get him, Sibomana was working on a piece about human rights violations. It was the last thing he wrote for a long time. 'The next day, I couldn't get into the paper: every time I went up to the door, someone shot at me. I had to take refuge in the nearby St Paul Centre until 12 April.

'The outbreak of the massacres came as no surprise. I had written about it in several editorials in *Kinyamateka*: said again and again that blood would flow. I knew about the threats President Habyarimana had been receiving. I knew the Presidential Guard wanted to kill him.

'Then RTLM (Radio-Télévision Libre des Milles Collines) radio *(Index 4&5 1994)* announced that a 'top brass accomplice' had hidden in the centre. They meant me. At 11.30am on 12 April, I left my hiding place; at 2pm, the soldiers came looking for me.

'In order to get to my parish in Kabgayi, I had to get past several roadblocks. At one of them I nearly got killed. I was saved by a girl, an *interahamwe*, who recognised me and whispered, "Abbot, they're looking for you, they want to kill you," before asking the man operating the barrier to let me through.

'I'd only got about 50 metres down the road when others recognised my car and started yelling that I had to be arrested. I put my foot down. They gave chase. At the next roadblock, a colonel I knew let me through with him. I owe him my life.

'I didn't spend a single night at the bishopric. They were looking for me. I went to the hills where I was born and managed to survive.

'The magazine *Kangura* and RTLM sent out messages calling for racial hatred and violence against the Tutsis and their so-called accomplices. They preached intolerance. Others, such as Radio Muhabura, the RPF radio station, broadcast propaganda, appealing for soldiers to desert, but they used the station to incite hatred. On the contrary, they denounced the actions of the *interahamwes*. Certain newspapers stood up for human rights, *Imaga* and *Kinyamateka* among them. But we were overcome.

'We made a mistake: we underestimated the force of the propaganda. That was a mortal error. Of course, we denounced it before the mass killings took place, but without the necessary vigour.

'They were very well prepared and had a lot of experience. Take Gaspard Gahigi, the director-in-chief of the radio station: he had been in charge of a newspaper in Togo, and then *Murwanashyaka* in Kigali. He was one of our most respected journalists and knew what he was doing. But as soon as he started work at RTLM he started to think with his wallet rather than his brain. He sold himself to the MNRD, the former ruling party.

'Habimana Kartano also had a great deal of experience behind him. We were fascinated by his broadcasts. They were very good indeed — until he started asking people to kill each other. Noel Hitidana was a long-standing employee of Radio Rwanda and very popular. It was unbelievable: people really loved him. He had a way of catching your attention. But when he started at RTLM, he became a different person.

'It was even worse in the French-language broadcasts. Georges Ruggiu, a Belgian, was scathing, acerbic and full of hatred.

'From mid-May right to the end, Radio Rwanda and RTLM broadcast the same calls for ethnic hatred: for people to kill, massacre and exterminate. Like RTLM, Radio Rwanda was also in the hands of Hutu extremists. They asked people to round up the "accomplices", or in other words, anyone who wasn't in cahoots with the Habyarimana gang.

'We talked about it. We looked at measures we could take against these "journalists". But they were beyond our control. It has mainly been human rights organisations that have denounced this sort of media abuse.

'Genocide was possible partly because of the general atmosphere of impunity. Killers risked nothing, and hadn't done so for years. And the press has to take its share of the blame: too many journalists were in cahoots with murderers and kept a lid on what was really going on. No one is above the law and journalists are no exception. Press freedom does not mean they have the right to say whatever they like.

'I don't think we'll have as many newspapers as we did before the war (over 70 titles). The people, like the authorities, no longer want to see extremism in the media, as they did in *Kangura* or RTLM. Also, lots of print works have been vandalised. Not to mention all the journalists who have been killed. We are going to need a great deal of courage to get back on our feet again. And a lot of help.

'I was asked to take over the administration of the diocese after the death of the bishop, the vicar and almost all his colleagues. But this is provisional: I don't want to spend the rest of my life as a bishop. I love journalism. That way I can serve the people and that's what I want to go on doing.' ❏

*Translated from* La Lettre *of Reporters* Sans Frontières *number 62 by Tom Nicholls*

**The press has to take its share of the blame for genocide: too many journalists were in cahoots with murderers and kept a lid on what was going on**

GENEVIÈVE HESSE

# Propaganda going cheap

*Germany's taxpayers finance the government's election campaign, and the journalists fall for it*

LUBOMIR MIHAILOV

When television ads and poster campaigns are no longer effective enough in persuading the voters, enlist the media proper. Germany's Christian Democrats (CDU) are well aware of this ploy. In 1993 the Bundespresseamt (Federal Press Bureau), which is directly financed by the government in Bonn, gave two specialised agencies a total of DM1.6 million (US$1 million) of taxpayers' money. The agencies use these funds to produce political commentaries supporting the CDU and criticising the opposition Social Democratic Party (SPD).

At first glance, the agencies — Hörfunk Fernsehen Neue Medien and Presseplan — resemble independent agencies in almost every respect, including their names: 'New Media Radio/TV' and 'Press Plan'. Christoph Schulte, a journalist who worked for one of them until June 1993, was taken in by the tempting offer of DM150 (US$95) for each radio commentary and a reliable guarantee of daily work. Until it was made clear that he ought to be showing a bit more enthusiasm for

the Christian Democrats if he didn't want to see his wages drop. Time and again, civil servants from the Bundespresseamt would openly ask him to praise the stance adopted by the CDU on international, social or domestic policy matters; the views of the SDP were either to be suppressed or held up to ridicule.

Not content with setting out to corrupt a few impecunious journalists, these agencies also appealed to radio stations by offering their products at rock bottom prices; broadcast ready 'news' bulletins for the price of a 'phone call. All for free. The offer was widely taken up by private radio stations, and the public station Mitteldeutsche Rundfunk has also broadcast bulletins on a regular basis, according to Schulte.

Chancellor Kohl's spokesman, the head of the Bundespresseamt, maintains that he knows nothing about pressures brought to bear on journalists by some of his civil servants. He will, however, be forced to explain things in court since the SDP have instigated legal proceedings in the Constitutional Court, accusing the Bundespresseamt of using methods which contravene the Constitution. ❏

*Translated from* La Lettre *of Reporters Sans Frontières number 61 by Carmen Gibson*

LUIS ROJAS VELARDE AND
CRISTINA L'HOMME

# Pious intentions

*Villagers take on the government in a fight against toxic dumping*

Wrapped in ponchos to keep out the bitter August cold, the inhabitants of Patacamaya, a village in the Bolivian Altiplano, have gathered to protest against waste dumping in their village. Their demonstration is unprecedented; it blocks the traffic on the Pan-American highway, the trunk road linking Bolivia's main towns. They want the government to remove what the Patacameños claim are 'toxic and radioactive' mineral waste dumps in open ground near their homes. The waste leaks a white powder that causes skin irritations.

Media interest was roused when Radio Pio XII — a privately-run Catholic radio station — took up the case. The station broadcasts from a village where the only economic activity is related to mining. From 1960 to 1970 Radio Pio XII had backed the miners in their struggle against the government. Last year, the national press joined forces with the radio to condemn a deal between Bolivia and Germany that allows the dumping of waste refused by other countries. The Chilian authorities, for instance, would not grant the waste convoys permission to enter their territory.

As a result of the fall in mineral prices on the international commodity market, several state-owned mines have been closed. The government turned to recycling mineral waste as an answer to the decline of the local mining industry and to prevent miners from uneconomical pits turning to the production of cocaine.

The government's first response to sustained criticism was a programme on public television justifying their decision on economic grounds, and 'demonstrating' that the infamous waste dumps were not toxic — despite the fact that they had been placed in special containers as a precaution against leaking. The broadcast was ineffective and the authorities finally decided to relocate the deposits. The outraged inhabitants of Siglo XX, a village near the proposed site, demanded the 'instant removal of the deposits to the most distant location possible'.

Things came to a head in August with the demonstration on the Pan-American highway, jointly organised by the two villages. The blockade threatened serious economic repercussions countrywide and was brutally dispersed. One person died in the ensuing riots.

The Catholic Church got involved when a local priest accused the authorities of lying about the nature of the imported substances. Radio Pio XII had supported the villagers throughout the conflict, despite the increasing politicisation of the dispute and government attempts to bring them to heel.

Jaime Villalobos of the mining ministry accused Radio Pio of 'hating mining, foreign investment and modern technology'. He alleged that Radio Pio's newscasts were at best selective, at worst hostile to the government. He further accused the station of backing mining unions that want pits to revert to state-ownership. At the start of the year, President Gonzalo Sánchez de Lozada, who has been in power since August 1993, had been forced to negotiate an agreement with the unions for the restructuring of Comibol, a public mining enterprise.

In August, Radio Pio replied publicly to continuing harassment from the mining bureau: 'If we were hostile to mining we wouldn't have been working in this area for the last 35 years. We are in favour of foreign investment, but there must be fair

play... so that financial gains find their way to areas which are having their resources exploited.'

Villalobos, alleging that the station could be fuelling subversive activity, asked the president of Radio Pio to provide detailed explanations for all news items on the waste dumping. The latter was also summoned to the mining bureau to listen to a defence of the government's integrity.

The radio station has asked the International Association of Radio Broadcasting in Bolivia to appeal directly to the President of the Republic on its behalf. ❏

*Translated from* La Lettre *of Reporters sans Frontières number 62 by Tom Nicholls*

LUBOMIR MIHAILOV

IRANIAN LETTER

# Faith in numbers

*An open letter signed by 134 Iranian writers living in Iran on 24 October 1994 and sent to the Iranian Ministry of Culture and Islamic Guidance, newspapers and magazines in Iran, International PEN and PEN centres and writers' organisations worldwide*

We are writers, but because of unresolved issues in the contemporary history of Iranian and other societies, the image of writers held by the government, sections of society and even some writers, has become distorted. In consequence, the identity of the writer, the essence of his/her writing and the collective presence of writers has become the subject of confusion and inappropriate reactions.

We Iranian writers, therefore, see it as our duty to elucidate the nature of cultural work and the raison d'être of our collective presence.

We are writers. As such we express and publish our emotions, imagination and exploration in different forms. It is our basic natural, social and civil right that our written work — including poetry, novels, short stories, plays, film scenarios, literary research and criticism and translations of foreign works — reach our audiences without any interference and impediments. Everyone is entitled to make his/her judgement about a literary work and is free to embark on its criticism after a work is published. But before a work is published, no-one nor any institution has the authority, under any pretext and excuse, to interfere with or create obstacles to its publication.

When, as individuals, we cannot overcome such impediments to our writing and thinking freely, we see no alternative but to resort to a collective, professional stand against these barriers. In other words, to realise our freedom of thought, expression and publication, we must stand together and act collectively.

We believe that by joining together in a professional association of Iranian writers, we shall, collectively, guarantee our individual independence. A writer should be free to choose how s/he wants to create his/her work and analyse and comment on others' works. The individual alone is responsible for her/his personal, political or social acts and thoughts; equally, a writer's participation in the common causes and issues of *'ahl-e qalam'* (those who write) does not make him/her accountable for the individual dilemmas, problems and predicaments faced by any other writers.

While this may seem obvious, rather than being seen as a writer and portrayed as such, s/he is often judged not by reference to his/her works but by an affiliation — or alleged affiliation — to a party, group or faction. As a result, by coming together in a professional, cultural framework, they are thought to be forming a political movement.

Governments, institutions and cliques affiliated to governments normally appraise and scrutinise the work of a writer in the light of political exigencies and the myopic dictates of day-to-day considerations. Furthermore, by fabricating ad hoc interpretations and allowing speculations which have no foundation in truth, the collective identity and presence of writers is attributed to specific political tendencies or seen as a by-product of conspiracies hatched inside or outside the country. Individuals, institutions and affiliated cliques then use the same fabrications as evidence against writers whom they attack, humiliate and threaten.

We want, therefore, to emphasise that our priority is to remove all obstacles to freedom of thought, expression and publication. Any distortion, any different interpretation of our aim is untrue. We deny any responsibility for such interpretations, the liability for which lies with those who fabricate them.

Accountability for anything written rests with its author and whoever signs it. The responsibility, therefore, for whatever is published and circulated inside or outside the country, agreeing or disagreeing with us, or signed by others, rests with the individual.

Everyone has the right to analyse and appraise any written work; this is not confined to a particular institution or group. Criticism is the prerequisite of cultural progress. But to invade the private life of a writer in pursuit of evidence to criticise her/his work, is a flagrant violation of individual human rights and personal privacy. To condemn a writer for her/his morality or ideological views is undemocratic and violates the writer's principles and dignity. The defence of the human and civil rights of any one of them is incumbent on all writers.

To sum up, our collective identity and presence is the only guarantee for our individual freedom and independence. The thoughts and acts of an individual, however, have no bearing on the collective identity of writers. In coming together in an independent professional association for writers, we are merely following the democratic process.

Signed:

*Manoochehr Atashi, Amir Hossein Arianpour, Daruish Ashoori, Shaheen Ahmadi, Massoud Ahmadi, Shiva Arastooi, Hassan Asghari, Mohammadreza Asslani, Jahanghir Afakari, Asghar Elahi, Maftoon Amini, Seyed Abdollah Anvaar, Mansour Ouji, Parviz Babai, Ali Babachahi, Mohammadreza Bateni, Reza Barahani, Shapour Bonyad, Mohammad Baharloo, Simin Behbahani, Mihan Bahrami, Mohammad Biabani, Bijan Bijari, Bahram Beyzai, Shahrnoush Parsipour, Rouien Pakbaz, Bagher Parham, Hassan Pasta, Alireza Panjeie, Ahmad Pouri, Hassan Pooyan, Mohammad Poyandeh, Changiz Pahlevan, Behrouz Tajvar, Ahmad Tadaion, Goli Taraghi, Faroukh Tamimi, Alireza Jabari, Kamraan Jamali, Hashem Javadzadeh, Mohammaad Javaherkalam, Shapour Jorkesh, Reza Joolai, Jahed Jahanshahi, Reza Chaichi, Amir-Hassan*

Cheheltan, Houshang Hessami, Ghafar Hosseini, Khosrow Hamzavi Tehrani, Zia-al-din Khalegi, Mohammad Taqi Khavari, Aliasghar Khebrehzadeh, Abotorrab Khossravi, Mohammadreza Khossravi, Azim Khalili, Mohammad Kallili, Simin Daneshvar, Ali Ashraf Darvishian, Mahmoud Dowlatabadi, Khashayar Deyhimi, Akbar Radi, Morteza Ravandi, Fariborz Rais-Daana, Nosrat Rahmani, Moniroo Ravanipour, Ghassem Robeen, Esmail Raha, Ebrahim Rahbar, Abass Zariab Kho'i, Kazem Sadaat Ashkevary, Freshteh Sari, Gholaam-Hossein Salemi, Mohammad-Ali Sepanloo, Jalal Satari, Faraj Sarkoohi, Alireza Seif-al-dini, Ahmad Shamloo, Mohammad Shari-fi, Mohammad-Taqi Saleh-pour, Sanal Sehati, Abdolrahman Sadrieh, Omran Salahi, Farzaneh Taheri, Masoud Toofan, Hooshang Ashourzadeh, Shirin Ebadi, Abdol-Ali Azimi, Mashiat Alai, Ghazeleh Alizadeh, Mehdi Ghairai, Hadi Ghairai, Soodabeh Fazaeli, Mohammad Ghazi, Mehdi Gharib, Azita Ghahremaan, Mehranghiz Kar, Media Kashighar, Manoochehr Karimzadeh, Bijan Kelki, Sima Kooban, Abdolah Kossari, Ja'far Koushabaadi, Mansour Kooshan, Lili Golestan, Houshang Golshiri, Shahla Lahiji, Shams Langheroudi, Javad Mojaabi, Mohammad Mohammadali, Ahmmad Mahmoud, Abass

Mokhber, Mohammad Mokhtari, Hamid Mossadegh, Mahmoud Mo'taghedi, Ali Ma'ssoumi, Shahab Mogharebin, Shahriar Mandanipour, Kiomars Monshizadeh, Elham Mahvizani, Jamaal Mirsadeghi, Ahmad Miralai, Mohsen Mihandoost, Keyvan Narimani, Gholam Hossein Nassiripour, Nazanin Nezam-Shahidi, Jamshid Navai, Sirous Niroo, Safoora Nayeri, Mohammad Vojdani, Esmail Hemati, Koroush Hamehkhani, Hamid Yazdanpanah, Ebrahim Yoonessi. ❑

Translated by Ahmad Ebrahimi

## How the Iranian government sees its writers

Published in Jomhuri Eslami, Tehran, a leading daily close to Iran's spiritual leader, Ayatollah Ali Khamenehi, in response to the open letter

I have enclosed my check for renewal of my subscription to *Periodica Islamica*. Congratulations on what I find to be an excellent publication. Indeed, I have argued with librarians and professionals, particularly those involved with Islamic/ Middle Eastern affairs, that a publication such as yours is far superior to data bases, which I also support and use. Publication such as *Periodica Islamica* is far more comprehensive and current than most data bases I have had access to...Keep up the good work.

SANFORD R. SILVERBURG
CATAWBA COLLEGE, SALISBURY
NORTH CAROLINA, USA

**P**eriodica Islamica is an international contents journal. In its quarterly issues it reproducers tables of contents from a wide variety of serials, periodicals and other recurring publications worldwide. These primary publications are selected for indexing by *Periodica Islamica* on the basis of their significance for religious, cultural, socioeconomic and political affairs of the Muslim World.

   *Periodica Islamica* is the premiere source of reference for all multi-disciplinary discourses on the world of Islam. Browsing through an issue of *Periodica Islamica* is like visiting your library 100 times over. Four times a year, in a highly compact format, it delivers indispensable information on a broad spectrum of disciplines explicitly or implicitly related to Islamic issues.

- - - - - - - - - - - - - - - - - - - - - - - - - - - >✂

PERIODICA
ISLAMICA
AN INTERNATIONAL CONTENTS JOURNAL

Editor-in-Chief: Dr. Munawar A. Anees ❏ Consulting Editor: Zafar Abbas Malik (Islamic Arts Foundation, London)

 Periodica Islamica, Berita Publishing, 22 Jalan Liku, 59100 Kuala Lumpur, Malaysia

## Subscription Order Form

Annual Subscription Rates:
☐ Individual US$40.00
☐ Institution US$200.00

Name:_____

Address:_____

City(+ Postal Code):_____ Country:_____

☐ Bank Draft/International Money Order in US$           ☐ 🏛 Coupons

☐ AMERICAN EXPRESS   ☐ MasterCard   ☐ VISA                Expiration Date_____

                                                          Signature_____

☐☐☐☐ - ☐☐☐☐ - ☐☐☐☐ - ☐☐☐☐

📞 BY PHONE                    📠 BY FAX                    ✉ BY MAIL

To place your order immediately,     To fax your order, complete this order     Mail this completed order form to
telephone (+60-3) 282-5286          form and send to (+60-3) 282-1605              *Periodica Islamica*

SUBSCRIBERS IN MALAYSIA MAY PAY AN EQUIVALENT AMOUNT IN RINGGIT (M$) AT THE PREVAILING EXCHANGE RATE

# WOLE SOYINKA

# The last despot and the end of Nigerian history?

There was once a thriving habitation of some half a million people in south-eastern Nigeria, the land of the Ogoni. It is an oil-producing area that had suffered much ecological damage. That damage has received world publicity largely due to the efforts of a feisty and passionate writer called Ken Saro-Wiwa, himself an Ogoni. A leader of the Movement for the Salvation of the Ogoni People, MOSOP, he exposed the plight of Ogoni to the United Nations Minorities Council, calling for the recognition of the Ogoni people as one of the world's endangered minorities. He agitated for compensation for damaged crops, polluted fishing ponds and the general destruction of what was once an organic economic existence of his people (*Index* 4&5/1994).

That at least was in the beginning, some two or three years ago. Now, Ken Saro-Wiwa is held in chains in a hidden prison, incommunicado. He is seriously ill — he suffers from a heart condition — and is totally at the mercy of a gloating sadist, a self-avowed killer and torturer of the military species, specially selected for the task of total 'pacification' of Ogoniland. Saro-Wiwa's people have taken to the surrounding forests and mangrove swamps to survive. Those who remain in townships and villages are subjected to arbitrary displacement, expropriation of their property, violence on their persons and the rape of their womanhood. Ogoniland has been declared a 'military zone' under the direct rule of a 'Task Force on Internal Security'. Within this enclave, reporters, foreign or local, are made unwelcome and in some cases, brutalised. In any case, the stable of an effective Nigerian press is being constantly reduced through illegal closures by the police on orders from the military. Before long, even those who penetrate the iron curtain of Sani Abacha's militarised enclave will have no media through which to remind the Nigerian populace of the atrocities daily inflicted on their Ogoni compatriots.

One ongoing actuality of repression very easily obscures another; it is a familiar and understandable pattern, one that dictatorships, especially of the most cynical kind, exploit most effectively. For the majority of Nigerians, Ogoni is only some localised problem remote from the immediate, overall mission of rooting out the military from Nigerian politics, rescuing the nation's wealth from its incontinent hands and terminating, once for all, its routine murders of innocent citizens on the streets of Lagos and other more visible centres of opposition. The massacres in Ogoni are hidden, ill-reported. Those that obtain the just publicity of horror, mostly in government-controlled media, are those that are attributed to the Ogoni leadership movements, such as MOSOP.

Yet the accounts of such

Ken Saro-Wiwa: 'feisty and passionate'

MAC DAVIS AJIBADE

incidents, and careful investigations, lead to more than mere suspicions of dirty tricks, of covert military operations designed to discredit the leadership, throw the movement in disarray and incite ethnic animosity between the Ogoni and their neighbours, thus instigating an unceasing round of blood-letting...

Ogoniland is the first Nigerian experimentation with 'ethnic cleansing', authorised and sustained by the Nigerian despot, General Sani Abacha. His on-the-spot operatives, Lt Colonel Dauda Komo, and Major Paul Okutimo are Nigeria's contribution to the world's shameful directory of obedience to orders over and above the call of duty. The so-called 'Task Force on Internal Security' is doomed to be Abacha's sole legacy to the nation, Nigeria's yet unheralded membership card of the club of the practitioners of 'ethnic cleansing'...

Ogoniland is, alas, only the model space for the actualisation of a long-dreamt totalitarian onslaught on the more liberated, more politically sophisticated sections of the Nigerian polity, which have dared expose and confront the power obsession of a minuscule but obdurate military-civilian hegemony. Ogoni people are, alas, only the guinea-pigs for a morbid resolution of this smouldering inequity that was instituted by the British as they planned for their departure. The beneficiaries remain, till today, a minority made up of a carefully nurtured feudal oligarchy, and their pampered, indolent and unproductive scions.

The carefully propagated myth of an uncritical, political solidarity within this section of the populace, the 'North', was only recently exploded however... In a sense, it was not until the national elections of 12 June 1993 that the collapse of that fiction became irrefutable, thanks to the conduct of those elections which was universally acclaimed a model of fairness, order and restraint.

The pattern of voting also made it abundantly clear to the entire world that the so-called gulf between the North and the South was a deliberate invention of a minor power-besotted leadership and its divisive gamesmanship. There is indeed a line of division in the North, but it was drawn between the workers, peasants, civil servants, petty traders, students and the unemployed on the one hand, and the parasitic elite and feudal scions on the other. These last, the beneficiaries of that ancient deception, are now traumatised. They cannot cope with this stark revelation of a nationalist political consciousness, so triumphantly manifested in the 12 June elections...

After the initial noises of realism and surrender to a popular, democratic will, the reprobates of the old order recovered their breath and recollected their endangered interests, regrouped, and ranged themselves behind a mouldy concept of an eternal right to governance and control. The latest instrument of their feudal, despotic will is General Sani Abacha, the last in the line of the reign of deception, of obfuscating rhetoric and cant in the service of a straightforward will to domination by an anachronistic bunch of social predators. Their notion of a historic mandate of power is not only warped and mindless; it may prove terminal to the existence of the nation if its most faithful facilitator to date, General Sani Abacha, succeeds in clinging to office for another six months, maybe less. That is our reading of this crisis of nation-being, and then Nigeria goes down as yet another forgotten smear on the geographical atlas of the world.

Of late, the Nigeria media have virtually waxed hysterical over the increasing arrogance and obduracy of this minority, thanks largely to the boastful performances of their most disreputable members. One notorious example is the lately returned fugitive Umaru Dikko, the Task Force specialist on rice importation, who barely escaped being crated back to Nigeria to face military justice under General Buhari. In denouncing the activities of this minority, described variously and often imprecisely as the Sokoto Caliphate, the Northern Elite, the Kaduna Mafia, the Hausa-Fulani oligarchy, the Sardauna Legacy, the Dan Fodio Jihadists etc etc, what is largely lost in the passion and outrage is that they do constitute a minority, a dangerous, conspiratorial and reactionary clique, but a minority just the same. But their tentacles reach deep, and their fanaticism is the material face of religious fundamentalism.

But it is not just the Nigerian free media — and perhaps, before it is too late, our nettled general of the occupation forces of media houses will be made to realise this. Public debate — in bars, bus stops, the markets, the motor garages, staff and student clubs, government offices etc etc, largely in the South, naturally — have catapulted the activities of this minority to the heart of the national crisis, resulting in questioning the hitherto assumption (and 12 June affirmation) of the nation as a single entity. And the military, by its sectarian alliance with these claimants of divine attribution of power, has lost the last vestiges of any claims to neutrality in all areas of the contest for civic power. On 23 June 1993, the day of the arbitrary annulment of the national presidential election, the military committed the most treasonable act of larceny of all time — it violently robbed the Nigerian people of their nationhood.

Those who still advocate therefore, that Sani Abacha has inaugurated his own programme of transition to civil rule from a 'sincere interest of the (Nigerian) nation at heart', are bewildering victims of a carefully nurtured propaganda that began with the erstwhile dictator of Nigeria, General Ibrahim Badamosi Babangida. It was this propaganda, waged on an international scale, and funded to the tune of millions of dollars, that enabled quite a few, normally intelligent analysts at the Africa desk of foreign powers to propose that the expensive, impossibly tortuous transition-to-democracy programme of Abacha's predecessor was a well-considered, disinterested programme that objectively recognised the peculiar nature of Nigerian politicians, to which abnormality the good General was merely responding...

But IBB was at least an original. What Nigeria is confronting today is a species of mimic succession that considers itself innovative. The

Ogoniland, Nigeria 1990: protest by Ogoni refugees

imposition of a Constitutional Conference by General Sani Abacha, as a 'solution' to the artificial crisis developed from a free and fair election, is really a pitiable compliment to IB Babangida, who at least played that con game with panache, milking it eventually to death. In Abacha's hands, it is a squeezed-dry, humourless patent for any would-be dictator. It is a fair assessment of the IQ of Sani Abacha that he actually imagines that this transparent ploy for self-perpetuation would fool the market woman, the roadside mechanic, the student, factory worker or religious leader of whatever persuasion. Even the village idiot must marvel at such banal rivalry of a disgraced predecessor.

Nigerians simply do not believe for one single moment in this conference, not even the propagandist who must churn out the government line; even less the volunteers and conscripts he has gathered together in Abuja for this non-event. The participants are mostly economically exhausted politicians, who cannot resist a six-month sabbatical without obligations, all expenses paid and some; they are chronic wheelers and dealers looking for a quick financial chance — from the inexhaustible (but drastically devalued) government purse; politicians seeking a free and painless venue for some horse-trading against the resumption of civilian party politics etc etc. There are, of course, also the anti-democratic die-hards, the aforesaid guardians of the very private precinct of power, for whom the very notion of an actualised 12 June election, that declaration of national unity, must be expunged from memory for all eternity...

Not to be forgotten — however academic it may sound, given the nature of military rule — is the fact that Abacha's administration is patently illegal, and has been thus proclaimed by the Nigerian law courts...

We have gone to court once again to obtain a separate declaration on Abacha himself. This move involves more than an academic exercise however. The Nigerian populace is being primed for a campaign of comprehensive civil disobedience. They are being reinforced in their conviction that their cause, and their acts, are backed by law; that it is an outlaw who presently inhabits Aso Rock; that his closures of media houses and confiscation of passports are illegal — nothing but plain thuggery; that his seizure and operation of the nation's treasury and revenues are nothing but acts of banditry; that his imagined authority to try anyone for treason is the ultimate ridicule of a judiciary that his very presence in Abuja (and contemptuous flouting of court orders) subvert; that his detention of any Nigerian citizen is nothing but the hostage-taking tactics of two-a-penny terrorists...; that, in short, he may exercise power through the gun, but he lacks authority even in the most elastic sense of the word, and that this emptiness must be made increasingly manifest in public acts of rejection...

Abacha's recent address to the nation, one which re-emphasised his determination to decide our destiny through this still-born conference, was, of course, not unexpected. This particular despot differs from his predecessor in his inability to cope with more than one line of thought, or anticipate more than one course of action or response in any given month. His address, however, fell short, for now, of the scorched-earth policy that we had expected him to declare — the proscription of the striking trade unions, imposition of a state of emergency, the closure of more media houses and yes, even detention camps for dissidents. *[Soyinka's fears were fulfilled in Abacha's September decrees. See p224.]*

**Abacha will be satisfied only with the devastation of every aspect of Nigeria he cannot mentally grasp, and that is virtually all of Nigeria**

The blueprint for these measures has been worked out, and military units — veterans of random slaughter of civilians — even deployed to opposition strongholds for a ruthless clamp down on the populace. The necessary decree was drafted — no, not from the Attorney-General's office, that misguided lawman had long been sidelined — but from the Presidency itself, where the Secretary to the Government, one Alhaji Aminu Saleh, an unabashed 'capo' of the notorious minority has taken over the functions of law-drafting, recruiting private lawyers to do the dirty work that the AG had shown increasing reluctance to undertake. The government prosecutors of the President-elect, Basorun MKO Abiola were, for instance, recruited lawyers from private practice, contracted not by the Attorney-General's office, but by Aminu Saleh. His bold, unchallengable incursions into the zone of authority even of generals within the cabinet are already public knowledge.

It is necessary to alert the world now that this plan has merely been shelved, not abandoned. Abacha, let no one be in any doubt, has resolved to subjugate the strongholds of opposition in an even more ruthless manner than he did last year when, as Babangida's hatchet-man, he succeeded in murdering over 200 pro-democracy demonstrators.... This time round, a far more systematic response has been outlined: Nigeria, especially the south-west and the oil-producing south-east, are to be 'Ogonised' in a thoroughgoing blitz. The trade union leaders, the intellectual and professional opposition are to be sequestered and subjected to absolute military control under the clones of the Dauda Komos and Paul Okutimos.

Abacha is resolved to spread the 'Ogoni' solution throughout southern Nigeria. A minuscule being and matching mind, but with a gargantuan ego, he feels personally insulted by the resistance to his delusions and has sworn, if it came to the crunch to 'wipe out the very oil wells those labour unions are using to blackmail us.' That statement is a very reliable quote. Abacha is out to out-Saddam Saddam's parting gift to Kuwait. Anyone who believes that Abacha will not kill the goose that lays the golden egg forgets that, in any case, the General's private barn is already bursting with a vast deposit from Nigeria's obliging goose.

Those who wish to understand the catastrophe towards which the Nigerian nation is being propelled will do well to study the personalities of the present and the immediate past Nigerian military despots.... Babangida's love of power was visualised in actual terms — power over Nigeria, over the nation's impressive size, its potential, over the nation's own powerful status (despite serious image blemishes) within the community of nations. The potency of Nigeria, in short, was an augmentation of his own sense of personal power. It corrupted him thoroughly, and all the more disastrously because he had come to identify that Nigeria, and her resources, with his own person and personal wealth.

Not so Abacha. Abacha is prepared to reduce Nigeria to rubble as long as he survives to preside over a name — and Abacha is a survivor. He has proved that repeatedly, even in his internal contests with Babangida. Totally lacking in vision, in perspectives, he is a mole trapped in a warren of tunnels. At every potential exit he is blinded by the headlamps of an oncoming vehicle and freezes. When the light has veered off, he charges to destroy every animate or inanimate object within the path of the vanished beam. Abacha is incapable of the faculty of defining that intrusive light, not even to consider if the light path could actually lead him out of the mindless maze.

Abacha has no IDEA of Nigeria. Beyond the reality of a fiefdom that has dutifully nursed his insatiable greed and transformed him into a creature of enormous wealth, and now of power, Abacha has no NOTION of Nigeria. He is thus incapable of grasping what is being said to him by some entity that speaks with the resolute voice of the Civil Liberties Organisation, the Campaign for Democracy, the National Democratic Coalition, the Market Women, Civil Servants, Student Unions, Labour Unions, the Press etc, etc. None of these could possibly be part of his Nigerian nation, and it is only by eliminating them in toto, by silencing such alien voices that Nigeria can bemoan the entity that he recognises...

Abacha will be satisfied only with the devastation of every aspect of Nigeria that he cannot mentally grasp, and that is virtually all of Nigeria. He will find peace and fulfilment only when the voices whose nation-language he cannot interpret are finally silenced, only when, like the Hutus, he cuts off the legs of the Tutsis so that Nigeria is reduced to a height onto which he can clamber.

These voices however, and the history that brought them into being, and with such resolve, have already ensured that Abacha is the last despot that will impose himself on the Nigerian nation. Of course, there will be others who will yield to temptation and attempt to tread the same path of illusion, but their careers will be so short-lived that they will hardly be noticed in passing. The strategy of the present struggle is such that the people are attaining an unprecedented level of self-worth within a national being that defines anti-democrats as treasonable conspirators, and precludes any future automatic submission to the sheerest suspicion of military despotism, even of a messianic hue.

The danger, the very real danger however, is in the character of this last torch-bearer for military demonology, the puny Samson whose arms are wrapped around the pillars, ready to pull down the edifice in his descent into hell. That hell that is Ogoniland today is the perception of nation compatibility of which Abacha's mind is capable. What does not readily yield to his obsessive self-aggrandisement both in power and possessions is alien and must be subjugated and 'sanitised'. In Sani Abacha's self-manifesting destiny as the last Nigerian despot, we may be witnessing, alas, the end of Nigerian history. ❏

9 November 1989: the first chink appears

# Post-Wall world

**The record of five turbulent years since the revolution of '89 is full of ambiguity: the joys of freedom v the pains of the market; new Communists v old liberals; democracy v nationalism. All still to play for**

# W L WEBB

# Media, market and democracy

**Getting the press out of the hands of state and Party and into private ownership was a key priority of post-Wall governments. That was the easy part: since then, things have not gone entirely as expected**

After five formative years, the influential press in east central Europe — at least in the 'big three' countries of the Visegrad group, Poland, Hungary and the Czech Republic — has not only continued to put its weight firmly behind representative democracy, it remains supportive of continuing economic reforms involving large-scale privatisation, the reduction of government spending and involvement in the economy and, generally, the aspiration to install modern market economies in place of collapsing, sclerotic command systems.

Even former party battleships like *Rude Pravo* (Red Right) and *Nepszabadsag* (Freedom of the People) remained almost as steady in this basic orientation as papers like *Gazeta Wyborcza* (Election Gazette) in Poland and *Lidove Noviny* (National News) in Prague, both of them born out of the *samizdat* traditions of the political struggle against bureaucratic socialism.

A corollary of this support is that there is relatively little regular and influential media backing for the forces that from time to time dissent from the culture of modern liberal capitalism. Things have been rather different in the electronic media. But there, too, except in election broadcasts and listeners' and viewers' grumbles about specific hardships, there have been few divergent views on how to run an economy.

What this commitment to the market economy seems to mean is that when the chips are down the papers' 'line' will oppose strikes and accept the argument of market imperatives, as practically all influential papers in Western Europe traditionally have done.

All this is not only remote from the days of state-party-directed media, it is not what might have been expected from the liberal-social democratic political culture in which many Western observers thought opposition to Communism was most securely grounded. To understand the origins of the present steady chorus of approval for economic liberalism, one must look at the culture of journalism and the deeper historical roots of today's politics.

A dapting von Clausewitz, one can see journalism as the continuation of history by other means, a fairly desperate attempt to separate out from the racket of events what will still matter in a year's or a century's time. When one looks at the recent history of journalism in the countries of east central Europe, it's necessary to see things in this light, just as it's necessary for journalists from the Western world to learn quickly that history is different, darker, more dangerous stuff east of the Elbe, alive and volatile, and frequently the clue to what otherwise seems enigmatic or simply irrational in contemporary politics. It was a Hungarian historian who said that in this part of the world 'the past is never idle.'

There are more up-to-the-minute formulations: for example, 'History speaks louder than the IMF.' This is the observation of Andre Hrico, an editor in the industrial city of Kosice, who in spite of the anti-Meciar, anti-regime stance of his paper goes on to remind us of one of the things Slovaks feel they know about history in their particularly impoverished corner of the poorer end of Europe: that after 1,000 years of oppression by Hungary, it was the Communists 'who delivered the Slovaks from village huts with mud floors into modern apartment blocks, steady jobs and an education for their children in their own Slovak language.' The Czech historian, Zbynek Zeman, from his chair of European history at Oxford, adds: 'In contrast with the chronic and murderous instability of Eastern Europe in the first half of the century', he writes in his study *The Making and Breaking of Communist Europe*, 'the second half stands out as a period of comparative achievement and calm.'

Even this measured judgement is not how we are accustomed to think of the fate of these nations in the years since Churchill and Roosevelt gave them to Stalin to look after. But it is a perspective which supplies part of the explanation for what has been happening in the opinion polls and the electoral polls in much of the region during the last unsettling year, reminding us that what they reflect is not entirely a kind of empty-headed peasant nostalgia for a time that never was. Memories here are longer and stronger than people in the West are used to, and not only the large cohorts of pensioners, but many to whom intellectual freedom is not an absolutely integral component of their professional identity weigh that time of 'comparative achievement and calm', with all its dour limitations, against the bruising rough and tumble of the rush to market which must often seem to be destroying far more than it creates. 'I'm afraid we have lost the fight for people's memory,' Bronislaw Geremek, one of the leading Solidarity intellectuals, then floor leader of Mazowiecki's party, was reported as saying in Lublin the other day. 'Freedom of the press, freedom of choice, elections: all that is important in the heat of a revolution. But in peaceful times, it is the material aspects of life that count.'

To understand what role journalists and media institutions have been playing in the transformation of their societies and economies since 1989, we need to know something of the history and cultures they emerged from. One of the practical problems about the decay of the sense of history that spread from America to Western Europe in the second half of this century is that when the West thought of Eastern Europe at all, it tended to think of its history as having begun at Yalta, or in the brief historical no-man's-land between the end of the Hitler war and the beginning of the Cold War.

At some time in the late 1970s I asked one of West Germany's best known poets and critics for his instinctive response to the word 'Dresden', and his reply was not, 'the ruined Florence of the North', nor, 'the place where Wagner and Bakunin might have met on the barricades in 1848', nor even, 'the place where the world first heard *Rosenkavalier* and where 33 years later the British and Americans incinerated nearly 100,000 German refugees'. No, what he said was: 'Dresden? A city in the GDR.' The danger now, I suppose, is that all too quickly the history of east central Europe will seem to have begun in 1989.

So, to have some sense of where these countries are up to in history, one needs to remember, for example, that the 18th/19th century partition of Poland between Prussia, Russia and Austria-Hungary had regionalising effects on the culture and economic development of the country that are even more visible today than they were in the

Communist years: that much of what was going on in Hungarian politics between 1989 and this spring's election was an attempt at a Restoration of the post-feudal politics left by the demise of the Austro-Hungarian Empire; and that the media battles so often at the centre of that politics had living roots in the old tensions between the *echt*-Magyar culture of the countryside and the cosmopolitanism of the Hungarian town, with its Jewish-German culture, above all of Budapest.

Through such educative encounters in history, one begins to understand the scale of what is being required of these new democracies. It is hardly more than five years since a time when every editor in eastern Europe and most of his senior staff could be appointed only with Party approval, and the larger journals had a higher proportion of police informers on their payrolls than most other institutions.

**The danger now is that, all too quickly, the history of east central Europe will seem to have begun in 1989**

Broadly speaking, privatisation — that crucial link in the argument that would establish a symbiosis between democracy and capitalism in the face of much discouraging evidence — began with the press. How this was done, how freely this press market actually operated, varied from one country to another, but in each of the three most developed countries of what Germans used to call *Zwischeneuropa,* the lands between Germany and Russia, it was clear that getting the press out of the hands of state and party-controlled institutions into private hands was among the highest priorities of policy. The case of the electronic media everywhere proved to be much more complicated, and the balance there between private or public ownership is still nowhere finally resolved.

The Polish press privatisation, the most rapid and systematic, was in various ways something less — or more — than a purely free-market operation. The commission set up to liquidate RSW–Prasa, the vast state press empire, had an eye not only to how much was bid but to where the bid was coming from, with a marked preference for editorial buy-outs, especially when they were backed by Solidarity-connected groups or money. One specific directive was that the process 'should not lead to the domination of the Polish press market by foreign capital', a formulation which would have reverberations later. At the time, it meant, in practice, that the commission must ensure that the newspapers of Silesia didn't fall

'Since the latest revelations about his past, Herr Müller doesn't show himself in public any more!'

into the hands of Springer, Bertelsmann, Gruener und Jahr.

The Czech way was different. Remarkably, considering the anxiety about any possibility of allowing claims to property by the descendants of former Sudeten German expellees, no great political fuss was raised when most of the regional papers owned by the big provincial towns in what had been the Sudetenland were sold off by the cash-strapped municipalities to the Passauer-Presse group.

In Hungary, too, there was far less anxiety about 'foreign domination' or indeed about any kind of hard currency investment, and large interests in the national press were bought up at bargain prices by various international groups, among them Bertelsmann, the French group Hersant, and the Murdoch and Maxwell enterprises. The most extraordinary coup in this first round of what has come to be known since throughout the region as 'wild privatisation' — the commercial culture of the Wild West reborn a century later in the Wild East — was pulled off between the two rounds of the general election that changed everything in the spring of 1990. In that brief hiatus Springer secured control of six regional dailies, five weeklies, 10 smaller local papers and 40 other titles.

It is interesting to compare what happened to the powerful central Party dailies in each of the three countries. In Hungary, a major, and later a controlling share in *Nepszabadsag*, was taken by Bertelsmann, part of the deal, as in nearly all these transactions, being that the investor would equip the paper with the new technology which had lately been revolutionising the industry in the West. Recently, when the paper's managing editor, Andre Kerteszy, left to organise the expansion of the former trade union paper *Nepszava* (People's Words), now in the hands of a Hungarian video shop tycoon, Bertelsmann put in its own man to replace him, but as manager more than editor. There have been no complaints of interference in editorial policy, and the paper remains by far the largest and most influential in the country. Its 'line', in so far as it has anything so unreconstructed, follows a fairly hard economic liberal course in its leaders, occasionally tempered by concern in other pages, especially the readers' letters page, about poverty, unemployment and other social costs of rapid marketisation.

When the Party which used to own and control it went perforce into opposition, *Nepszabadsag*, now under the editorship of Zdenek Porybny, its talented and energetic former Washington correspondent, added to its masthead, as a parting gesture, the line 'a socialist daily'; when the post-Communist successor party to the old Hungarian Socialist Workers' Party (HSWP) won its famous victory this spring, the line was dropped and replaced with 'a nationwide daily'. But it clearly has the best connections still to the corridors of power, and is unchallengeably Hungary's best informed paper, a necessary daily read.

Prague's *Rude Pravo* also retains the largest circulation in the country and remains well-informed and full of news, putting its sources of information to better, and certainly more mischievous use than it was ever allowed to in the past. *Rude Pravo* — now more right than red — has the role of opposition paper rather more to itself than it should have for the health of Czech journalism and politics; and the rump Czech Communist Party at least found it independent enough to feel obliged to start its own daily, *Halo Noviny* (Hello News). *Rude Pravo* thinks both personal taxes and especially taxes on business profits are too high, deplores the weakness of the bankruptcy laws, runs a manager-of-the-week column, and is generally very positive and sympathetic about the situation of the Czech entrepreneur, of which the dynamic editor, who owns a large slice of his paper's shares, is indeed a notable specimen.

The case of the former Polish Party paper, *Trybuna* (formerly *Trybuna Ludu*, Tribune of the People), is different and not without a certain irony. It never had the absolute dominance of *Rude Pravo* and *Nepszabadsag* because the press in Poland was always more diversified; it faced real competition even before Solidarity and the underground press further undermined its position. After the Restoration or reformation, it was briskly ejected from its fine offices on Aleje Jerosolimskie which were given to *Rzeczpospolita* (The State Gazette), the still partly state-owned former 'government paper' that has a role as the established 'paper of record'.

A t this point, it's relevant to consider the Polish results of a large survey of 'Elites and Continuity' whose findings were described and discussed in March in *Gazeta Wyborcza* which was allowed to Solidarity in the run-up to the country's first free elections. The paper is now both Poland's best-selling and most politically influential national daily, a rare combination. The survey, conducted last year in Poland, Hungary and Russia, showed that as much as 45 per cent of the new business elite in Poland formerly belonged to the PZPR (the former Communist Party), and only 43 per cent had never belonged to it. The authors of the report, Jacek Wasiliewski and Professor Wnuk-Lipinski, describe Poland's present managerial culture as the product partly of 'a brisk duplication of the former business elite', partly of a phenomenon which could justifiably be termed 'a deputy manager's revolution'.

One might add that pre-election polls showed that the SLD — the reconstituted PZPR — had the largest proportion of small businessmen among their supporters. Three years ago the owner and editor of *Nie!* (No!), one of the most remarkable, scandalous and commercially successful of all the new publications, told me where his support and large readership mostly came from. This corpulent, jug-eared and slightly sinister champion of certain strata of the new economic elite is none other than the former Communist vice-premier and minister of information, Jerzy Urban, notorious for the scurrilous wit of his treatment of Solidarity politicians and the Church in his regular press conferences during the years following the imposition of martial law. In opposition, his well-edited scandal sheet has continued to attack the same targets. 'I keep loyal', he says, 'to the Establishment of which I was a member, and defend the former authorities against attack.' His readers, he told me in 1991, were the new rich class, among them certainly many of the nomenklatura capitalists, while others represented a different recruiting ground of the New Class — successful survivors of what he called 'not the political, but the economic underground of former times, the "Change money?" business'. A member of the latter class provided financial backing for the paper for the first three months while it got on its feet.

Much of the new economic elite seems to combine a self-interested enthusiasm for free market ideology with a certain loyalty, or sense of kinship with the more reconstructed survivors of the old political elite. And here is a significant part of the explanation for a striking feature of the present-day press, which is a near unanimity in the way it addresses its readers about the essential questions of economic policy. This general 'line' on economic policy can be observed not only in the Czech Republic, with its strict and particular monetarist administration, but also in countries like Poland and Hungary which have lately voted into power coalitions in which much the more powerful partner is a party which calls itself social democratic but whose historical roots are in the Communist parties which were so soundly defeated and rejected just five years ago.

It is difficult to hear of views in the national press, at any rate outside the letters pages, which dissent significantly from certain propositions about economic policy. All the papers (except in the case of the Czechs, with their proudly balanced budget) tell you that there must be a lower budget deficit, severe monetary control, and 'reform' of the social services, although when it comes to specific proposals for cuts, the consensus may dissolve into temporising generalisations.

Press support for continuing and, where possible, speeding up privatisation, is practically as general; in Poland, the press have been making this the litmus test of whether the post-Communist government is going to stick sufficiently to the straight and narrow, and Prime Minister Pawlak's hesitations over the third tranche of privatisations and his interest in the half-way house of 'commercialisation' were followed daily with the beadiest attention. Any real back-tracking on privatisation would have the press chanting in unison with the former prime minister Jan Bielecki: 'The third way leads to the Third World.' It's true there has been a lot of ironising from Adam Michnik's *Gazeta Wyborcza*, which speaks for, indeed from, the heart of the old intellectual leadership of Solidarity, about this sea-change among ex-Communist politicians, but *Gazeta* too accepts, as it has to, the retort of Grzegorz Kolodko, the coalition's minister of finance, whose 'Strategy for Poland' has been endorsed for its generally orthodox intentions by several of Poland's international bank managers: 'All right, guys. But do you want us to continue with the reforms or not?'

Jerzy Bacinski, editor-in-chief of the Polish weekly *Polityka,* was interesting about this broad economic liberal consensus among senior journalists, pointing out that since privatisation most of them were appreciably better paid than before. Journalists, for the first time, weren't just part of the relatively status-privileged 'service intelligentsia', but now themselves belonged to the economic elite, and had the most practical of reasons to see and share its point of view. One can guess at other reasons: for example, that to journalists in early middle age the tough-mindedness of born-again economic liberalism is still pretty dashing in its repudiation of all that went before — the excitement of an intellectual world turned upside down again.

It seems that some part of the mind of east central Europe, having escaped from that post-Yalta time when the clock of history stopped for a couple of decades, had now got stuck at another time — the moment at the end of the 1980s of the eternal triumph of liberalism and 'The End of History', from which, elsewhere, the world had begun to move on.

It was true, Bacinski had said, that there was a gap between the opinions on the economy expressed in the press and the opinions expressed in the polls, which amounted to a vote for slowing down the marketisation process. 'But if the main job of a political elite here and

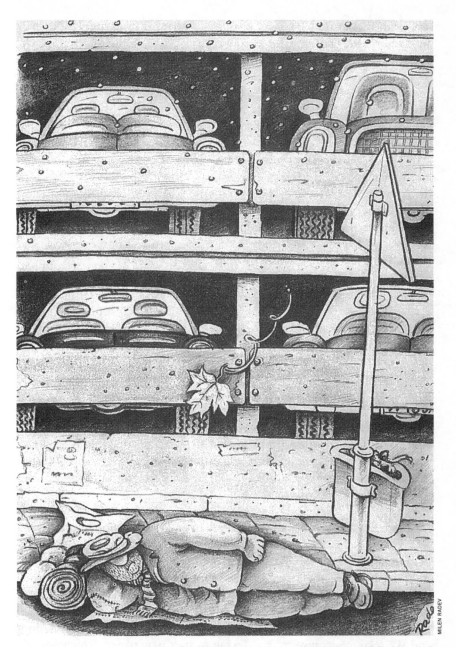

'In peaceful times it is the material aspects of life that count'

now is to modernise,' Bacinski went on, offering a justification as well as an economic explanation for the consensus, 'then the press has a role in that too.' Parenthetically, except by observation, one doesn't easily come by information about what kind of people journalists are in eastern and central Europe. What the Survey of Elites reported on by Wasiliewski and Wnuk-Lipinski has to say about the cultural elite — in science, culture, the media — is that about 25 per cent of it consists of people who were similarly placed in 1988 in the old order, with a 5 per cent addition of former senior state or party officials now living on their pens and wits. Otherwise, new people firmly dominate, most of them (as in the new political elite) being of the relatively highly qualified intelligentsia. It's difficult to say how representative journalism's share is in this. Veteran journalists, like Ernest Skalski of *Gazeta Wyborcza*, Andre Kerteszy of *Nepszava*, and *Rude Pravo*'s rather younger Porybny, complain about the lack of professionalism among the newer entrants. So do people involved in the various Western agencies still offering help and training to journalists in the post-Communist world. An adviser at the Prague Centre for Independent Journalism described a profession in a condition rather different from that reported in Warsaw by Jerzy Bacinski. There was considerable turnover in the trade. Some newspapers, like *Telegraf*, had changed hands several times, and bright young people were hard to keep. Young journalists were poorly paid, and tended, when trained, to defect quickly to foreign commercial firms as analysts and local advisers. She reported also a rather touching reluctance, especially among recruits with roots in the old opposition, to take on editorial hiring and firing jobs, seeing the editing function as a sort of censorship, which made for baffled relations with new foreign owners to whom readers were not a congregation of citizens to be addressed, but just another class of consumer.

There now emerges a kind of correlative consensus among politicians, left as well as right, about the media. In government the old right resented bitterly the fact that so much of the press was in the hands of the political liberals, the heirs and collaborators of those oppositionists, writers and intellectuals, who had the best connections to Western journalists and through them to the foundations providing aid: these were the people who tended to be at the head of the queue for privatisations and Western media investment. Trying to start new papers which nobody wanted to read, they turned their attention to the electronic media, still largely state-owned, suspending the independent chairmen of television and radio, and putting in their own, who then suspended whole production and editorial teams of people thought politically unsympathetic. At the height of the Hungarian media wars, hotly fought on the other side by the press, there were more than 400 of these people in a kind of limbo — 'the gulag', they called it — still paid, but never called to make a programme (*Index* 3/1994). The scandals continued into the spring election campaign, which was marked by pervasive distortion of the news.

As media manipulation goes, it was hardly of the same order as that reported from Kiev during the recent Ukrainian presidential election, when the television commentator at a football match interrupted the flow of the game to bring viewers the news that each member of the Kiev Dynamo team had personally assured him that he would be casting his vote for President Kravchuk. Such stories remind me that in considering the state of the media, as in all other matters political, it is necessary to distinguish between the condition of the countries immediately to the east of Germany, with a modern tradition of independent nationhood to which they have returned, and that of their eastern neighbours among the CIS states. In Belarus, for example, the established press is under government control. 'The government finances it and appoints the editors of the newspapers', Ihar Hiermancuk, the editor of *Svaboda*, a small independent biweekly journal in Minsk, told *Index on Censorship* recently. 'Every editor knows that if he gives space to opposition views, he won't be editor much longer.' Whatever the unresolved problems of the media in Poland, Hungary and the Czech Republic there is no comparison between the freedom of access to arguments and facts there, with the conditions that prevail in the countries immediately to the east.

Still, people working in television throughout the region will recognise ruefully the force of a joke a Polish editor told me last month. 'Journalists say that working in television is like working in the mines. There can be an explosion at any time, and you never know why.' In Poland, the Independent Broadcasting Council has its third chairman in not many more months, the first having been summarily sacked by President Walesa when the council granted a licence for the country's first independent television station to someone the president didn't approve of.

The latest explosion in the media mines, demonstrating the consensus among politicians, has also occurred in Poland, where the politicians of a government of the left have been complaining almost as loudly about media bias as those of the right once did and proposing to do something about it. Part of the declared ground for this is a concern about foreign domination of the media.

Some months ago, Adam Halber, an SLD Sejm deputy (MP), proposed the institution of a National Press council, along the lines of the existing Broadcasting Council, to be embodied in a press law that would impose a limit on the extent of foreign ownership of newspapers.

That it may not be such an unpopular policy is suggested by the finding of a Demoskop poll reported during the summer by the daily *Nowa Europa*. The poll — taken soon after Adam Halber's proposal — showed half the respondents fearing foreign domination of the Polish media, while a third said that foreign firms should be barred from setting up newspapers, magazines, or radio and TV stations in Poland.

The news kiosks — many of them still located at the convenient street corners where the appropriate authorities of the three partitioning powers of Poland in the nineteenth century set them up for the easy confiscation of offending editions in times of crisis — now fairly bulge with Polish carbon copies of foreign, especially German, girlie magazines, women's magazines and comics. And, as *Nowa Europa*'s reporter, Miroslaw Szacillo, didn't fail to point out, 'Skalski's praise of the free market notwithstanding, *Gazeta Wyborcza* is not exactly delighted to see that out of the total circulation of 50 million copies of colour magazines, 20 million are carbon copies of German magazines.' Ernest Skalski, *Gazeta*'s managing editor, and a journalist as well as vice-president of the company's executive board, had attacked Halber's proposals vigorously, and chosen to defend press freedom by referring to 'the cardinal principle of democracy which is the freedom of concluding contracts.'

As to the reality of foreign domination of the press market, as opposed to this fairly ugly dumping of largely lowest common denominator entertainment weeklies, the poll report quoted the opinion of Dr Bajka of the Jagiellonian University's Press Research Centre, that Hersant's Socpresse group alone controlled 20-25 per cent of Polish daily papers, and that 'what we know about the share of foreign capital in the Polish media is surely just the tip of the iceberg.' A later *Nowa Europa* report gave Hersant control of roughly 40 per cent of the Polish press, but added that the French magnate was heavily in debt and might sell his Polish interests — as he had lately sold Budapest's *Magyar Nemzet*. Indeed, by the end of September it was reported that most of Hersant's holdings had been acquired by the German Passauer-Presse, giving a combined circulation of 2.2 million from papers published in Poznan and Katowice in the once-German west, as well as in Cracow, Gdansk and Lodz. This is the group that already controls most of the provincial press in northern Bohemia; its deep penetration of the Polish market gives an altogether new flavour to arguments about concentration of ownership. It also marks the end of the first stage of the new, post-1989 era for the press in Eastern Europe, being only the largest of several retreats of this kind. The next stage, given the shortage of investment capital, especially in Poland, may be difficult.

Psychological reasons for opposing regulation are not hard to find. It is unsurprising that the experience of the older generations of journalists and of those recruited from the underground press should make them ultra-sensitive to any suggestion of government control, and that most of them so far lack any experience that would sensitise them to the dangers of commercial concentration of ownership and control. They lack, for example, the experience of a Murdoch able and willing to cut down the opposition with a ruthless price war and a marked lack of interest in the desirability of a diversified press. Generally, the region's small-time Murdochs — the Schlees and Kudlaceks, to take two lurid Czech examples — have not yet got their hands on serious political papers.

Another immediate inhibitor is that the proposals indicate arrangements roughly parallel to those already made for the electronic media that have produced such a horrendous mess of uncertainties. Perhaps when the new Polish constitution is established and some of the loopholes that exist in so much of the hastily drafted and enacted legislation of the past five years have been sewn up, journalists will have more reason to consider that a press law can also usefully include provisions that are protective of press freedom.

Meanwhile, in September, the Polish government made its relationship with the media even more difficult with the publication of a very widely drawn bill on state secrets and punishments for those who would leak or publish them. Not only was the legislation regressive in itself, it was peculiarly rash and ill-advised from a government of its particular political ancestry. Faced with trenchant condemnation not only by the liberal and right-wing press, but also by papers more friendly to it, a month later, the Communist successor party — half of the coalition government — did a sudden about turn: the bill was voted down in the senate by an overwhelming majority.

It was said that this change of heart and mind immediately followed a meeting with the editors of the old Party organ *Trybuna* and the influential weeklies *Wprost* and *Nie!*, both of them edited by former Communist politburo members, all of them adamant that the bill was unworkably bad. Cynics, however, thought that another reason was to rob the President of the opportunity of vetoing an unpopular measure.

Today, no government in this part of the world that wants to carry on along the road towards a fairly full-blown modern capitalist society will find itself opposed in this programme by the opinion-shaping media. What one won't so easily find in this press, however, except perhaps as an occasional provocation in smart or academic discussion, is much debate of what an interested bystander like Anatol Kaletsky of the *Times* was calling, a year ago, 'in post-Communist politics... the issue that dare not speak its name... should the economy be freed before or after the political system? To put it more starkly: is democracy always compatible with capitalism?' I have the strong impression that such blunt questions touch the raw nerve of history too painfully in central Europe to be trotted out for speculative inspection in a newspaper article.

The last five years has been a great learning experience, in which people have emerged from confusing times with clearer heads: not without some nostalgia for the stodgy stability and simple educational and welfare benefits of the old regime, but rejecting, nevertheless, any idea of returning to a system that had been imposed on them from the east, from not-Europe. And rejecting, also, both the old feudal-nationalistic politics of between the wars and dreams of a Utopian capitalism purer or redder in tooth and claw than any version still practised elsewhere in the world. And in all this, the better half of the newly constituted free press has frequently played, as they used to say in these parts, a leading role. ❏

*An edited version of a contribution to the American Social Science Research Council and Polish Academy of Sciences conference on Democracy and Marketisation, held in Warsaw, September 1994*

# IVAN KLÍMA

# Freedom and garbage

**The profound transformation in the former Soviet Union, in central and eastern Europe, has not only affected political and economic conditions, it has made deep inroads on the way of life, the value system and the culture of these countries**

It may seem paradoxical to speak of 'culture' in connection with a totalitarian regime. One would have thought, after all, that the intellectual sterility, the dogmatism, the censorship, the central control of education and the arts as well as in the life of the church, would leave no room for culture. In reality, however, the situation was not quite so straightforward. Books came out; television programmes were broadcast, and not all of them were contemptible, even in the worst of times. Prague television broadcast marvellous productions of classical plays, nature films, wonderful animated films for children, and so on. Exhibitions were held, and theatres were full. The book market was a narrow one, with few titles available, and the same was true of the repertoire of theatres and cinemas, or even of tours offered by state travel agencies. On the other hand, books and tickets to cultural events were cheap, since everything permitted in culture was heavily subsidised. What was written in the papers or broadcast on radio or television news was, of course, deliberately mendacious and, in fact, mendacity reached into many spheres of life, from what was taught to children to the very act of elections.

Censorship was practised on the broadest possible basis: it not only shielded people from everything that was ideologically suspect, from everything new and potentially disturbing; it also protected them from the worst trash. The pornography or perverse and bloodthirsty thrillers that inundated free countries could be smuggled across the borders on videotapes, but were denied access to the mass media. An exhibition in which an artist kills a sheep before the eyes of his audience and then creates a work from its blood and innards would have been unthinkable.

When thinking about the culture of the so-called socialist era, we should also remember that most people were not longing for things of real value, for change, or even for novelty. In fact, the rapid rate of change in modern life tends to encourage conservatism and supports the notion that art should entertain rather than disturb and provoke. From this point of view, the cultural policies of the totalitarian system corresponded, to some degree at least, to the taste and opinions of the average person, and if there was something wrong with it, it was in not going far enough to meet that average taste, in being too didactic, in not surrendering its basic requirement that art should first of all educate, that is, serve the political system.

**Trash began its victorious march through all spheres of culture. Curiosity had been satisfied, mediocre viewer taste came to the fore**

The totalitarian system created its own way of life, its own hierarchy of values, by which I mean not the values it declared but its actual values. The way of life under totalitarianism at first glance had much in common with the way of life in Western societies: it was aimed at a limited consumerism, it had its own sports heroes, popular singers or favourite hockey teams. Among the values it inculcated were loyalty, obedience, measured optimism, discipline, a positive attitude towards work, egalitarianism. Officially it rejected racism, nationalism, colonialism; officially it declared solidarity with the poor, the oppressed, the non-white. The system cultivated an antagonism towards enterprise, excessive wealth, criticism, towards any kind of deeper thinking; which means it was antagonistic towards the creative intelligentsia, particularly those in the humanities. At the same time, it guaranteed work and wages (even for effort which was more simulated than real), free education (which, however much the system tried to control it, was sometimes a real education) and free health care, the level of which may have been constantly dropping, but which nevertheless was part of the total social security system.

The police state controlled the movements of every citizen, and secured the borders of the country with barbed wire. While this frequently kept decent citizens locked inside, it also kept the worst aspects of international crime out. The knowledge that the state was looking after him, that it was its duty even, became a profound part of people's consciousness and the average loyal citizen could even feel somewhat safer than he feels today in a democratic society. Regardless of how people rebelled against the system and its culture, they unconsciously accepted many of its features and, I would even say, with a certain simplification, that they deliberately developed qualities in themselves that were different from qualities in people who had grown up in free circumstances.

People who refused to accept this way of life, who saw through the mendacity and the falsehood of the system, were usually persecuted. They suffered materially, but perhaps even more they suffered intellectually and spiritually: from a lack of freedom, a lack of information, from a wide variety of restrictions that touched almost every level of their lives. The realisation that they were cut off from the free world — which from a distance appeared in exaggeratedly attractive colours as a world of unlimited possibilities, plenty, affluence, and total freedom — infuriated them and made them feel that their lives had no future, chiefly because the entire social system in which they lived had no future.

This state of mind led to more than just a contempt for the totalitarian system; it led to the perception that a free society (despite the regime's propaganda attempting to persuade them otherwise) was capable of solving all human problems, that it was a model for a perfect arrangement of affairs both social and personal. The USA, as a symbol of such an arrangement, became as well a symbol of that perfection. Everything made in the USA seemed admirable. Alertness to the pseudo-values of the consumer life, resistance to the invasion of mass culture that was

MILEN RADEV

Repeat slowly after me: 'The market economy is good for me...'

typical of cultural life in the free part of Europe — these, to say the least, were not aspects of the cultural climate in the unfree part of Europe. Most people east of the former Iron Curtain entered the new, freer conditions after 1989 culturally unprepared, with none of the antibodies against the chronic infections the value system of the market society and its mass culture concealed within itself (as indeed any human effort does).

In the first few months after the revolution, it seemed that the greatest boom would be enjoyed by things the former regime had forbidden. In literature, for instance, both the work of the dissidents and of Western bestselling authors like J M Simmel or Stephen King, or utter trash that simply reproduced westerns or action stories, became immediately popular. In theatre, it was the work of Beckett or Ionesco as much as plays like the musical version of *Les Misérables*.

The public was simply curious. There was a queue a kilometre long for Václav Havel's first book. The work of dissident writers came out in print runs of 100,000 in a country with 15 million inhabitants. But Beckett soon disappeared from the repertoire of half-empty theatres and the work of even the most famous domestic authors sank to print runs in the thousands. Trash, on the other hand, began its victorious march through all spheres of culture. Curiosity had been satisfied, and mediocre viewer taste, no longer prompted or guided by anything, came to the fore.

**A public unprepared for the sudden explosion of choice appears not to know its own mind; it is a fickle market**

These revolutionary changes touched all spheres of culture, including the value system. Nothing of what used to hold true yesterday held true today. Things considered a sin yesterday are considered meritorious today and vice versa. Even though most people accept this transformation, not everyone is capable of adapting and a form of culture shock affects all levels of society.

People accustomed to the simple schemata and precepts of the former regime (and in any case people always have a tendency to listen to slogans and simplified solutions) often subconsciously search for substitute ideologies, new superstitions to cut through the confusions of the current situation. One such popular superstition is the repeated declaration that the market will solve all essential problems by itself. I am not an economist and cannot judge how far that claim will get you in the economic field, but I know that it will not get you very far in the field of culture.

The changes in our country were, to a considerable degree, the work of intellectuals, but artists themselves played an important role in these changes as well. They now have what can be considered the most important things in any creative work, that is, complete freedom. Nevertheless many of them, along with a part of the cultured public, feel uneasy with the recent changes, if not disappointed.

Many non-conformist artists had become used to exceptional respect from the educated public, despite the fact that they were persecuted by the regime. They were considered spokesmen for the people, often the only ones who would express what others thought but were afraid to say. That rather privileged position vanished after the revolution. Exceptional courage was no longer necessary to express truths about society, and the former spokesmen for the people became what artists are everywhere in the free world: simply artists.

Most artists — even the conformists — during the former regime used to dream about the things they would accomplish if they ever lived to experience freedom. Actors, directors, writers, potential publishers, film-makers and television workers all had this dream. It was one aspect of the vaguely articulated notion of a 'third way': after the fall of the regime, the state would continue to be a patron of the arts, but at the same time it would grant complete freedom to creators and invent ways to limit the spread of the worst forms of trash. Few realised that, if complete freedom came to them, it would come for everyone else as well. Very few reckoned with competition, or realised that decisions about what would be bought, and thus produced and sold, would be made with the tastes and interests of the average reader or viewer in mind.

Suddenly, almost overnight, society found itself in the free conditions of a market economy and everything was quite unlike what the dreamers had imagined. Instead of the dreaded but familiar enemy — the censor — came the marketplace. The marketplace has no use for dreams, it requires capital, experience, courage, enormous effort, good judgement, talent. Most of those who dreamed about freedom had none, or almost none, of those assets. They looked on in shock as they watched their grand dreams of art, of freely created and eagerly awaited work elbowed

MILEN RADEV

From Wall to Wall Street

aside by trash (trash, moreover, of foreign provenance), as the audience on whom they had pinned illusory hopes turned its back on their authentic creative work, preferring the most banal consumer items.

The present developments have undoubtedly meant some cultural losses. Czech animated and puppet films that were once among the best in the world have been forced out by Disney megakitsch. The same may be said for Czech children's literature, including the tradition of children's illustrations, created over the decades by the best Czech artists. Czech cinema, one of the best in Europe during the 1960s, is vegetating and mostly just producing a hybrid of silly comedies, pornography, and action films. The theatre is trying to survive on a diet of shallow, trashy comedies, and musicals. Cultural magazines are dying, deserted by their readers. Many publishers of the 2,000 or so that came into existence after the revolution, specialise in publishing trash and are enjoying huge market success.

A public unprepared for the sudden explosion of choice appears not to know its own mind, and is a fickle market. Academics in the humanities, who might have bought serious works, are so badly paid they have no money left for culture.

The situation has its positive side: illusions about the third way are fading and those who are creating culture can, for the first time, determine their true standing in the contemporary world. On the other hand, it is unfortunate that we have been able to learn so few lessons in the cultural sphere from the experiences of free societies: that television screens are dominated by violence, that village shops which only recently offered, along with the rest of its merchandise, editions of a classic book or work of children's literature now offer only Harlequin Romances and comic books, and thus are not only depriving the customer of choice, but degrading his tastes as well.

Society will, one day, recover from its culture shock. Even today, many publishers and booksellers are focusing on the production and sale of serious literature, just as one of the two channels of public television is concentrating on programming for sophisticated viewers. Funding organisations are also being set up, both state and private, who have set as their goals support for the development of serious works of art.

Unlike censorship, the marketplace offers free choice. This does not mean that those who give thought to the future of art, who are persuaded that the main meaning of human life does not lie in mindless, time-killing entertainment, do not have the right — the duty even — to do everything to win over as many supporters to their side as they can. ❏

© *Ivan Klíma. Translated by Paul Wilson*

# INTERVIEW

## RYSZARD KAPUSCINSKI

# The last empire

*Ryszard Kapuscinski, Polish journalist, writer and traveller extraordinary was born in Pinsk, then on the border of Poland, now a part of the new Republic of Belarus, in 1932. He graduated in History from the University of Warsaw in 1955. He worked as a journalist in Poland in the late 1950s but lost his job at Po prostu when the journal was closed down in 1957. In 1962 he joined the Polish Press Agency (PAP) as their sole correspondent for Africa and Latin America. He has also travelled widely in Asia. Kapuscinski has written 13 books, published in over 30 languages. Six titles are available in English — including the latest,* Imperium *(Granta, 1994). He spoke to Irena Maryniak in London shortly after its publication in September.*

'It may be that in our world — so overgrown, so vast, so chaotic, elusive and unmanageable — everything is moving towards a huge collage — a loose collection of fragments — a Lapidarium.'
*Ryszard Kapuscinski*, Lapidarium, *1990*

IM: *It has often been said that the underlying purpose of your writing was to draw political parallels between African or Latin American countries in crisis and the situation in Poland under Communism. Was that the intention?*

RK: I wanted to watch history in the making, its vital processes formed by people and societies, civilisations and cultures. I wanted to find the sources of new historical phenomena, to observe the rise of new classes, ideologies, conflicts, and alliances. I was fascinated by the Third World because I come from Polesie: a very poor part of Poland, a kind of European third world. I feel more at home in environments where there is poverty, hunger and underdevelopment. I can't seem to get used to 'comfort'.

*Does comfort create barriers? Are you trying to overstep social or economic frontiers in your work?*

It seems to me that the outer limits of modern literature are being stretched all the time. Polish literature was always so polonocentric. These days we should be thinking globally. No country, no nation, no culture in the contemporary world can function without the others. Isolation has become an agent of destruction. Dictatorships have always sought to keep their societies in isolation. The deepening and broadening of the thematic space of literature — which is what I am trying to do for Polish writing — is important and timely. And the desire to know the truth, get there, be there and see it, is a strong motivator. It gives one's writing tremendous power.

*What prompted your trip to Russia and the former Soviet republics — the subject of* Imperium?

In the mid-1980s I realised that a historical watershed was before us and it seemed incumbent on me as a reporter to be there. My books were banned in Russia until *perestroika*. But with *glasnost* they published *The Emperor* and I got a bit of money. That paid for the trip. Travel is still cheap there and so I made the gargantuan journey which became the theme of *Imperium*.

*How did your own sense of nationality, your 'Polishness', affect your perceptions?*

It is very hard for us to write about Russia. As a people we were exposed to particularly rough treatment from the Russian state and, subsequently the Bolshevik state. You could argue that the Poles suffered most. No other nation outside the Soviet Union proper faced as much loss, destruction and persecution. Our account with the Russian state is vast, and one could keep touching upon it. But that's a dead end. My role as someone who knows the territory and the language was to write a book which would be understood by societies which are not burdened with this kind of experience. I tried to write a book without reference to all our losses and wrongs. So I had to be very conscious of what I was writing. It would have been easy to write about the Polish uprisings or Katyn. I was deported myself and escaped with my mother and sister. My father was an officer who got away while he was being transported to Katyn. For a year, he was a marked man. But all that doesn't get us anywhere. We should analyse these things and become more familiar with them. Russia won't go away. We should think about getting to know it better.

*You quote Nikolay Mikhaylovsky's dictum that 'the main characteristic of the Russians... is the incessant pursuit of suffering.' You remind us of Elena Bonner's remark about the Russian 'spirit of expansion and domination'. You seem to suggest that the Russian nation is intrinsically dangerous. Is that really true? The Russians live in an extraordinarily harsh and difficult environment. Survival has to be a struggle.*

And the price is very high. Life is hard. It always was and it will be in years to come. It's a retarded country and the world doesn't have the resources to develop it quickly. It's a country in which no political system has been fully shaped. The future of Russia remains a riddle for everyone including the Russians themselves. It's easy to talk about democracy and the free market. But what is that? Russia is a powerful country with a vibrant culture. The kind of thing which assumes that it will adopt the American tradition and life-style is very naive. The culture is too independent, too individual to allow anything to be easily imposed upon it. Russia will have to work out its own social, political and cultural model.

*Daniel Yergin and Thane Gustafson suggest in their book* Russia 2010 and what it means to the world *that the economic miracle which the Russians call* chudo *may be around the corner.*

When? A century hence? For people living there the time scale makes a difference. Things won't be better tomorrow that's for sure, or in five years time. In the distant future, perhaps. And meanwhile efforts are being made to recreate the Soviet Union in a different form, with a more federal, decentralised structure within the old borders except, most probably, for the Baltic States.

*What implications would this have?*

We don't know; it's an open problem. Russia is going through a *smuta*, a 'time of troubles' — which is a familiar scenario in Russian history. The first *smuta* came in the early seventeenth century. It's a time when the state infrastructure and old institutions collapse, while there is nothing firmly established in their place. Because it's such a vast country, with a massive population which is culturally, linguistically and religiously diverse, and because communication is poor and technology underdeveloped, the pace of change is very slow. Russian academics say that a *smuta* is generally an extended period. It lasts years or decades. This is only the beginning. We will probably see some form of stabilisation and strengthening of the state. But the rest of the century is bound to be unclear and full of nebulous conflict. People talk of capitalism. But capitalism isn't something you pull out of a hat. It needs a middle class to sustain it, and Russia hasn't got that. Educating a middle class is a lengthy process.

The past 10 years have seen three phases. There was Gorbachev's attempt to reform Communism from April 1985. That failed and led to its collapse and that of the Soviet Union in December 1991. There followed a brief period of disorientation and shock. Russians had traditionally been the subjects of a Great Power. Suddenly that had ceased to exist and in its place was what the Russians themselves called *prostranstvo* (empty space) — not even a state. This lasted until about 1992-3 when the political doctrine of the 'near abroad' was promulgated. The Soviet Union had ceased to be, but the Russian state stood in its place. And for historical reasons, it regarded everything which came within the territory of the former Soviet Union as its own exclusive sphere of influence. It introduced the notion of the Commonwealth of Independent States and seemed to be trying to draw the non-Russian republics into an alliance in which, as before, Russia was playing the leading role.

*In* Imperium *you talk of the pre-eminent battle between the forces of integration and fragmentation in Russia.*

At the moment the integrating tendency is stronger. There is pressure from Russia to try and recreate the structure of the old Great Russian power, with modifications, in the territory of the former Soviet Union. But the present condition of each republic, and their historical and political experience, is very different. The Transcaucasian attempt to separate in the early 1990s undoubtedly failed. Georgia, Azerbaijan and Armenia have lost their fight for independence for the time being. They have turned back and signed the Soviet agreement. In Lithuania, Latvia and Estonia the situation looks better; they have moved much further away from Moscow. Belarus is closer; Ukraine may be slipping away.

*You write about the dangers of nationalism, racism and fundamentalism, the 'three plagues, three contagions which threaten the world'. Don't they relate, perhaps, to a need for community and identity in a fragmented world?*

Global ideologies like Marxism have been defeated and have left a social vacuum which has to be filled. Their place has been taken by ideologies which have the highest mass appeal. They demand little reflection and are driven by emotion, reflex or stereotype. This is what now dominates the mentality of the man in the street. It relates to the need to believe and belong.

*It may also reflect a desire for group diversity. The need to identify and emphasise that which makes one community different from another: ethnicity, race or religion. One is left with a dialectic between the impulse both to integrate and to diversify.*

Those are the conflicting forces in the contemporary world. Every social process is packed with paradox. You can't say that it's one thing and not another. It's both; it's variegated. There are six billion of us. There is no single ideology which could encompass six billion people motivated by different interests and needs. We live in a post-modern world of untamed diversity. There is no single truth; no single tendency; no single school of thought. There are only remnants of taste and history. It's a world which will not tolerate final solutions; every thought demands constant reappraisal.

*You have written a lot about political power. How has the significance and the face of power changed over the years? It used to be about tyranny, dictatorship, totalitarianism. Where does it lie today?*

I think its significance has grown. The dominant tendency is towards democratisation and pluralism. The weakness of this direction is that democracy assumes the existence of strong institutions to secure itself and its constitutional values. In the new democracies these institutions do not yet exist. So democracy is often a mood, a declaration of intent. But it isn't yet an established state of things. The crisis of tyranny and dictatorship seems evident. In the 1960s and 1970s effectively all African countries were single-party states. Now the majority are multiparty. Today a dictatorship such as Amin's in Uganda or Stroessner's in Paraguay would find it hard to survive in isolation.

The mechanisms of modern power are very intricate. There's economic, social, institutional power, the power of the armed forces, the power of information. Every group calls for power when it organises itself. There is state power, the power of non-governmental organisations and of global institutions. These are all very different things. There are groups which are very strong economically, but lack power. And there are groups, like the army for example, which have no economic assets but wield a lot of control. A coup in Sierra Leone will be conducted by a group of officers with no economic clout who then become the sole rulers of the estate. Power in the modern world is an indefinable abstraction. Rather like the notion of good. ❑

We just sat and stared at our new partner from the East: we couldn't believe our eyes. He was
amazingly good with a knife and fork

# TIMOTHY GARTON ASH

# A more civil world

**Five years on, the author of *We the People* takes another look at his account of the revolution of '89 and asks what has gone right — and what has gone wrong**

I recently received a copy of the Croatian edition of *We the People*. Croatian — I suppose we can no longer say Serbo-Croat — is the thirteenth language into which this book has been translated. It is, of course, good to have so many editions. Yet the very idea of an account of the 'velvet revolutions' appearing in the middle of a post-Communist war also prompts darker reflections.

Does the free word still have any power amidst such a morass of carnage, intolerance and lies? What price now those central European dreams of civil resistance and civil society? Does not Bosnia show up the naivety of the euphoria of 1989?

A German critic recently argued that, looking at the flaming ruins of former Yugoslavia, one had to conclude that the idea of central Europe, as revived in the early 1980s by writers such as Milan Kundera, György Konrad and Czeslaw Milosz, was a 'short-lived utopia'. But one can also turn his argument the other way round: what has happened in Bosnia, and, for that matter, in Georgia, shows that there is an important difference between central Europe on the one hand and eastern or south-eastern Europe on the other.

To be sure, we must beware oversimplification and cultural prejudice. The vehemence of post-Communist populist nationalism in Catholic Slovakia, and, on the other hand, the more impressive progress towards democracy in largely Orthodox Bulgaria, should be sufficient caution against any simplistic correlation between a Western Christian past and a Western democratic future. And even in what we now call eastern rather than East Germany, closest to the West geographically and most helped by the West in every way, there have been flarings of social unrest, scapegoating and racial violence.

Nonetheless, in the heartlands — and great cities — of central Europe the hopes of '89 have not all been disappointed. True, no brave new style of consensual 'forum politics' has emerged. True, the antipoliticians have found it more difficult to reconcile morality and politics in power than they did in opposition. Beside many inspiring speeches and noble gestures, Václav Havel has made compromises — notably by signing the so-called 'lustration' law enacting the blanket decriminalisation of former secret police collaborators — which are difficult to defend by his own earlier standards of morality. Meanwhile, the glinting Friedmanite Václav Klaus, weighed down with no such moral baggage, has taken to the professional partisanship of party politics, but also to the hard business of government, with triumphant gusto.

Wandering down Wenceslaus Square in Prague early in 1990, I bumped into the Hungarian playwright, Arpád Göncz, whom I had last met as a wry, avuncular witness to the last weeks of Communism in Hungary. 'We seem to have found a compromise on the candidate for the presidency,' he told me over a coffee at the Café Europa. And who, I enquired, might it be? 'It seems', said Arpád, 'it will be me.' And sure enough, he has since become a wry, avuncular President of Hungary. Unjustly neglected in the Western media, Göncz's role has actually been quite as important as that of Havel or Walesa. Yet he, too, has found himself being dragged into the undignified melée of party politics, with — as in Prague — the sharpest cuts often coming from those who themselves risked least in the Communist period.

As for Lech Walesa, he threw himself into the melée, displaying his most erratic, populist and autocratic side in his campaign for the presidency. Yet, despite the dark warnings of Adam Michnik and others, the result has not yet been dictatorship. Poland's problem is that it has too many political parties and a Parliament that really does matter; not too few, and one that doesn't.

In his *Reflections on the Revolution in Europe*, also written in early 1990, Ralf Dahrendorf foresaw that these countries would have to pass through a 'valley of tears': that is, through a very painful period of economic, social and political change. Down in the valley, in the dark, the tangled thickets and the mud (and mud-slinging) of traumatic change, even the most seasoned campaigners for human rights and democracy have been heard to emit cries of despondency and alarm. Not least when the West has failed to practise what it preaches (for example, free trade) or has preached what it does not itself practise (for example, purely free market economics). But someone who went into a deep sleep in January 1989, and awoke again in Warsaw, Prague or Budapest (not to mention Berlin) today, would find these cities a great step closer to the West, for good and ill — in consumerism and crime, in politics and pornography, in a free press and unemployment, in television programmes, in the book market, yes, even in the slowly emptying churches.

Of course, much of the old, much that people in the West still automatically associate with 'Eastern Europe', remains in place. And there is no guarantee at all that this progress will continue. The transition from Communism is by no means necessarily the transition to democracy. Yet the heartlands of east central Europe have a more than even chance of making the transition *from* as the transition *to*. Or, as Bronislaw Geremek puts it, of converting the bright passion for liberty into the steady attachment to democracy.

In one respect, moreover, the hopes of '89 have actually been surpassed. Rereading what I wrote in early 1990, I notice the anxious warning of a possible backlash in Moscow. Well, it happened: in the attempted coup of August 1991. But it was also defeated. Eleven years after the Polish August of 1980 we had the Russian August. The crowds in Moscow and St Petersburg were every bit as brave as those in Leipzig or Prague. And perhaps, in our age of tele-war and tele-revolution, those Russians had watched the Czechs and Germans on television?

For years, many in the West argued that fundamental change in the Soviet empire could only come from the centre and from above. Solidarity in Poland tried to change things from the periphery of the

Economic pimps and prostitutes

empire and from below. In fact, it needed both. Gorbachev and Solidarity conditioned each other.

The former Soviet foreign minister Eduard Shevardnadze pours scorn in his memoirs on the idea that *perestroika* caused all the changes in what was once Soviet-dominated eastern Europe. There was Solidarity long before there was *perestroika,* he says, and both Poland's half-failed revolution and Hungary's half-successful economic reforms made a real impact on people close to Gorbachev. But then, without the policies of Gorbachev the peaceful revolution of 1989 could never have succeeded. But then again, without 1989 in eastern Europe, 1991 in the Soviet Union would have looked quite different. And the former East German leader Erich Honecker might say: 'I told you so.' For the most radical yet also most logical conclusion of this central European decade was: no Berlin Wall, no Soviet Union.

**The heartlands of east central Europe have a more than even chance... of converting the bright passion for liberty into the steady attachment to democracy**

This is a great gain, also for the security of the fledgling democracies in east central Europe. But this does not mean they are safe. Far from it. Besides an aggressive Russia re-emerging from the post-Soviet turmoil, they also face the new security challenges of possible mass immigration, terrorism, frontier disputes and minority agitation. And they face them alone. At the time of writing, they may have what in the polite parlance of international relations are called 'friends', but they still have no allies.

Now the problems of giving guarantees rather than vague promises are not small. Once you extend the Nato line beyond the new eastern frontier of Germany, where do you stop? How can you define east central European states as allies without redefining their eastern neighbours, and above all Russia and Ukraine, as adversaries? Does it make sense militarily in any case? But none of this makes living in a security limbo any more comfortable for the Poles, the Czechs or the Hungarians.

As with Nato, so also with Europe. If in 1994 there is some disillusionment with the idea of the 'return to Europe', then this may partly be due to the unrealistic, idealistic, even starry-eyed quality of the original expectations. But it is also a result of the way in which Western Europe has actually behaved. One should not facilely dismiss what has been done. There has been in western Europe, in the West altogether, a genuinely idealistic (as well as a sincerely opportunistic) response to what happened in central and eastern Europe in 1989. Moreover, it is actually more difficult than you might think to 'help' sensibly and effectively.

Nonetheless, too much of the public money designated for central and eastern Europe has either not been disbursed at all or has been recycled into the pockets of Western consultants — benefitting, at most, the Marriott, Forum and Intercontinental hotels in Warsaw, Prague and Budapest. The spectacle of a bank specifically designed to help post-Communist Europe, the European Bank for Reconstruction and Development, spending more than a million pounds on new marble for its lavish London headquarters, almost beggars belief. Measured by the European Community's own previous standards, the so-called 'Europe agreements' which the EC signed with Poland, Hungary and (then still) Czechoslovakia in December 1991 were generous. But on close examination you find that up to 50 per cent of Polish, Hungarian and Czech exports are treated as 'sensitive' goods subject to special import restrictions.

As with goods, so also with people. Again, one should not simply dismiss what has been done. Western Europe has abolished visa requirements for Poles, Czechs and Hungarians. This is a big step towards the Europe of which Jiří Dienstbier dreamed in his boiler room in the mid-1980s. (The book he wrote then has now been published as *Dreaming of Europe*.) The real Europe has always been made by the meetings of individual men and women, not by regulations or treaties. So this allows Europe to happen. But at the same time, western Europe in general, and Germany in particular, have edged towards an immigration policy which places on the fragile democracies of east central Europe the burden of either looking after, or themselves keeping out, the refugees and migrants from the Balkans and the former Soviet Union.

To say, as many do, that the West is building new Berlin Walls is a rhetorical device that I dislike, because it trivialises the real Berlin Wall. The statement 'no Berlin Wall, no Soviet Union' also holds the other way round: 'no Soviet Union, no Berlin Wall.' The West is building no walls to keep its own people in. But it is true that, in security, economic and immigration policy, the Poles, Czechs and Hungarians keep knocking their heads against west European walls which are all the more frustrating because they are invisible. There are no snarling alsatians, only regulations; no automatic shooting-devices, only the smiling 'yes' that in fact means no. And in western Europe the pressure of lobbies, special interest, taxpayers and voters make for more covert protectionism, less openness from Europe to Europe.

Now these may just be the passing concerns of the moment. But east central Europe has certainly not made it to stable democracy yet. And here, in this region delicately poised half-way between Maastricht and Sarajevo, the West can make the difference between success and failure. Not that success will necessarily bring any great new inspiration or revelations. Five years on I am more inclined than ever to say that most of the particular qualities I discerned in the 1980s were, indeed, the uses of adversity. That means, alas, that they have largely disappeared with the adversity. The Round Tables, too, have long been dismantled or packed away. The age of chivalry is gone, that of sophisters, economists and calculators has succeeded — as Edmund Burke famously observed after 1789. But it by no means follows that, as Burke concluded, the glory of Europe is extinguished.

One of the glories, perhaps the greatest glory, of the revolution of '89 in Warsaw, Budapest, Berlin and Prague, was its peaceful, civil and civilised nature. Civic forums organised civil resistance to rebuild civil society. For all the recrimination and mud-slinging and even ethnic taunts of post-Communist politics in these cities, those politics have remained, in conditions of traumatic change, almost entirely non-violent. That may sound like a modest achievement, but if you look at the history of earlier European revolutions, or at the former Soviet Union and the former Yugoslavia today, then you realise that it is actually a very large one.

Certainly my Zagreb editor, Vesna Pusic, seems to think so. In her preface to the Croatian edition, which she has called *We the Citizens*, she suggests that the story of central Europe's velvet revolutions may have lessons even for those places where things have gone more traditionally wrong. And she concludes that there too the future depends on the rediscovery of civic responsibility. In the midst of this century's third Balkan war, that may sound like whistling in the dark. But who are we to dismiss such a hope, however faint, from our safe distance? ❑

©*Timothy Garton Ash*

# Which magazine broke this year's top London news stories ?

We were the first to name the Stoke Newington police officers at the centre of the biggest **police corruption** scandal since the 1970s.

We first revealed the **failure** of London councils to follow their own **equal opportunities** policies.

We were the first to expose London's illegal trade in the **dangerous** East African **drug** Khat.

 **London · Every Detail · Every Week**

# Staying on

Havana, Cuba 1993: time to shout out Revolution

**The following letters were sent to *Index* by a young writer living in Havana, known as *El Lugañero* (The villager). He is part of a movement of writers — all born since the Revolution — known as the *Novísimos***

### 26 February 1994

...I'm part of a generation that reads, or tries to read, *everything*, all that is published in this country and all that is not; that wants to know the truth about everything, everything that's spoken and everything that's stifled. But we are isolated from everything published abroad as well as from local authors who are 'politically difficult'. Above all, we are cut off from those Cuban writers who, though in exile, are nevertheless a vital part of our literature and culture, and whom we *must* read.

Sometimes, these few who travel abroad send back money so we can buy books, which we read in turn, read in record time because others are waiting to read them after us...

There's very little respect for the work of writers and artists any more. In the last few years the number of magazines has been cut to just one or two, bi-monthly, with only a few copies printed because of the cost of paper. Film production is down to one or two a year. Directors have to make extraordinary efforts to secure co-productions with companies abroad. Radio and television are loaded with political slogans all day. They repeat the same news you get in the press. Radio, television, papers, all have the same political content...

**9 June**
...To give you an idea of the absurd level to which life in my country has fallen: a bus-boy or a chambermaid, with tips, can earn more than any professional — doctor, journalist, engineer — because they have access to dollars. They are part of the new social class that, without going to university, with scarcely any education, has overnight become the most privileged because of the decriminalising of the dollar. Someone like me, on the other hand, earns 198 pesos a month which, on the black market, comes to about US$2. As much as a prostitute earns in about two hours.

Food, clothing, and other essentials are practically non-existent. The little food we can get goes off immediately in the heat. In terms of transport we have returned to the last century. There's no petrol, so cars have been replaced by horses. No medicines. One has to perform veritable pirouettes just in order to live. Even more so in order to live and to write. That, along with the problems of censorship which you already know about, should give you some idea of the reason for the exodus of artists and intellectuals abroad; why only a few of us crazy individuals stay and carry on writing, delving into our country; why young people drop out of university to get jobs in the bars or restaurants where tourists go...

I have lived for 32 years in a country and under a regime in which, at times, even smiling could constitute a 'political problem'. Where politics, the Fatherland, socialism, the freedom of the people, the happiness of the masses, the imperialist enemy, the spies from North America and the Far East have been our daily bread: the great lie, the blindfold with which they covered our eyes.

In this country you just can't eat by writing. And yet it's impossible to stop writing, that is something I cannot do...

## 23 August

This is the third letter I have written you in the last 10 days. I have no idea whether any of them will actually reach you, but it's so good just to talk to you.

Reflecting on the situation of writers, journalists, or on freedom of expression in general, is very hard: it's like asking a sailor in the middle of a storm, to evaluate the force of the wind, the strength of the rain. What is freedom? What is freedom of expression? I know nothing of these things. I know only the right, as a writer, not to betray the truth, not to betray myself. Even though you have to live with the knowledge that even your friends might be spying on you, that your personal correspondence can be intercepted and read, that it probably won't reach its destination; that you won't get published and your books will sit gathering dust for five or six years. This is preferable to prostitution, to writing and telling lies to get some job, or travel abroad, or win prizes.

We have become third-class citizens in our own country: the glorious utopia of the Revolution has become the most terrible burden. The fact is, Revolution and Fatherland mean nothing to most of my generation any more. They only think of getting themselves on a raft and fleeing. A while ago the navy shelled and shot at a launch full of women and children, but every day dozens, hundreds of young people get on rafts, most of them never reaching the US. They die in the attempt, food for the sharks...

## 15 October

...There's a growing feeling among our writers of fear, apathy, scepticism. The older ones know better than anyone how high the price of political dissent can be. The younger ones, perhaps simply because we are young, have been a little more daring at times. We have managed to force a little more openness: authors, themes, things that could not be touched before, saw the light of day thanks to us. Writers like Dulce María Loynaz, José Lezama Lima and Virgilio Piñera, who had been silenced for a long time, were rediscovered and read by these young writers, but from a new perspective.

This has opened up new narrative possibilities, new thematic and aesthetic horizons: alienation, hippies, drug addiction, homosexuality suddenly burst into our literature for the first time in works that earned more than a scolding for their authors. So it's a pity that our only writers

Cuba 1994: return to horse-power

well known outside Cuba are Guillen, Carpentier and Lezama Lima: as if the rest of our literature had been put behind bars, prevented from bearing testimony to the reality of life here.

In the last few years my generation has started to wake up, wanting to know the truth that has been hidden from us. The writers they never let us read because they weren't part of the Revolution or had left the country, but who are just as Cuban as we are. Because no political system can justly say it's the only system, or sacrifice the lives and the destiny of millions in the name of its principles...

Compared to the young people in your country, those of my generation here must seem culturally deformed. For my father, who was a Communist, tape recorders and videos, all these things were bourgeois possessions. I was never allowed to learn English: they taught me Russian because, according to my father, the man of the 21st century would belong completely to socialism. All this is vital to understanding the work of my generation: the pessimism, the nostalgia, the sadness of betrayal. Often, they talk of their childhood as a cruel hoax, searching for the paradise they were promised.

So many tracts, hymns, marches, slogans in which we believed. Reading a literature (socialist realist) in which man was perfect, idealised. We wanted to be made perfect, like robots. But what of the heart, the contradictions of the soul? And my anger, my hatred, my imperfect loves, all that is impure in me? And my fears, my loneliness, my sexual preferences? Do none of these have a place in literature? Of course they must. These are the questions that these authors ask, this is what they are trying to talk about. And they must be read with the heart... ❏

*Translated by Adam Newey*

## ALEX DICK-READ

# Hustling in Havana

It is hard to imagine that there could be a more powerful censor in Cuba than the state, but the forces of want and decay now seem to be just as effective in stifling Cuba's artistic and literary expression as the Party machine.

For anyone without access to US dollars, everyday life involves queueing for hours, only to be told there is no more bread; houses and cities are literally crumbling; and, in a country known for the best state health care system in the hemisphere, even the sick are going without medicine. In times like these, artistic priorities fall way down the list.

Amid the sullen chaos of several Cuban towns and cities I met many writers and artists, all bursting with inspiration but frustrated in the face of overwhelming economic need. It is long past the time when Cuba should have been talking openly about its misery: they all seem to know it and despite everything manage to remain dedicated to their vocation.

'The most important thing for a writer to do is to write about his time', said one young novelist. 'All the time I'm trying to write for anyone who will publish.' In order to live, though, he has to hustle cigarettes on street corners. There are some, painters in particular, who have broken into the dollar economy by selling their work to foreigners in hotels and art galleries. But only rarely do these works contain even the subtlest hint of the political and social realities of life in Cuba.

In central Havana, where the dollar economy has affected people's lives more than anywhere else the atmosphere seems more permissive. Juan Carlos draws on the decaying colonial splendour of Old Havana for his paintings. In his vision the downtrodden Cuban is crowned by a halo even as he sleeps among the rubble in a darkened doorway. His pained brow rests on a pile of back issues of *Granma*, the government's organ of official good news. When his exhibition opens in November at the Provincial Centre of Painting and Design, Juan Carlos doesn't expect any trouble from the state. 'After all', he says, 'this is the dollar economy and the gallery gets half of what I sell.'

Juan Carlos's share of any sales will keep his family fed and supplied with the basic necessities for a few weeks. It will also open the door to a world where there are, at least, possibilities. 'I can only buy my materials in dollars,' he says, 'and painting is my life.'

Outside the capital, where the dollar economy is not so well developed, things are different. Whereas some cars are still running in Havana, the streets of the southern port of Santiago de Cuba echo with the sound of horse-drawn carriages. People's clothes are obviously older, shops which accept pesos are empty and the food supply has dwindled to a trickle. Santiago, like most of the country, is governed by more conservative revolutionaries than those in Havana. Every block has its vigilant representative from the Committee for the Defence of the Revolution and the three cultural organisations in these parts do not encourage free thought. What little material they print or display is always 'safe'.

Havana, Cuba 1993: revlutionary transport

TIDDY MAITLAND TITTERTON/CAMERA PRESS

In this stifling climate Iginio earns a living on a black market street, while trying to complete his sixth book. He has already spent six months in prison for what he calls his 'tendencies towards liberty', and was hounded out of his job as sub-director of the municipal House of Culture by a group of Party activists who ostracised and taunted him until he was unable to work. Now the secret police are examining one of his articles which he asked a foreigner to take to Miami. 'I know they have it at the police station,' he says. 'I'm expecting them to come for me any day.'

There have been other practical problems, too. Iginio won a place on a top journalism course in France, but the cheque they sent him never arrived. He won a writing competition in Mexico's cultural magazine *Plural*, but the prize never arrived. Neither has the payment for the articles he sent to Argentina. For Iginio and others like him, sending anything which could be deemed 'politically difficult' through the postal service is out of the question, and foreigners are their only means of reaching the outside world. 'Outside Cuba we are not known,' says Iginio, 'and inside Cuba we don't even know each other.'

Another writer, El Lugañero, was lucky enough to have one of his books published last year. He has no copies to give away, because only six were printed. His lucid and profound poetry goes unread by his peers, his compatriots and the rest of the world. Certainly there is no money to be had from this kind of 'success'. He has had some work published in the Mexican magazine *Critica*, although again money is slow in coming in. He waits, too, for £45 from a British publication. The transaction has failed several times in the last six months. In Cuban pesos, £45 is more than four years' pay.

Most would have left by now if their obligations to family and friends were not so strong. Those who have left are sometimes spoken of with respect and envy, symbols of the apparent possibilities overseas. Then there are the friends who just disappeared, presumed to have left the country, but of whom no word comes for years.

'Mexico, Jamaica, anywhere!' says Iginio. 'I've often thought of trying to get to Jamaica, or even trying to swim around to Guantánamo.' Many of his friends have done it, and artists around the country are planning things like this all the time. But Iginio says he knows he will never go. 'I couldn't keep my manuscripts dry on the raft, and I can't possibly leave them behind.' ❏

# MINORITIES

## DAVRELL TIEN

# In search of Veps

**Within 100 kms of St Petersburg a tiny, isolated community, all
but destroyed by Stalin and now threatened with extinction,
battles for recognition of its language and culture**

Some languages are more equal than others. In the countryside outside
St Petersburg live a people called Veps. Their language is related to
Finnish and Estonian. Several related Finno-Ugric tribes vanished from
the area earlier this century. So, when the first team of post-War Russian
ethnographers set off in the mid-1980s on an expedition to find them,
there were worries that Veps had already been assimilated.

In a village where Veps were known to have lived before World War
II, everyone seemed to be Russian. But then one of the expedition
overheard a strange language with the heavy first syllable stress typical of
Finnic languages. An old woman explained that they were *Chukhontsy* —
a pejorative Russian term which, roughly translated, means 'Finn-nigger'.
The scholars didn't know whether to laugh or cry.

The repression of Russia's ethnic minorities began in Tsarist times.
Publication in 'ethnic' languages, many of which lacked written forms
anyway, was forbidden. After the Bolshevik revolution, however, Lenin's
government encouraged literacy in native languages under the banner
'national in form, socialist in content'. By 1935, 120 nationalities had
some form of primary school education in their own languages. Veps
acquired a Latin transcription: primary school began with ABCs instead

of ABVs.

But in 1937, in the tide of Russian chauvinism unleashed by Stalin, the Veps language was banned: all the primers disappeared and people feared to call themselves Veps. In the search for 'enemies of the state', bureaucrats needed to peruse everything written; simply proscribing obscure languages may have been easier than translating them. Whatever the reasoning, the result, in the words of one Russian official, was that 'under Stalin, Veps were not considered human, and only in the last 10 years did it become possible to declare oneself a Veps.'

Terror, though, comes from more than a book ban. 'If they burned the books of course the scholars who wrote the books were repressed,' says Nikolai Abramov, co-editor of *Kodima*, a newspaper with a circulation of 1,000 which speaks for the Veps nation. He cites the example of Stepan Makarev, a Veps folklorist who was executed in 1937 for unpatriotic attempts to publish his work in Finland. To be active in Veps cultural life was to risk extinction.

> **Under Stalin, Veps were not considered human; only in the last 10 years did it become possible to declare oneself a Veps**

The attitude of Russian speaking immigrants was another factor in Veps's decline. One middle-aged man writing to *Kodima* explained why he never learned his parents' tongue: 'Once, while riding a bus, my mother and her sister were carrying on a lively conversation in far-from-perfect Russian. Forgetting themselves, they suddenly shifted to their native language. The other passengers immediately began staring hostilely at them. A man in a respectable suit and tie demanded that they stop speaking Veps because it was uncivilised. At the age of 12 I wanted to sink into the earth. I begged my mother to forget that language forever and to shame me no further...'

When the writer of this letter went to the militia for his first Soviet passport at the age of 16, he feared the word 'Veps' would be branded in this all-important document. To his relief, however, the woman filling in the forms serenely informed him that no such nationality any longer existed.

Do Veps officially exist today? At the passport desk in Podporozhe, a town in which half the residents have some Veps roots, a passport clerk admitted that Veps had been forcefully assigned Russian nationality in the

Veps village, pre-1945: dehumanised by Stalin

1970s, but maintained that they may now re-establish their nationality if they so choose, as long as they present a document proving they are Veps. 'We can't allow people simply to take whatever nationality they like.'

Despite this new freedom, few Veps have gone to recover their nationality. An old woman in Vinnitsy, a Veps logging town, said that her 18-year-old grandson who wanted 'Veps' in his passport was refused, not by a Russian official, but his own father who refused him the necessary documents.

Merely adding 'Veps' to one's passport is considerably easier than learning the language, which has 28 cases. Why master a language which offers so little in the way of information or entertainment? Aside from a few hours weekly on radio from neighbouring Karelia, Veps is absent from street signs, the library and television. The few ethnic Veps officials scrupulously avoid speaking their native language in public.

One way to raise the prestige of any language is to give it official status, but in Russia this is political dynamite. Higher education in the humanities is only available in two non-Russian languages, in Tatarstan and Bashkortostan and nowhere do schools require Russian-speaking immigrants to learn any of the Russian Federation's 150 recognised minority languages. 'Immigrants [Russian speakers living in minority areas] should learn local languages but only on a voluntary basis,' said Evgeny Galskov, director of Minority and Regional Programme development at the Ministry of Education in Moscow.

Under ministerial guidelines, however, the education authorities in Podporozhe district (population 43,000) this year introduced Veps classes in three schools as a regular option. A total of 25 pupils signed up. In other schools, Veps is only available as a conversation class, twice a week after school has finished; just 132 pupils attend. Such low numbers disappoint Veps activists.

Even in areas considered Veps heartland, such as Vinnitsy where Veps make up 1,500 of the town's population of 3,900, Veps is dying out. In summer the town comes alive with visitors, mainly Veps emigrants from St Petersburg, who come back for the high point of the Veps cultural calendar — a musical folk festival. But in the local school, although 10 out of 40 teachers can read and write Veps, parents remain unenthusiastic.

**'When I speak to God in my native language it pleases Him'**

Headmaster Viktor Yershov says it is hard to convince parents to allow their children to attend Veps classes. He consoles himself that there are isolated villages where three generations still speak the language. Yershov writes poetry in Veps, perhaps less out of talent than wonder that the language is in him: 'Not being wholly Veps or Russian, we are uncomfortable in life... . But when I speak to God in my native language, it pleases Him. After all, we don't ask Him for wealth but for help with our problems. Our ancestors demand that we not stand aside, and broaden our children's intellects.'

When Yershov campaigned for Veps classes in schools, parents called on his wife to ask her opinion. Would Nadezhda Yershova the headmaster's wife — an ethnic Russian — have her own grandchildren learn Veps? 'I am convinced that it's a fad that will pass,' she told them, reasoning that Veps has no higher culture, no scientific vocabulary and, therefore, no future. 'When the older generation passes, that will be the end,' she said, to her husband's dismay. To her mind Veps scarcely merits being called a language: 'It has no grammar and half of its vocabulary consists of loan words from Russian. I could learn it easily but what would be the point?' she said, looking at bookshelves full of fine Russian classics.

The headmaster concedes that great knowledge is impossible through a small language. The remedy, he hopes, will be a standard literary language based on the Bible. Nina Caitseva, co-editor of *Kodima*, has already translated parts of the New Testament, which were then published in Finland. Where Veps lacks a word, Caitseva invents one out of a Finnish root. Yershov spoke of her work enthusiastically: 'It seems like old Veps, just as our grandmothers spoke it.'

The influence of Finland may yet affect the fate of Veps. When the Finnish troops took Veps villages during World War II, Veps didn't feel the same dread as Russians. Today, Finnish intruders are back in the form of humanitarian aid workers. At the sight of their Russian neighbours crowded round the trucks, fighting over old clothing cast off by their capitalist relatives, some Veps step back and chuckle to themselves. And when the Finns lack an interpreter, someone is likely to push an old Veps forward to stumble through a conversation of common words.

A chance to study Finnish is a key promise made to parents who send their children to Veps lessons: fluency in Finnish means a good living. The first group of young women who have agreed to become primary school teachers are also studying Finnish at the university in Petrozavodsk. Some doubt they'll ever return to their villages.

The future for Russia's Veps is far from certain: from the Russian point of view, raising their cultural identity and ambitions constitutes a dangerous kind of nationalism. But Nikolai Abramov believes that Russia's Finno-Ugrics (Chuvash, Mari, Khants, Mansi, Udmurts, Komi and Karelians) who happen to live where there is either coal, gas and oil or gold, furs and forest have been ruthlessly exploited by the Russian centre. Moscow, he notes, is full of BMWs and Mercedes bought with profits which originate in minority regions. What sort of economic rights Veps — and minorities in general — should have in Russia's new and lawless market economy is an open question.

Veps started to take overt political action in January 1993, when the first Veps national congress was held. Unfortunately, they elected Anatoly

Bakulin, an established local politician and an ethnic Russian, to be their lobbyist. Bakulin, who subsequently gained control of the federally financed Northwestern Fund for the Revitalisation of Minority Languages and Cultures, then disappeared. Rumour has it that he went into business, founding the Finno-Ugric Insurance Company in St Petersburg.

But in post-*perestroika* Russia such things are run-of-the-mill. If Veps are going to save themselves, then they will have to take action by themselves. As one Russian put it: 'Who is going to do something for a minority at a time like this when the country is in such a state?' ❏

Veps folk festival Vinnitsy, 1993: 'highpoint of the cultural year'

# SUBSCRIPTIONS 1994
## United Kingdom & Overseas (excl USA & Canada)

INDEX ON CENSORSHIP

Lancaster House, 33 Islington High Street
London N1 9LH, UK
tel: 071 278 2313 fax:071-278 1878

| | | | | | | |
|---|---|---|---|---|---|---|
| **1yr** | **UK:** | £30 | **Overseas:** | £36 | **Students:** | £23 (Worldwide) |
| **2yr** | | £55 | | £66 | | |
| **3yr** | | £80 | | £99 | | |

❑ I enclose a cheque* or money order for **£**...............
(*Sterling cheques must be drawn on a London bank)

❑ Please charge **£**........ to my

      ❑ Visa/Mastercard

      ❑ American Express

      ❑ Diners Club

CARD NUMBER...............................................

...............................................................

EXP DT.................

❑ I have instructed my bank to send £..............
to your bank account 0635788 at Lloyds Bank,
10 Hanover Square, London W1R 0BT

SIGNATURE..................................................

NAME.........................................................

❑ I have sent £.............. to your Post Office
National Giro account 574-5357 (Britain)

ADDRESS....................................................

...............................................................

...............................................................

❑ Also, you can send **Index** to a reader in the developing world — for only £18! These sponsored subscriptions promote free speech around the world for only the cost of printing and postage.

---

# SUBSCRIPTIONS 1994
## USA & Canada

INDEX ON CENSORSHIP

Lancaster House, 33 Islington High Street
London N1 9LH, UK
tel: 071 278 2313 fax:071-278 1878

'Index has bylines that Vanity Fair would kill for. Would that bylines were the only things about Index people were willing to kill for.' **BOSTON GLOBE**

| | | | | |
|---|---|---|---|---|
| **1yr** | **US$** | $48 | **Students:** | $35 |
| **2yr** | | $90 | | |
| **3yr** | | $136 | | |

❑ I enclose a cheque or money order in US$ for **$**...............

❑ Please charge **$** ........to my

      ❑ Visa/Mastercard

      ❑ American Express

      ❑ Diners Club

CARD NUMBER...............................................

...............................................................

EXP DT.................

SIGNATURE..................................................

NAME.........................................................

ADDRESS....................................................

...............................................................

...............................................................

❑ Also, you can send **Index** to a reader in the developing world — for only $27! These sponsored subscriptions promote free speech around the world for only the cost of printing and postage.

Index on Censorship
Lancaster House
33 Islington High Street
London N1 9LH
United Kingdom

---

Index on Censorship
c/o Human Rights Watch
485 Fifth Avenue
New York, NY 10164-0709
USA

# Nikolai Abramov

Nikolai Abramov is one of the few Veps in Podporozhe to have formally restored his nationality. He wrote an essay about the experience entitled 'How I Became a Veps', which describes his contest of wills with the state bureaucrats at the passport desk.

At the age of 10, like many rural minority children in the Soviet Union, Abramov was sent to an *internat* (state-run boarding school). Speaking Veps was prohibited there, but the pupils, 90 per cent of whom were Veps, spoke it among themselves regardless. As soon as he was old enough, Abramov escaped to Leningrad. Working at odd jobs and feeling lost in the big city, he attempted suicide at the age of 18 after an unhappy love affair. While lying in hospital with broken legs he began to write poetry, which turned out to be publishable.

Nikolai Abramov: poet

All these adventures have a distinctly Soviet Russian flavour. Indeed, Abramov didn't think of writing in his native language until he met the linguist Nina Caitseva who urged him to submit some verse in Veps to the Finnish-language newspaper in Karelia.

'Not having written anything in Veps in the last eight to 10 years, I wrote a few lines of poetry with great difficulty; it didn't come well at all; it was like writing in a foreign language. But after the first piece it became easier. Veps comes to me easily since I spoke it in childhood,' said Abramov.

Turning to journalism, Abramov worked for several years at the Podporozhe Russian paper *Severny Ogni*, but was dismissed after leaving work suddenly to defend Yeltsin and democracy at the White House siege in August 1991. *Kodima,* the paper which Abramov now writes and edits, exists thanks to a subsidy from the Republic of Karelia which provides Abramov with a minimal salary. To save money on postage he passes out papers to Veps on the streets.

Does Abramov think that Russians may be willing to learn Veps? He reveals that some already have, especially the 101ers (former convicts forbidden to live within 100 kilometres of St Petersburg), who have since settled among Veps. ❏

KRÓLOWO POLSKI SZEŚĆ WIEKÓW JE[...] POMOCĄ KU OBRONIE NASZEGO NARODU

# State-church or Church-state?

**Five years after Poland's first free election, Church and state are joined in battle for hearts and minds.**

**A report from Poland by Irena Maryniak**

JAN SVAB/CAMERA PRESS

Left: Shrine of Jasna Gora in Czestochowa: 'Queen of Poland you have defended our nation for 600 years'

# IRENA MARYNIAK

# Idols and demons

**Shaken by the loss of its old enemy, and its own reduced status, the Catholic Church moves back into authoritarian mode**

'*Education?*', the bookseller said, incredulously. 'For *democracy?*' He sniffed. 'Idols and demons', he muttered cryptically into a wispy beard.

'Education' (*edukacja*) is a comparatively new, western word in the Polish lexicon: its 'purer' equivalent (*oswiata*) is fringed with connotations of wisdom and spiritual enlightenment. Say 'democracy' (*demokracja*) and the erstwhile German Democratic Republic springs to mind, or rock culture and Disneyland at best. And so... 'Sorry,' the bookseller said, peevishly. 'It's not the sort of book we hold in stock.'

I had been looking for a collection of interviews with some of the more liberal figures in Polish public life, including one with Wiktor Kulerski, of the Foundation for Education for Democracy (an organisation which helps promote the practical skills to sustain democratic political cultures in central and eastern Europe). The interview was about the mechanics of Church-State relations in Poland.

It is a delicate topic these days, for — five years after Poland's first free election in half a century — the interests of the Catholic Church and the Polish state are beginning visibly to diverge. The Church hierarchy is clinging hard to the role it held under the Communist order. Then it was the voice of public opinion, protector of cultural identity, defender of the right to hold religious beliefs, sanctuary for political opposition. It was an umbrella organisation sheltering all shades of non-conformist thinking. It nurtured creativity. It provided a forum for philosophical and political discussion. It negotiated freedoms from the government which made the country one of the most liberal states in the Eastern bloc. For years, its clergy risked imprisonment and death.

Today, Poland is emerging into a Europe it finds very foreign. The country is, effectively, monoethnic and monoreligious; it is also economically very ambitious. Unfamiliar with modern diversity, it seems surprised at the sudden fragmentation of vision within its own borders. After two hundred years of conspiracy and resistance, how *does* one find a common language in the market place?

The Catholic Church has been shaken by the changes: its position no longer demands that it should act as a surrogate state; it is no longer responsible for representing the majority of the country, or for mediating between the state and the population. It is unwelcome in politics and education, and distanced from the arts. Once its power lay in the moral thrust of allegations against a reluctant and insecure Communist nomenklatura, trapped in a sense of its betrayal of the national and religious values so immovably embedded in the Polish tradition. The Church was strong because everyone — apparatchiks included — felt subliminally that, when push came to shove, the Church had got it right. The weakness of the ruling regime lay in a conviction of its own duplicity.

The technique of dealing with opponents by exerting moral pressure levered by underlying beliefs, which has been the Church's stand-by in politics for the past 50 years, is still often applied. 'The Church and the Communist state were so firmly locked in combat that it has been impossible to separate them,' Wiktor Kulerski says. Former Communists

ALFRED GREGORY/CAMERA PRESS

Rural procession: one Church, one faith, one people

are now among the most ardent supporters of Church policy.

The new, independent state, which the Church regards as its brainchild and natural successor, must — in the view of the current hierarchy — be grounded in Christian ethics. The Polish Church's ethical idealism, its reluctance to recognise the value of compromise in opening channels of communication, and its traditionally political self-image has prompted clumsy incursions into politics, the media and education. The abortion question — so high on its political agenda — symbolises its refusal to defer in the face of impending secularisation. It has become an emblem and a rallying cry for devotees of anti-secularism, and public evidence of the Church's consistency in defending 'absolute' truths and rejecting moral relativism. The issue is seen as an opportunity to cry out, once again, against ideological rationalism and social engineering in defence of the silenced. 'I'd like to suggest', one priest told me with a degree of satisfaction, 'that these people should also legislate for children to kill their parents once they are infirm and non-productive. Parents are killing their unborn children for material reasons; children should have the right to do the same.'

**People are being choked by democracy and freedom. They think everything is allowed...**

**A Jesuit priest**

It all reflects the underlying belief that to soften the line on abortion, and indeed on contraception, would be the first step in capitulation to all those atheist policies which the Polish Church was fighting off after 1945. It would, Polish Catholics say, imply going back to a Communist way of thinking and Communist legislation. This is true as much of the Church's stand on the issue in Poland as of the Vatican's position at the Cairo World Population Conference in September. Secularism is viewed by the Catholic hierarchy as the first step to a kind of global totalitarianism: the absolute rule of pragmatism and expediency in the control of birth and death, pain and distress. The Church sees all these as experiences which can cement human relationships, encourage more subtle discourse and act as equalisers, opening the way to a better understanding of other people's experience and the ability to transcend one's pettier egotistical interests. Because the end is not to make people more comfortable; it is to make them more in tune with the Divine Order.

Evidence that women are willing to take serious health risks and have abortions done illegally is likely to leave the Church unmoved. A doctor in Czestochowa committed suicide recently, after performing an abortion on a woman who subsequently had to be hospitalised. In newspapers gynaecologists advertise 'a full range of services', at a price. It can be cheaper to take a special bus east, or — if you can afford it — to Berlin or Amsterdam. Some women return from these trips within hours, frequently with complications. Others try to provoke self-induced abortions or seek amateur help in villages. Many end up in hospital. The number of recorded infanticides has risen. Some are presumably unreported.

But the Church will not sanction the obligation a secular society feels to control the effects of choices which desperate women make in any case. The teaching of a belief culture encourages absolution from responsibility: a willingness to go with the flow and a posture of absolute trust in the positive outcome of events. It encourages a psychological frame of mind which presupposes that *Another* will carry the can. The danger is what Dostoevsky might have called the Grand Inquisitor Syndrome. You make the assumption that choice is actually the greatest source of human misery. The grey mass of humanity just isn't ready for it. Consequently, it is the obligation of the Great and the Good to take away the options and free people from the unhappy obligation of making their selection. Religious fundamentalism, like totalitarian ideology, makes people free by releasing them from the burden of responsibility and choice.

Polish intellectuals opposed to the political gesticulations of the Church in the past five years say that the long-term intention of the Vatican and the Polish hierarchy is to protect the interests of the priesthood as a privileged caste; to train it into being one of the organs of state power; and to root the institution so deeply in the public mind that it will have the power to affect legislation and high level posts in the professions, business and politics. This, they argue, will be sanctioned by the Concordat, an impending international agreement with the Vatican which guarantees the Church's autonomy, its position in public life, its right to own schools and its access to the media. Not so, critics say. The Concordat will guarantee the privileges gained by the Church since 1989, ensure its dominance in education and legislation, encourage a mood of religious intolerance and reduce the country politically to a state

Old market, Warsaw 1992

dependent on the whims of Rome.

More loyal Catholics tend to lay the blame for the Church's political mistakes at the door of right-wing political parties; they complain that religious beliefs have been hijacked by right-wing ideologies, and emphasise the Church's overall respect for the autonomy of the state. They acknowledge some 'over-enthusiasm' on the part of individual bishops and priests, but emphasise that the hierarchy as a whole takes a moderate view. The problem is that official statements of intent are often lost in that sermon-induced stupor Catholics know so well. The effect of individual instruction from a father confessor is considerably greater; as are potential administrative measures which will officially record whether a marriage took place in Church or whether a child is taking religion at school. Given the atmosphere many people still remember, where Party membership determined one's career, anxiety that the Church may have the power to influence or undermine job prospects is high. In education, administrators and teachers are careful not to express controversial views for fear of incurring clerical displeasure. A complaint from the Church is likely to mean a professional reprimand or even the loss of a job. The introduction of the teaching of religion in schools has given the Church the opportunity to play a supervisory role as regards teaching methods in general. Textbooks available in school libraries and used in classrooms are submitted to an indirect form of Church censorship. A translated Western textbook on sex education which promoted the use of contraception to prevent the spread of AIDS was translated by the Ministry of Health but failed to receive a recommendation from the Ministry of Education for use in schools. Although legally there is nothing to prevent its use in teaching, the certainty that a priest would object ensures that it does not appear in the classroom.

A well-placed member of the Church hierarchy, who asked to remain anonymous, argued that parents seem to make the mistake of expecting teachers to offer their children a service. 'They make demands', he said, 'and have little sense of what educational upbringing really means. They don't know about hard work, discipline, organisation and Good Causes. Polish society lacks a sense of "authority" and hierarchy. It is a vestige of the Communist notion of universal equality.'

There is in the Polish Church a stultifying mixture of complacent patronage and intellectual poverty. Priests tend to be poorly educated, with inflexible views and authoritarian attitudes. Among Catholic intellectuals there is a tendency to regard the remainder of the population as politically immature, narrow-minded, easily lead, undiscriminating and unable to recognise the benefits of Western capitalism. This complacency may have contributed to the reported statistic that 70 per cent of the population feel that the Church should think of winding up its political activities. A strong Catholic presence in the media, with special radio channels; an information agency; frequent religious programmes on television; wide reporting of Church ceremonies; a range of impressively-presented publications; and the vastly superior fleet of cars owned by Church dignitaries, may have added to the disgruntled mood of congregations. But Church representatives say that that the right message is still not getting across: reporting by secular journalists can be misleading and, too often, misunderstandings arise over conceptual terminology. The Church is also keen to promote its grass roots activities and to emphasise its role in social welfare. Meanwhile non-Catholic writers complain that it is increasingly difficult to publish attacks on Church policy, and that if publication is agreed it is frequently on condition that anything likely to offend is removed or rewritten.

Why the Church should feel vulnerable enough to have created this kind of atmosphere is a thorny question. 'People are being choked by democracy and freedom', a Jesuit priest told me. (He too preferred not to be named.) 'They think everything is allowed. Just after independence sex shops became the symbol of democracy and freedom. These are perhaps a young democracy's childhood ailments. In private, we often say that it's a current coming from the secular, anti-Catholic climate in the West. There are left-wing, secular currents, and masonic ones too.' Masonic? 'Currents which are against the Church. But you can't prove it. The Church isn't threatened in the sense that it has a concrete opponent as it used to. But some secular currents and scientific views undermine religious, supernatural values. It isn't only the Catholic Church which is suffering.' He describes reporting of the Church's role in politics as 'provocative'. 'Certain political groupings need it...' Secularism and the left again.

Predictably, the left-wing coalition government elected in September 1993 has been accused by the Church of intending to bring back the Communist system. When it was proposed that the constitution should be passed prior to the final signature of the Concordat, the Primate, Cardinal Glemp, is reported to have said that Parliament was 'the sick foetus of a sick state' and that the constitution in preparation was doubtless Leninist. Some priests seem to be trying to foment a mood of fear among congregations with talk of enforced atheism and the return of Communist ideology. In one Warsaw church, I heard a sermon in which an analogy was drawn between present-day Poland and ancient Israel: 'a country surrounded by enemies who rob, betray and manipulate it.' There were references to external attempts to dictate Poland's internal policies and to another imminent partitioning of the country.

Just how deeply all this penetrates the minds of congregations is hard to say. The country, though fiercely loyal to the Vatican, is also sensibly sceptical. Practising Catholics — in town and country — are often surprisingly anti-clerical: they don't like to be told how to live; they don't support official Church policy; they have altercations with parish priests and bishops; they are critical of the Pope. But they observe the Church calendar all the same, participate in the ritual and partake of the sacraments. Every Easter they will go to Confession. It has been estimated that the Church remains a moral, cultural, and, by extension, political authority for at least 30 per cent of the population.

Catholic intellectuals from the more liberal enclave of Kraków speak of vestiges of pre-Vatican Council II attitudes. They explain that there is prejudice against the West inculcated by the Communist regime. There is fear of finding oneself in a world where the rules are unclear, they say. In the new political context, the Polish Church is uncomfortably divided. Pulpit-thumping conservatives see a dualistic split between themselves and the world: their role is the defence of the homeland against the onslaught of evil (read secular) forces. Subscribers to the post-Vatican II vision take a more holistic view, inclined to dialogue with other religions and 'even with the non-religious'. The tensions between the two underlie many of the attitudes in Poland today. In 1963, Vatican II failed to penetrate far outside the hermetic circles of the Catholic intelligentsia. Consequently traditional attitudes and antagonisms continue to exert a stronger hold than modern notions of polyphony and discourse.

Kraków intellectuals may talk of a need for the Church to enter into dialogue with a pluralist society, to encourage authentic philosophical thinking, to make a sorely-needed cultural contribution by encouraging a deeper knowledge of local history and a respect for the environment. But in a country where old habits die hard, where training in the workings of democracy often becomes a new kind of ideological indoctrination, and where there is talk of a Catholic 'mission' to save the West, a tough sermon with the requisite ingredients — enemies, invasions, infanticide — is likely to be more readily received before Sunday lunch than thought-provoking invitations to dialogue and inner exploration. The time for self-discovery is past. The way is open for stylish living, designer clothes, fast food and — if you survive long enough to see it — an easy life. ❏

SVEN SIMON/CAMERA PRESS

Open air dialogue

## JACEK FEDOROWICZ

# Polish
# paradoxes

Man in car to journalist:
'Now get this down: ruin and destitution. Next thing we'll be on the streets!'

The Poles are citizens of that least 'socialist' country in the former socialist bloc. Not only did they manage to salvage private farming and retain a bit of private enterprise, they preserved a dollar exchange rate though the currency was officially barred. Over the five years which have passed since the fall of Communism, Poland has travelled furthest along the road to capitalism: it was the first country in the former bloc to record significant economic growth. But in the course of those five years, opinion polls have consistently shown that people were opposed to capitalism, that they thought the country was going in the wrong direction and that economic reform was ruining it. Asked when life was best, everyone would respond in harmonious chorus: why, under socialism. They then promptly pick up their pens and carefully write out their personal details in order to take part in the US visa lottery in the hope of winning the right to live in that most capitalist of capitalist countries, the United States of America. Every year hordes of these admirers of socialism flooded the requisite Washington department with their applications. As a result, the US visa lottery — once envisaged as an opportunity for migrants the world over — became an internal Polish affair. The Poles traditionally hogged the pool. No one else stood a chance. What kind of inner impulse prompts these people to seek solace in the very place they least want to be?

Financial health checks on the Polish population — especially those carried out by international organisations specialising in the exposure of poverty — consistently show that people here live below the poverty line, with 37 per cent of the population in abject misery and on the verge of starvation (so states a report released in the first quarter of 1994). Yet foreign visitors will observe a remarkable phenomenon. Travelling to any corner of the country they will consistently see only 63 per cent of the population: those *not* in extreme poverty. The poor are there to be found, of course, but attempts to seek out the starving, all 37 per cent of them, are bound to end in failure. Which will confirm the foreign tourist's conviction that traditions associated with two centuries of resistance to successive occupiers have turned the Poles into masters of conspiracy.

The average local will tell you that things are bad, very bad or desperate. A statistical analysis of salaries will confirm this assessment. Poles don't earn much. But a passing glance at data on non-essential goods people buy will show that they have spent far, *far* more on them than they actually earn. Western companies selling luxury cars, cosmetics, clothing or drink have made so much here that they still can't believe their luck. A glance inside Polish homes will tell you that every family has a fridge and a television (colour in about 80 per cent of households). Nearly half of them will also have a video. The number of cars has risen by five million over the past few years; this in a nation of 30 something. The most striking feature of the landscape these days is the satellite dish, and at every step you can see evidence of the activity of tens of thousands of prospering private building firms, which the Poles call a disastrous state of stagnation in the building business. Among the answers to questions put by inquisitive pollsters about the worst aspect of nascent capitalism the most frequent reply is unemployment. Yet in areas riven with job shortages it is impossible to find anyone interested in mending a leaking tap, cleaning a stairway or doing a bit of baby-sitting. The unemployed have no time for extra work because they are working. To complete the picture of a country in which everything is topsy-turvy, there is the party in government: a coalition between the peasant party (private farming) and the former Communist party (with 40 years of hard socialism to its credit). In this coalition the Communists battle for a speedier privatisation of the economy, while the peasants procrastinate.

So are the Poles a nation of schizophrenics? Has everyone gone mad? By no means. It can all be rationally explained if one bears in mind the circumstances and accepts the traits common in most — apparently irrational — aspects of Polish behaviour.

The circumstances are, above all, historical, and conspiracy hits the nail on the head. Twenty decades under occupation have taught the Poles that when they make a request they should lie; when they seek to acquire something, they should mystify. It has taken generations to perfect this stance towards invigilators of every ilk. Just as grandad once

**Two centuries of resistance to successive occupiers have turned the Poles into masters of conspiracy**

hid his cow in the woods so that it wouldn't be requisitioned by the Tsarist army, the Red Army, the Nazis, or *kolkhoz* (collective farm) supervisors, so today his grandson answers the questions: 'How much are you earning? What do you have in your home?' with the lowest possible estimate, barely restraining his urge to hide the telly in the cellar. He does so atavistically, out of habit, out of a sense of tradition and just in case. What's more, the pollster will have been sent by the authorities and whatever you tell him will get through to them.

The Poles understand the advantages of capitalism but see no reason to say so in public. What have they to gain if they do? On the other hand, you can get quite a bit by making nostalgic noises about socialism. If you niggle the authorities with sufficient lamentation, you might just screw something out of them. It is widely assumed that competition is

Warsaw 1990: an end to Solidarity

exclusively a feature of capitalism. Not true. There is intense rivalry in a
Communist set-up between different people all seeking to persuade the
authorities that their own needs are greatest. In capitalism everyone is

JACEK FEDOROWICZ

trying to prove he's the greatest; in socialism it's the other way round: that he's a wimp.

And another thing. Every Pole takes a pretty poor view of his compatriots' intelligence. When the first non-Communist government in Eastern Europe — Poland's Mazowiecki government in 1989 — was formed, politicians who found themselves in power knew perfectly well that the Communist infrastructure had to be dismantled with all possible speed and capitalist principles brought in. But they were convinced that only they knew it and that ordinary people didn't. They began to introduce capitalism without ever using the word in public, while loudly proclaiming their sympathy for an electorate they were wronging so badly. The people instantly picked up the convention and burst into a chorus of complaint. And because — as I've said — every Pole thinks that his compatriots aren't very bright, the electors decided that post-Solidarity politicians were introducing capitalism without any belief in its superiority over socialism. Consequently, in the last elections, they voted for anybody who was available, so long as it wasn't one of those who, four years earlier, had helped to overthrow Communism. Because since they had overthrown something they knew nothing about, without knowing why, there was nothing to be got out of the situation. In this way the so-called Left came to power, firmly convinced (because they take a poor view of the electors' intelligence) that it was elected because people wanted socialism. And now it's having a lot of trouble persuading public opinion that what it is doing is not a straightforward continuation of the Leszek Balcerowicz's market reforms (which it is) but something quite different. All in all everyone is thinking that everyone else is thinking what they aren't thinking at all.

And what do people really think? Capitalism, they think, is here to stay because, alas, no other system has proved itself better. Socialism, they think, would be the most pleasant solution if it didn't contradict the greatest Polish desire of all. This — with the greatest respect — is extremely prosaic: Poles want to be rich. And so they shall be. Years of watching the increasing prosperity of a part of the world to which they couldn't belong has given them an appetite for affluence. It will help them get rich a lot quicker than anyone imagines. Though what we don't know is whether (out of habit) they will hide their growing prosperity from everyone else or merely from the taxman whom they regard, of course, as none too bright. ❏

# BARBARA STANOSZ

CAMERA PRESS

# The greatest Pole of all time

## The choices people make in personal and collective behaviour depend on their perception of their own interests or values

The laws, morals and customs upheld or recommended in a society, can provide the basis for a reconstruction of its world-picture and of its mythology: that largely unquestioned and subconscious system of beliefs relating to different social phenomena and their causes which are treated as truths equal to the laws of science. They are expressed in loose, at times quasi-poetic language, and accepted either as God-given truths or on ill-defined 'intuitive' grounds without scientific verification or correction when experience undermines their credibility.

In my own cultural tradition, one of the most powerful myths links the notions of woman, family and nation. Versions of this myth function in the cultures of many societies, particularly those which have been heavily influenced by the Catholic Church over the centuries. History and its present political or cultural composition make this myth especially vigorous in modern Poland.

The idea that the family forms the basic unit of society is like a slogan, repeated at every opportunity with ceremonial emphasis, suggesting that it is not a straightforward descriptive device, but something deeper, a fundamental truth which individuals and whole societies must respect, under the threat of hazy but disastrous consequences. 'The family' is strictly defined: it is a marriage (monogamous and heterosexual), sanctioned by civil law and a Church sacrament, with children sprung from that union. The functional division of roles between members is firmly established: the man bears the main responsibility for its subsistence, the woman for the upbringing of the children and for 'running the home' which entails the provision of a range of daily services for husband and children. Children should be blindly obedient to their parents, and essentially have no voice at all ('silent as fish', the Polish saying goes). The man is 'head of the family'; he has an unwritten right to the 'final word' in all matters in which he chooses to voice an opinion.

At the social level, this model is obligatory and natural, even though for several decades at least life has forced people to encroach upon its very foundations: the division of roles. In the 'People's Democracy' Polish women achieved full equality before the law and easy access to education. Differences between men and women in education and training were erased with relative speed. In education women began to be more successful than their male colleagues; in medical schools and universities women have long had the advantage. All this motivated women to professional activity, the more so as in a socialist economy, the man's income was generally inadequate to keep a family. This continues to be true today. In effect, women began to share the burden for their family's material welfare equally with men. But this didn't lead to an analogous expansion of the male role. Men did not make any significant contribution to household duties nor to the upbringing of children (except in the case of an insignificant number of young 'partnerships'). The myth of the 'normal family' has decisively shaped legislation. This is true even though the equality of women before the law helped to level the start men and women had in life. But no more than that: custom ensured that women's professional careers were and are harder to build, regardless of their qualifications.

All this happens with the tacit consent of women who succumb to the pressures of custom no less than men. They are exhausted by working double time — professionally and at home — and, on the whole, they are resigned. They treat their position as something assigned to them by

**As a result of intensive religious indoctrination, divorce is now surrounded by a thickening aura of transgression**

Central Warsaw: troubles shared

God or nature. Few rebel and break the stereotype. Feminism made its appearance in Poland very late and did not penetrate outside the intellectual elite.

Nor does one see young women breaking free of institutional family ties. On the contrary, women marry young (in 70 per cent of marriages the woman is under 25); they have children young (42 per cent of births are to women under 25); and the number of children per family is comparatively high (an average of 2.3). In Europe the figures are higher only in Albania, Ireland, Spain and Romania.

The mythology of the family incorporates the dogma of the indissolubility of marriage. Divorce is treated as something profoundly nefarious, associated with a grievous fault, to be prevented even at the cost of the greatest renunciations. Divorce figures are consequently low, while the number of broken marriages and families (caused particularly by male alcoholism) is huge. In 1988 there were only 195 divorces for every 1,000 marriages. These figures have decreased since new legislation made divorce even more difficult. Furthermore, as a result of intensive religious indoctrination, divorce is now surrounded by a thickening aura of transgression.

The most serious mythological incursion into the lives of modern Polish families has been the anti-abortion law passed less than two years ago. It allows the termination of a pregnancy only in the event of rape, threat to the woman's life and heavy damage to the foetus. Resistance to the new law was fairly high: 1.5 million signatures were collected in a petition calling for a national referendum. This demand was rejected by the previous parliament which was dominated by the pro-Catholic Right. In June 1994 the present parliament passed an amended law, permitting abortion in cases of 'extreme hardship'. But President Walesa, unstintingly loyal to the Church, refused to sign and parliament was unable to overthrow his veto. The prohibition still stands. The number of abortions has not fallen; the number of births has remained steady; neither contraception nor sex education have been made more widely available. But the costs of illegal terminations performed by doctors have risen radically and the number of unprofessionally stimulated artificial miscarriages has grown, with disastrous consequences for the health and lives of women. Unless abortion is legalised soon, the dogma that abortion is 'the murder of innocents' may lead to a considerable increase in the number of births within the context of growing impoverishment in a large sector of the population. This will deepen the poverty crisis to catastrophic levels, while turning the difficult lives of many Polish women into unmitigated hell.

The political changes since 1989 have not raised living standards for the majority of people, nor led to improvements in the state of education, but they have exposed people to Western cultural influences. While this may eventually help people — women — to break customary stereotypes, there are grounds for pessimism. The increasingly strong position of the Catholic Church — despite the change of political parties in government — may lead to the formation of a religious state with a legally sanctioned Catholic social and moral doctrine as the successor to Marxism-Leninism.

In contrast to other East European countries, the national and historical traditions of Poland would create an auspicious climate for this: the age-old myth of every 'true Pole' as a Catholic; or the myth of the 'Polish mother' as a woman whose vocation it is to sacrifice herself boundlessly for the good of family and nation. It is favoured too by the malicious twist of fate which combined the fall of the Communist system with the aggressively conservative pontificate of John Paul II. He has been built up by the Church hierarchy and a large section of the victorious anti-Communist opposition in Poland as an unassailable moral authority and the Greatest Pole of All Time. ❏

## KRYSTYNA KOFTA

# In thought, word and deed

There she sits, facing me. Weight: 145 kilos. Her thick hair is tied in a plait crowning her large, flat, white face.

She talks without cease. Lost in flab, her jawbone moves mechanically. The voice emanating from the depths of her massive belly is full of rancour. As always. Every utterance is a trap, it's all pure provocation. Even the apparently friendly: 'I bought you some cigarettes' — even that contains an element of unspoken hatred, there's a sub-text saying, 'but you never ever think of me.'

And that simply isn't true. I think of her a lot. In our two years of enforced cohabitation I've thought of

'the voice emanating from the depths of her massive belly is full of rancour.'

her more than of myself. I've devised a special way of thinking, a subtle technique for survival.

Now she's raving on about her misfortunes: how hard it is for her to walk with all that weight, it's such an effort, she's so weak, and there I am wanting her to get up, wash and go out for a walk — I'm so cruel to her...

Now she's shouting. In a short time she'll suddenly quieten down and move on to words filled with pain, 'as if I don't exist'; it's well-rehearsed, brilliant acting. A bit over the top, perhaps. We're into the second hour of prattle now. It's the full performance with no interval. My thoughts about her always get rather less refined when she starts to shout.

An axe with a keen, heavy blade, rounded like a cup. Its wooden handle is brightly polished, so smooth it could never stab a splinter into the hand that holds it. My trusty axe. I raise it high and strike a blow; like a plummeting falcon down it comes onto that great big head, down onto the gabbling lips. The gabbling goes on in two voices. The words pour out in a flow of real blood: 'You never say a thing to me by choice — it's all forced.'

She goes on sitting there, her head split in two right down the line of her profile — I'm amazed by the precision of the axe's bisection. Alright, it's a fantasy axe, but it didn't fall with such a heavy blow.

I sin in thought, but thanks to that I'm not in prison for premeditated murder.

Now she's eating. She reaches for a potato. 'You never tell me what you're thinking, you never do.' She's accusing me again.

Perhaps I will, though, maybe one day I'll tell you what I'm thinking. I'm committing a sin, it's true. But just by sitting at the same table with her I'm paying for all my crimes. At first sight you might think I'm performing my Christian duty by taking care of an old woman. You might well look at it like that if you couldn't read my thoughts. I could bugger off out of it — she's a stranger to me, she's only my stepmother, who got rid of me as soon as she got the chance, who set my father against me and beat me. Now she's all alone and I have to look after her. It was imposed on me by an alien morality which I cannot share. I just can't come to terms with it.

I ended up in her world by accident. My father took a shine to her when she wasn't quite so fat, just large, and two years after my mother died she moved in with us. She consumed everything that came her way.

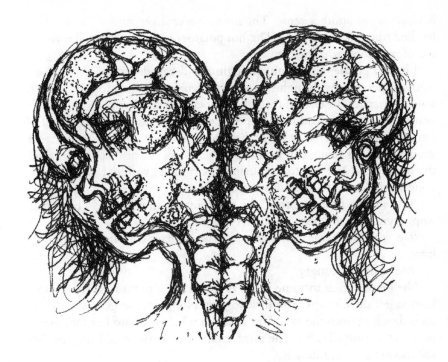

'I'm amazed by the precision of the axe's bisection.'

My father got thinner and thinner, until finally, gaunt as a shadow, he died. She's devoured him, I thought at the time. But before he died he said: 'Please look after Nina, she just can't manage on her own...' So now I must look after her when she can hardly creep along, heaving herself about.

Every day I escape from her podgy embraces into the world of the man with whom I spend my nights making love. I share myself out fairly, but not willingly. I'd rather eat with him, I'd rather sit by him all afternoon.

But in the morning I have to go and get the fodder ready. I serve God with a hatred in my heart that I can only rid myself of by murdering my stepmother 10 times a day. I recede to the far end of the table. I'm repelled by disgust.

Now she has stopped talking. She can smell the food. It hypnotises her. She imbibes the smell with all her senses, even her brain, which in her case is just another sense. The mood has changed now — it has levelled out and brightened. The hot potatoes in the pot have absolved me of my emotional frigidity.

I let her guzzle, but it's not enough. She demands emotion too. She wants to devour my thoughts, swallow down my imagination, be party to my experiences. Instead of that I heap potatoes onto her plate and pour sauce on top. A cartload fit for a peasant after the ploughing. One half of her split-open head hangs lower than the other. She's shovelling potatoes straight into her brain, still steaming. There's not much that's hotter than the middle of a hot potato. Its burning flesh mixes with her slightly congealed blood. It's a curious artistic effect.

'I do so love fresh potatoes,' she says, quite calm now, like a baby that stops crying the moment it touches the teat.

'Do you like them?' She wants to make contact with me at any cost now.

'Me? I'm not hungry.'

She helps herself to some meat. A large chunk of meat. Fatty. It's so hard to get these scraps. You have to wait a long time to get them. The fat is dangling from the side. She stabs the whole bit onto her fork and gnaws at it from all sides. The intervention of a knife would only put off the moment of engulfing it.

Her head is back in one piece again. She's the same as she was before I chopped her in half with my axe.

While she's guzzling I start cutting up smaller and smaller pieces, as if eating were an obscene function. Never eat like that — that's my motto. Never wolf it down. Eat with due elegance.

'This is such a tender bit of beef... you can tell... it must have... been a

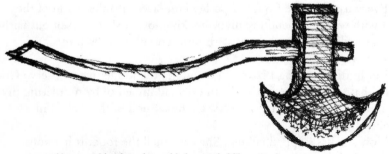

'An axe with a keen heavy blade rounded like a cup.'

... very young... animal...' she says, taking pauses to swallow.

She rips the young cow apart with her teeth — that's not in the imagination at all, like my splitting her head in two, no, she's right before my eyes, gassing on about a young cow, gnawing at it with her false teeth; if she can't cope with grinding it up she swallows the chunks whole, without chewing or even biting them, as fast as she can, as much as she can. She'll never quench her appetite. Feed the hungry, water the thirsty, so up I pipe: 'A glass of fruit puree, perhaps?'

'Yes please,' she says, 'I'd love some.'

I chuck a spoonful of cyanide in the puree. I don't stint on the shining white powder. She won't notice. She downs the lot in great big gulps.

Now she's dead, instantly. A good old traditional poison works wonders. There she sits, stiff and fat. She's going blue. In angular movements she sticks another piece of meat on her fork and chews.

'Yes, it must have been a very young cow,' she says.

That's what she'll be saying to me even as she dies. She'll never stop. Bitter saliva rises to my mouth. I can see the young cow — only yesterday it was still skipping about the meadow. Green grass. And today it's green peas. I saw that meat before it was cooked. That was no young cow — it was a tasty old ox. I don't eat meat. Because of her. For her sake.

'It's an old chicken, it'll have to have a long time cooking, but what wonderful stock it'll make,' she once said to me.

A chicken as old as the hills. Its dead eyes were cast skywards, dull little buttons among the grizzled feathers. Its comb flopped like a lolling tongue.

I watched her cutting up the stringy flesh of the aged chicken breast. She could suck her own breast without any special acrobatics. She'd only have to lift it up a bit. It could come to that. If there's a famine, it won't be impossible. The torment of famine is getting ever nearer.

While I was thinking about the chicken she's come back to life and grown pink again. She's examining a bit of fat, yellow as tallow. She sprinkles it with salt. That's an unfair comparison — not tallow; just one slap against the palate and it's swallowed. Quickly I bring her medicine for constipation. She drinks it down in one great swig. 'I've got poor metabolism, that's why I keep putting on weight — after all, it's not as if I eat much,' she's always telling the impassive 'phone receiver.

Forgive thy neighbour, the catechism taught me. I know it's not true.

People should love — love thy neighbour as thyself. And if you can't love him, you've got to hate him.

She's had her food, she's had her drink; only a few paces to the sofa and she lies down. The sofa groans and sags beneath her, poor thing. I feel for it. I feel for all the chickens, cows, oxen and pigs she's eaten, I feel for the water she drinks, for the chairs she sits on. I feel for everything this monster touches. But isn't the whole world created by the same force? How can it be possible that she and I were created by the same force, by one and the same thing? If so.... Sometimes I feel for myself, having to commit murder every day.

'Stuffing oneself full is the only tangible proof of existence,' I say to you in the other world, as I have removed myself from the world of hatred and duty into the world of love and whimsy. A summer supper in the late sun, as it goes on being light for ages. Fish, procured with great difficulty on hunting expeditions in town. The severed head of a smoked trout. Baby sprats tightly packed in a flat tin. The symmetry of the alternating heads and tails. Brown bread with a crisply baked crust on a bright wooden board. Butter and cheese on the same little plates, yellow, like brother and sister; even the white wine is in harmony, transparently dark yellow in colour.

In a carved wooden bowl, showing the chisel's craft, lie colours somewhat removed from the muted range of the bread and fish on the far side of the table: lettuce, always green as spring with an anaemic verdure, and two cucumbers, serpentine dildoes with shiny skin like a semi-precious stone clash with the vulgar, unnatural colour of tomatoes; radishes, purple as a cardinal's cloak, with bleached-out, ratty tails, amaranthine, lie scattered here and there, bringing it all together like a musical motif.

'Why don't you just bugger off out of it? You can always leave her — she's not ill, she's just fat. It'd do her good to move around a bit,' you say, and kiss me with your warm, dry lips. 'Come and live with me.'

'No', I reply, for what am I to say? Who on earth would fail to fulfil a dying father's last wish?

So don't you tell me she's a stranger, who never wanted me, don't remind me of what I already know, that at every opportunity, even without one, she'd pack me off to strangers in the countryside, don't tell me that again, because I never forget it for an instant — I hate her, but I loved my father and I'm doing it purely out of duty. And don't go telling me I've got an obsession with her obesity, because I know I have. Better not to talk to me on that subject.

But you keep on coming back to it, saying it's perverse for me to be looking at all that every day, that it's crippling me and that I've only to give the word and you'll poison her — yes, that's just what you said the other day when she had stomach-ache after eating half a goose and I couldn't come to you. I can remember exactly what you said: 'It won't be any loss — what with all these food problems it'd be a benefit for society.'

'I recede to the far end of the table. I'm repelled by disgust.'

And there was no note of fun in your voice, although it was meant to be a joke — I could hear hatred in your voice. It has passed from me to you. I'm feeling much better now — watch out or you might have to commit murder, just like me. You're being specific, like an engineer, you're already thinking how to do it, a mushroom, perhaps. We're eating supper together, and you chuck one separately-cooked killer toadstool into her food — it has no flavour, she can't taste anything, she won't suffer any more than from her usual blow-out... you're just as cruel as me in your plans. I must stop you from fantasising. I promise that in three months' time we'll be together, in three months I'll move in with you.

That's a surprise and a bit of a shock to you. Why in three months' time? Just don't try anything on your own, you're a bit too sensitive.

I'm amused by what you say about my sensitivity, although it's true. 'What do you want to do?' you ask again.

In three months I'm taking her to the airport. On the seventh of September. The plane will sag when she gets in. In Chicago her rich emigre brother will be waiting for her, the owner of some dubious hotels. I've seen him in photos. A fat smile of satisfaction and a longing for his homeland in his eyes. And overtones of guzzling. A wealth of different kinds of meat.

Now we're drinking the wine. I'm looking at you through my full glass. You kneel down and push my knees apart. Your head is hot, as if you had a temperature.

'You promised we'd eat our supper in peace,' I say.

You're not listening. Maybe you are, how should I know? You cast off your things, flinging them all over the place. You're like her — you throw yourself on top of me the way she threw herself onto the meat. I can't rid myself of her image. I must be patient. Give me a little time. You can never be as greedy as her, or as rapacious, not even in your love-making, no.

I push you away. You start to settle down. We drink the wine. You've calmed down, you know I won't run away. I'm not thinking about her any more. There's no place here even for the thought of her. What you say is not for repetition; what you do is not for description; what I think is not for sale.

The world of love is made up of secrets, just like the world of hatred. In some corner of my subconscious I forgive her, that poor, lonely barrel of lard, whose spiritual life consists of chunks of meat she's eaten; I want to be good to her until the seventh of September.

You'll help me to wait it out. I've only got a little bit more killing to do, just a little, and then I'll do nothing but love.

The sad secret of love as a tool for survival; I feel relief and absolution in both my mixed-up worlds.
*March 1981* ❏

*Translated by Antonia Lloyd-Jones*
*Illustrations by Geoffrey Keeling*

# 'My name is Adam Michnik'

J GUMOUSHII

Punctuality is not his strong point. He is brusque, explosive, irrepressibly blunt and impatient with the subtler nuances of manner. 'They say I'm a complete thug,' he remarks brightly; then he kisses your hand.

Adam Michnik, former political prisoner and controversial underground activist (once suspected of harbouring political ambitions) is now the editor of Poland's best-selling daily: *Gazeta Wyborcza* (Election Gazette). Launched in 1989, it prints around 500,000 copies, with additional local editions throughout the country and a weekly colour supplement. The basic format is still heavily reminiscent of underground publishing: 24 pages of cheap paper crammed with barely legible print. It is variously dismissed as 'a cheap tabloid' and lauded as 'the most readable paper in the country'.

Michnik is notoriously hazy about the administrative workings of the enterprise he heads, although his personality dominates in *Gazeta*'s challenging and provocative tone. He continues to project the image of the worker-intellectual and protests at the suggestion that he has finally joined the ranks of the press moguls. 'But consider the way I *look*. Compare my style with Rupert Murdoch's. It must say *something* about me. An intellectual is there to form the critical conscience of a democracy: that's exactly what I'm trying to do.'

His old preoccupations: sovereignty, resistance, literature, Christianity and history, have been translated into concerns about democracy, anti-Semitism, the Church, the art of compromise and the presidency of his erstwhile friend and ally, Lech Walesa. At any mention of the Communist order he still bristles and prepares to launch into a diatribe made perfect by years of practice: 'It was a concentration camp,' he bellows. 'There was no access to information, books or films. You couldn't travel, change your job, say what you thought or write what you wanted. And the economy... I mean... *loo-paper*. Getting hold of it was a major achievement. You went to the black market specially because someone was selling a few rolls of the stuff. We've made a great leap forward for civilisation. It's a different country.'

No nostalgic hankerings then, no sense of the loss which some former underground activists diffidently describe? And what about all those complaints one hears from people in the street about how much easier life was under Communism? 'The Poles have lost what they'd have lost anyway: their sense of security. We now have unemployment and all that. But look at Cuba. Poverty, empty shelves in the shops, and 33 years after the revolution Cuba is living off American tourism and prostitution — the two things in the name of which Castro fomented revolution against Batista. There's the end result of the system for you: deprivation and demoralisation. You can see the consequences in mafia operations in Moscow, Warsaw, Prague and Budapest. The horrors we are witnessing today are just ways of "getting by" which Communism taught us.'

Michnik's parents were active Party members who grew disillusioned with its ideals after World War II. They loathed officialdom and doctrine, and were deeply sceptical of the triumphalism and phobias of Polish nationalism. Michnik's own non-conformist manoeuvres have always elicited a mixture of respect and vitriol among Polish observers.

'I think I have retained my system of values,' he says. 'The idea that freedom and pluralism are preferable to domination and monopoly; that tolerance is preferable to the enforcement of an ideology on people with different views. I don't believe that what I write now conflicts with what I wrote then. Although many of my antagonists think otherwise. People say that I have betrayed my calling.' How? 'In the sense that I was a hard-line anti-Communist and am now speaking out in defence of former Communists. But there is a kind of inner logic in all this.'

He doesn't refer to it, but in May 1981 he intervened to stop a mob preparing to lynch a policeman in Otwock, near Warsaw. 'Listen to me,' he is reported to have said then, 'my name is Adam Michnik and I am an Anti-Socialist Force.' The boldness of his rhetoric knocked the crowd sideways. They let the policeman go.

Polish attitudes to authority are marked by a mixture of rebelliousness and childlike trust, stemming from a history of partition, occupation and puppet rule, and a far longer tradition of patriarchal ecclesiastical leadership. Today, in the wake of the Catholic Church's unpopular political incursions, Pope John Paul II may not have the clout he once had in his home territories but, Michnik emphasises, he remains 'an integrating, moderating factor in Polish society'.

There is a strong inherent desire for a ruling father figure, and a tendency to mistrust the notion of representation. ('Ah, "homo

Warsaw 1992: McDonald's can damage your culture

sovieticus",' Michnik muses, 'that epitome of rootless insecurity seeking refuge in dictatorship.') And indeed, people here expect to be taken care of — largely because they have never known anything else. Since the partitions of the late eighteenth century, power and responsibility have lain either in the hands of authoritarian governments or in the Church. And it is the hallmark of both to try and rewind the clock.

Michnik acknowledges that it is potentially a serious problem. 'We suffer from the prison-security syndrome. In prison the windows may be barred, there may be no handles on the doors but there are certainties. You know what you'll be eating and where you'll be sleeping. Then all of a sudden you're free. You can do anything, but you've no idea where you'll eat or sleep. So you begin to pine for security... for prison. I've always thought that the Poles needed three things: sovereignty, political democracy and economic freedom. I was wrong. People also have one other deep-seated need: security. It's encoded in us. There are people who create their own reality, of course. American democracy is based on the philosophy of people condemned to self-sufficiency, to their own merits and resources. The American won't get help from anyone. But America is a country of immigrants: people who chose to take the risk. Europe is more complicated, and the welfare state provided some kind of guarantee. But that idea has collapsed, and evidently high Thatcherism is no solution either. I expect modern democracy will seek a balance between the two.'

The need to feel safe is encapsulated in the image of a huddling national community under seige, watched over by a beneficent Church and enfolded by the heavenly cloak of the Mother of God. In popular religious tradition she is depicted as Poland's 'Queen'.

MATUSZEWSKI/CAMERA PRESS

Language of the new culture

But national solidarity is associated with a 200-year struggle for identity. 'It has been a specific kind of solidarity, in response to something negative. I don't know whether the Poles will stay with it. But I'm sure there's no danger that Polish culture will undergo a major change. If anything threatens, it is a kind of cultural americanisation: McDonald's and Mickey Mouse. But be conscious of the problem and model your own culture within the new language. The alternative is a kind of slow suicide. We'll be so afraid of foreign ways that we'll become closed and provincial and unable to offer the world anything of interest.'

The introspective side of the Polish experience, the ingrained assumption that there are no positive political choices available, still encourages the belief that because the world outside is stronger and more powerful, the only possible way forward is by obsessive introspection and self-delusion. The desire to 'privatise' is overwhelming: to run your own affairs, to keep within a closed circle of friends, to watch out for the others. And it is transposed to the national level. To an outsider the Polish manner can seem Byzantine. There seems to be an inconsistency between declared and actual intention, and a home-grown tradition of verbal abuse when referring to outsiders. But immoderate language does not necessarily imply immoderate behaviour, as Michnik hastily explains.

> An intellectual is there to form the critical conscience of a democracy: that's what I'm trying to do

'Poles behave better than you'd think from what they say or write. Perhaps it's a feature of the transformation. Perhaps there's a discrepancy between their "collective consciousness" and the behaviour which is forced on them by the demands of daily life. If you heard all those parliamentary speeches you'd think the country had never seen such hard times and that they're all about to commit murder. But when it comes down to it they find ways to compromise... It all looks far worse when you examine it sociologically and better if you simply observe... In the years just prior to the collapse of Communism, sociological tests showed that the population loathed the regime. But the country was quiet. There were no major strikes or demonstrations. Sociologists dubbed it "delayed radicalism": people thought in radical terms but their behaviour was peaceful because there was no room to bring the radicalism into effect.

Conversely, I'd say that what we are seeing now is a "delayed tolerance". We are living tolerantly, but have not yet learned to speak the language.

'If you told people that tomorrow the borders would close and things revert to what they were under Communism, no-one would want that. On the one hand there is the fear, on the other the certainty, that the Westbound train is already on the move. There's nothing to be done. For better or worse, it has already happened. For the present I can think of no mechanism better than the free market for the creation of prosperity. The question is how we are going to divide it up once we have it. That's where the argument begins.'

And what of Europe, its borders and pockets of national culture scrambling for supremacy? How important is the nation state for its future? 'Personally I need to be rooted. One lives out in the world, but one needs to have a home where one can be oneself. Where the chairs, the bed and the bookshelves all have their place. That's national culture. The nation-state most certainly isn't dying, irrespective of the question whether or not it's really necessary.'

The suburban urge to own a home which welcomes guests but fears thieves, and is, above all, filled with the familiar and the pleasing is what motivates a country which is mistrustful, unsophisticated, politically incorrect and determined to prove itself. In this context Michnik — once idolised by some — is now, at best, described in public as a nice man to talk to: 'clever, with a sense of his own limitations'. At worst he is dismissed as a 'Communist collaborator' and 'a Jew' (these days, more often than not, a political term meaning 'liberal'). But despite the patriarchs and the prejudice, the Poles can't resist buying his paper, if only to rubbish it in the office. A guarded sense of national privacy and a posture of uncompromising loyalty to one's tradition is one thing. The temptingly varied intellectual and political hamper *Gazeta* offers is another. But some people are worried. A right-wing tabloid recently accused *Gazeta* of initiating 'overtly anti-Polish propaganda' and published 'genealogies' of its senior staff pointing an accusing finger at their former Communist Party credentials.

Adam Michnik is unlikely to be concerned. Sales are up and a new printing house is well on its way to completion. The market impulse to diversity and choice, the consuming curiosity of the readership and the grip he has maintained on the public imagination, are bound to ensure his survival. ❏                        *Interviewed by Irena Maryniak*

# DAWID WARSZAWSKI

# Whatever happened to Rabbi Weiss?

**A member of Poland's tiny surviving community of Orthodox Jews examines the catalyst that unleashed a long pent-up debate on anti-Semitism**

Until World War II, the Jewish community in Poland had been the world's largest, best organised and culturally and politically most active. Almost all Israel's founding fathers came originally from Polish lands. At the same time, anti-Semitism, always rife in Polish society, was more and more explicitly endorsed by the state. The Church was unambiguously anti-Semitic; it took another half century for this to be denounced from the top.

All this, plus a continuing economic crisis, led to a steady exodus of Jews throughout the years following the end of the war. They carried with them — and left — few fond memories. Approximately three million Polish Jews, over 90 per cent of the community (and 50 per cent of Poland's total loss) were exterminated during the Nazi occupation of the country from 1939-1945. The Polish population, itself suffering tremendously, was unable or unwilling, to succour its Jewish compatriots. Hundreds of thousands of Poles moved into premises 'vacated' by murdered Jews, and took over their belongings. Some actively participated in the murder of Jews, others saved Jews at the risk of their own lives. In subsequent polemics each group would be cited as representative of the entire community.

In the general climate of post-war lawlessness, exacerbated by a bitter civil war against the Soviet-imposed Communist regime, Jews were an easy target. At least 300 were murdered in 1945 alone, as they tried to return to their homes, or recover their properties. Organised pogroms were again commonplace: one of the cruellest took place in July 1946 in Kielce where 44 Holocaust survivors, including women and children, were murdered by a Polish mob. The exodus continued.

At the same time, Communists of Jewish origin were nominated, as elsewhere in the Eastern bloc, to prominent positions in the Party and state apparatus. The regime could both count on their untrammelled loyalty, and, when it seemed expedient, use them as convenient scapegoats. During de-Stalinization for instance, the only secret police functionaries tried for 'excesses' were of Jewish origin. In 1968, the authorities resorted to anti-Semitism in an inter-party faction struggle, and again in a bid to win popularity with nationalist circles. The exodus of some 20,000 Jews in the late 1960s extinguished organised Jewish community life for almost two decades. The re-emergence of Jewish identity coincided with the growth of the Solidarity movement and merged into it, causing some nationalist activists to question its 'Polishness'.

Nothing of Poland's long history and reckoning with its Jews could be openly discussed under the Communist regime: the subject was sealed. Issues and accusation that had remained taboo for half a century exploded into the open for the first time in August 1989 when Rabbi Avraham Weiss arrived from Brooklyn USA.

He had come to stage a protest in Auschwitz against the presence of a Catholic convent within the perimeter of the former German camp, now a museum.

Rabbi Weiss's demonstration, his rough handling by local workers and the anti-Semitic undertones of the Church's condemnation of his protest, became front-page news. For two months the 'Weiss Affair' along with its attendant discussions of the state of Polish-Jewish and Christian-Jewish relations and frequent allegations of Polish anti-Semitism and Jewish anti-Polonism dominated the media to the virtual exclusion of all else. Rabbi Weiss became symbolic of 'the Jews' just as the workers who had roughed him up came to represent 'the Poles'; Primate Cardinal Glemp, in a sermon on 15 August, not only attacked Weiss, but also the Jews for inducing Poles to alcoholism in the past and controlling the world media today. And this was the summer of '89 — the demise of Communism, Poland's first non-Communist prime minister, throughout Eastern

Poznan 1992: anti-Semitic grafitti

Europe old taboos and barriers crumbling — Europe's most exciting summer since 1945.

Five years later, Rabbi Weiss returned for another demonstration. In his absence, the convent had been removed but, contrary to earlier agreements, a huge crucifix remained. The Rabbi also protested against the presence of a church near the perimeter of the adjacent camp in Birkenau.

But even though the summer of 1994 was somewhat dull, the Rabbi got no more than a token two days on the news agenda. The Church refused to get involved, and the public remained unmoved. What had changed?

After the years of silence, Weiss's first visit had broken the barriers and released the pent up prejudices and emotion of half a century and more. It allowed the discussion of concrete issues and addressed accusations unresolved since the end of World War II; it dragged skeletons out of murky cupboards and began the exorcism of Poland's Jewish ghosts. What began as a rabid exchange of abuses and primitive stereotypes developed into a rational debate ending with the unequivocal condemnation of anti-Semitism and its manipulation by politicians. By the time it was all over, the subject had been exhausted: anti-Semitism was no longer 'respectable' and, with the exception of *Gazeta Polska*, a right-wing weekly published in Warsaw, the press routinely condemns anti-Semitism and is vigilant in denouncing local incidents and the appearance of grafitti. By 1994, the Rabbi and what he had incited were non-issues.

Not that the process was without setbacks. Nationalist passions were revived and inflamed when the Jewish card was played during the presidential election campaign of 1990. Solidarity leader and ultimate victor Lech Walesa launched an undistinguished appeal to the anti-Semitic segment of the electorate when he proclaimed himself 'one hundred per cent Pole' and called on Jews 'to stop concealing themselves and reveal their identity'. His chief opponent, Prime Minister Tadeusz Mazowiecki, was crippled electorally by unsubstantiated accusations of his supposedly Jewish origins.

**Three million Polish Jews, over 90 per cent of the community, were exterminated during the Nazi occupation**

The debate returned again to the media. Mazowiecki supporters accused Walesa of tolerating and fostering anti-Semitism. Partisans of the Solidarity candidate accused their opponents of being unpatriotic and of slandering their country. Catholic theologian Michal Czajkowski summed up the tenor of the discourse: 'What is characteristic of Poland today is "Jews by nomination". It would seem that the opponent on any issue necessary has to be a Jew... the word "Jew" has become an insult.... For the average Catholic Pole this word still has pejorative undertones and a huge emotional load.'

But a year later, during parliamentary elections, although seven parties ran on distinctly anti-Semitic platforms, not only was the 'Jewish question' not aired in the media, no anti-Semitic candidate was elected.

There is still an impending matter that could test the 'normalisation' of the media's treatment of Jewish issues; confiscated Jewish property. Potentially covering vast areas of real estate, this unresolved matter not only threatens Poland's forthcoming privatisation law, but is so explosive that no-one has yet dared address it. ❏

# CAMERA PRESS

# Secret state

**Behind government allegations of bogus
asylum seekers and illegal refugees hides
a shadowy network of detention centres
of dubious legality**

Refugees are not criminals. But in Britain, unlike elsewhere in the European Union and in contravention of the UN Convention on Refugees, innocent people, who have escaped persecution in their own countries, are being detained in increasing numbers without charge, without trial, with no fixed term and with almost non-existent rights to bail, on the capricious say-so of individual immigration officers. They can find themselves in prisons in Britain for up to 18 months, in an atmosphere of secrecy and with an almost total absence of explanation. Most are then deported.

Just a year ago, in November 1993, some of us in Oxford woke up to this hidden shame only when the government opened an immigration detention centre at Campsfield House, just north of the city. While the government said its aim was to reduce the number of asylum seekers in prisons, the numbers held in detention centres and in prisons roughly doubled between July 1993 and March 1994. There are currently 700 'asylum seekers' in detention centres and prisons under the immigration laws. Campsfield House has 200 of these. Others are held in a semi-clandestine network of similar places across the country: in a decrepit detention centre at Harmondsworth near Heathrow airport, first used in 1970; Haslar near Plymouth, a former barracks run by the prison service

Campsfield, March 1994: exposing the hidden shame

since 1989; at various airports, ports and police stations; and nearly 200 asylum seekers in ordinary prisons. Apart from a few east Europeans, they are all from the Third World, particularly Ghana, Nigeria, Zaire, Algeria, Ivory Coast, Angola and South Asia.

Campsfield House is a refurbished youth detention centre, with new 20-foot metal fences, electronic gates, video cameras inside and outside and, the most recent addition, rolls of razor wire. Campsfield is run by Group 4 Security, whose low-paid staff have two weeks' training and range from the sometimes kind to the malicious. Detainees suffer a barrage of tannoy announcements relayed into each room, frequent early morning 'fire alarms', and other more or less petty harassments. They have hardly any organised classes or other ways of passing the time. Medical facilities are minimal. Detainees are normally not locked into their rooms; visitors are admitted to special lounges to see named prisoners. However there is now a list of undesirable visitors about whose visits, and visitees, immigration officers must be informed; at least two visitors, both known campaigners, have been forcibly evicted.

The asylum seekers committed to this carpeted hell are there solely on the 'administrative' decision of immigration officers. According to the Home Office, about one in 75 asylum seekers is thus detained; the rest are given 'temporary admission', usually on condition that they live in a particular place and sign on at police stations. Of those detained, over half have gone straight into detention from their port of entry. Within a few days they must answer a long list of standard questions, usually without a lawyer. After two or three months in detention, they are summoned to receive the immigration officers' decision, normally (especially for detainees) a refusal of asylum. Of the 22,370 people who applied for asylum in 1993, 1,590 were granted asylum, while a further 11,125 were given the insecure status of 'exceptional leave to remain' (ELR); by the fourth quarter, only 150 of the 5,650 applicants were granted asylum and 520 exceptional leave — down from over half to a little over 10 per cent.

Only legal representatives, interpreters and immigration officials are present at the 'hearings', which last about half an hour. The asylum seekers are given seven days to appeal and the date of their flight back to the country they escaped from. This is cancelled only when they appeal. Appeals, which usually take place after two further months in detention, are heard in front of an adjudicator, appointed by the Lord Chancellor's Office. The adjudicator can make life and death decisions; witnesses and others may be present and give evidence. Should the adjudicator come to a different decision from that of the Home Office, the latter may appeal and detention continue. Lawyers may appeal against refusal on points of law, but not fact, to higher courts and detention, again, may continue. Those who fail in this process are deported.

Once asylum has been refused, an adjudicator can grant bail. The sureties are prohibitive, £4,000 (US$6,000) or more, and bail is often refused. A handful of detainees at Campsfield, who have been offered accommodation by visitors, have achieved temporary admission. But

> The combination of muzzling and secrecy enables the government to portray the prisoners as 'bogus asylum seekers' and illegal immigrants

immigration officials have the power to grant or withhold temporary admission at any time without giving reasons for their decision or evidence for their supposition that a detainee 'will not comply with the conditions set', on the grounds that 'we are not a court of law'.

The only discernible pattern of refusal is that those detained tend to be from countries of a nationality for which immigration systematically refuses asylum. In 1992, for instance, both refugee status and ELR were refused for 99 per cent of Zairens and Angolans, 98 per cent of Ghanaians, 97 per cent of Indians, 95 per cent of Pakistanis, all well represented at Campsfield. Forty per cent of those granted refugee status were from Iran, Iraq and Sudan. But even as between the nationals of particular countries, decisions appear arbitrary and incomprehensible.

Immigration officers do supply written reasons for the refusal of asylum. These may include questions on the refugees' identity, nationality and the accounts of their escape. One African refugee was told, incorrectly, that he could not have escaped across a river because it was full of crocodiles. Refugees are systematically disbelieved; frequently they report their despair at the refusal of officials to listen to them or try to understand. When they have been misunderstood by interpreters or misrecorded by immigration officers, the latter accuse them of deception or inconsistency.

The most common reason for the refusal of asylum is the official denial of political persecution in the refugee's country of origin. In a letter responding to a visitor's appeal on behalf of a detainee, Michael Howard, home secretary, told Douglas Hurd, foreign secretary, that assessment was based on information from 'our embassy in Kinshasa where the chargé d'affaires and her staff are well placed to provide objective assessments of political developments... although there are sporadic arrests of political activists there are, in fact, very few political prisoners and the widespread opposition to President Mobutu and his government is usually tolerated.' Not only is this untrue, it fails to explain the refusal of asylum to those who *have* been political prisoners in Zaire.

Group 4 use the threat of transfer to ordinary prisons as a means of maintaining discipline in detention centres. But since refugees are often political activists who have resisted tyrannies elsewhere, they rebel. In March this year, after 10 Algerians from Pentonville prison and another 10 from Campsfield had won release after going on hunger strike, 180 prisoners at Campsfield, and others elsewhere, went on a mass hunger strike. The Campsfield strikers, ignoring a tannoy warning not to expect the same treatment, issued a declaration stating that Campsfield 'is a prison', that 'we want to be free while our cases are going on', and suggesting that the British government should 'withdraw its signature to the Geneva Convention and refuse to accept asylum seekers at all rather than put men and women through the trauma and uncertainty we are experiencing in detention.'

Group 4 staff put meals in their rooms and, some alleged, tried to push it down their throats; immigration officials made false promises of release if people ate: detainees were locked into their rooms and corridors; some visitors, 'phone calls and letters were stopped; medical attention, when it occurred, seemed more of a threat than a help. Between 10 and 20 hunger strikers were transferred to prisons. The Home Office issued a press release accusing them of being 'ringleaders', causing *The Voice*, for example, to report, quite incorrectly, that the

MIGRANT MEDIA

Rooftop protest 1994: giving the lie to propaganda

prisoners had become violent and 'smashed furniture'. On arrival in prisons they were, as usual, not charged and were put in isolation. Most of those transferred were among a group of 100 or so prisoners who escaped into a courtyard, climbed onto a roof and exchanged shouted communications with demonstrators outside. At least one of them was subsequently granted asylum.

The hunger strikers did not win their freedom. But two months later the Campsfield prisoners rebelled again. On 5 June there was a mass uprising at Campsfield House, triggered by the deportation of an Algerian without notice (contrary to promises made by immigration officials that proper notice would in future be given). Group 4 and immigration officials locked themselves into their offices and the prisoners took over the centre for several hours; many escaped into a courtyard and several climbed the fence using a Group 4 ladder. Eventually some 200 police, some in riot gear and with dogs, entered and put down the rebellion with considerable force. The Home Office has so far failed to account for the number of detainees who were observed leaving in ambulances after the police had gone in.

By thus giving the lie to the notion that detention is humane and bearable, the prisoners won more publicity than the efforts of their supporters and campaigners had achieved. The latter are reluctant to publicise individual cases for fear of the vindictiveness both of the Home Office and of the prisoners' governments. Two of the Algerians released after their hunger strike were detained again after they took part in a demonstration outside Campsfield and appeared on television; a Ghanaian was re-detained after he was interviewed on television. The combination of muzzling and secrecy enables the government to portray the prisoners as 'bogus asylum seekers' and 'illegal immigrants', and to promote its counter-images — such as condoms stuffed with heroine in the sanitation system at Campsfield.

Charles Wardle, the now-sacked immigration minister, dismissed the critics of government detention policy as being confined 'within a narrow band of public opinion' and the campaigners as 'a motley collection of the far left and liberals'. However, the detention without trial of innocent people is not only shocking, but calls into question the whole repressive system of immigration controls. ❏

*By a resident of Oxford and member of the Campaign to Close Campsfield*

# BABEL

**Continuing our series focusing on the voices of those silenced by poverty, prejudice and exclusion**

## SABINE GOODWIN

# 'We shall never get Jerusalem'

During a brief ceasefire in the 1987 camp siege of Bourj Al–Barajneh in Beirut, Josef, now 34, sits drinking coffee in the sunshine with his family. Suddenly a shell fired by the Amal militia lands next to him. He, his father and his brother lose both their legs, five others in that small group lose their lives. 'There is no future for the Palestinians in Lebanon.

So many people died, so many people were injured, so many people were imprisoned. The massacres, the sieges, all for nothing. The whole world has deserted us: the PLO, Israel, America, Britain.'

As the architects of peace in the Middle East receive their Nobel accolades, and the international community applauds the creation of a Palestinian homeland in the narrow confines of Gaza and Jericho, three million Palestinians outside their country reflect bitterly on their exclusion from the process. Officially, though estimates by those working in the camps put it much higher, 320,000 of these refugees wait in Lebanon, the majority since the exodus of 1948 that followed the creation of the state of Israel. It will be at least two years before their fate becomes part of the peace agenda: first resolve the thorny question of Jerusalem, and only then the return of the diaspora.

Palestinians in Lebanon live without basic civil rights in recognised and unrecognised Lebanese and Syrian army-controlled camps. One in three is not registered with the UN Relief and Works Agency (UNRWA) and is denied the material support this brings; financial aid from the PLO that funded the Palestine Red Crescent Society, the equivalent of a health department for the refugees, has dwindled to nothing following the Gulf War and the cut-off of Arab subsidies.

In the south of Lebanon, the refugees still live with the constant reminder of the presence of Israeli forces. Shelling and 'sound bombs' are the norm since the Peace Accord.

They survived Lebanon's long civil war; endured the sieges of their camps; lost thousands to starvation and massacre — the most notorious that of Sabra and Shatila in 1982, the most devastating, they say, that in Tel al-Za'atar in 1976. Morale has never been lower than now: for the camps of Lebanon, the peace has failed to deliver. Twenty-seven thousand refugees have recently been offered Lebanese citizenship. Some have refused to take it, but many in the south feel it is the only realistic option.

But for most, the status of 'refugee' is central to their rights as Palestinians: the only guarantee of their ultimate right of return home.

'I used to get reparation from the PLO for my injury,' Josef explains in the summer of 1994, wheelchair-bound in the small grocery store he runs. 'I relied on it. Now we get nothing from the PLO. I am registered with UNRWA as a "hardship" case. They lent me some money to help me open this shop, but I hardly make enough to feed my three children.

'We cannot work properly in Lebanon. We are only allowed to work in labouring jobs. These are badly paid and now there are less and less of them. There are more and more Syrians coming to work here.

'I want our people to have human rights just like any other people. Are we not human beings? Do we not have rights like any other people? Because we are Palestinian should we live like this? When we were starving during the camps war, when we had nothing else to eat but dogs and cats, you in the West cared more for the dead animals than us.

'I am from Acre. Everyone knows about Acre. I went there to visit once. We can sometimes get permission if we have a relative in Palestine. It was just for a few weeks, but I saw Acre. I would rather live in Acre again than have a million dollars.'

Not far away, through the cramped alleys of the camp, Um Walid lies all day in the bed from which she cannot move. She cries: 'There is no-one here to look after me, no-one.' She has no family in the camp. Her son was killed by the Israelis in 1982. Sometimes some money might come from her surviving son in Germany, 'Sometimes.'

**'Abu Amar, he will never get Jerusalem. It is impossible. Israel will never allow it'**

Sumeira comes from the Cabri region of Palestine: 'My family, my parents, one sister, four brothers and I lived here in Bourj through every little thing. We lived here through every siege. When the war was over we moved to Saida for my father's health. When he died last year we came back to the camp. A week later, my sister went missing. That was 27 July 1993, she was 11. Now she is 12 and we still cannot find her. She went missing from inside the camp. She was playing with a friend, then she was gone. At first I felt she was still here in the camp. Now no. Another girl was taken when she was with her family at the beach. She came back a few months ago, but she wouldn't speak to us. Her family wouldn't tell us anything. Now they have moved away.'

Rola, Sumeira's friend: 'In 1990 my husband went missing near the entrance to the camp, near the Syrian checkpoint. I do not know if he is alive or dead. I am sitting, waiting. I take care of our two children.'

A young computer technician complains: 'I was born in Kuwait. I lived all my life in Kuwait. I came here for the first time to visit my

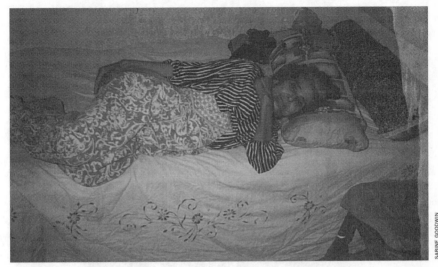

SABINE GOODWIN

Um Walid: Bourj Al-Barajneh

grandparents just before the Gulf War. We could never go back. I cannot go back to Kuwait because I am a Palestinian, but I am a foreigner here. People think I am Kuwaiti, I can find no place here.'

Samia lives along the frontier of the camp: 'This was no man's land all through the camp wars. I was shot here once. One of the men was brave enough to venture out during a short ceasefire to try to get some food. The Amal shot him dead. I tried to retrieve his body and was shot in the leg. I had to lie still for three hours before crawling back to my house. That man's body was there for three weeks before we finally got him. The smell had become unbearable.'

Fatmeh has lived all her 30 years in the camp: 'We are afraid of this solution. This solution is not for us. We will not go to Gaza or Jericho; we will go to our land, to our country. This peace is not for us. This peace is for the economies of the governments of the Middle East. Where is the justice in this peace?'

A former Fatah leader living now in the unrecognised camp of Quasmiah in southern Lebanon: 'It is part of a process to minimalise the refugee problem, but any lasting peace must be based on something real, something truthful. If the Palestinians do not have the right to go back to their land and their homes, I do not think there will be real and lasting peace in the Middle East.

'At first Abu Amar (Arafat) spoke to the world about a democratic Palestine for Palestinians and Jews alike. This is the real solution, to find a democratic land for all these people to live in peace. But Israel refused this, so the solution we have now is the only one.

'No-one can know what will happen to we Palestinians in Lebanon. All we know is that there are negotiations and the Palestinians in

Um Tawfiq: Bourj Al-Shemali

SABINE GOODWIN

Lebanon are part of those negotiations.

'Abu Amar is a great leader. He is struggling to find a solution for his people. His greatest quality is that he is a patient man. History will speak for itself.'

A devout Muslim living and working in Quasmiah: 'This is an unjust peace. This is peace by force. I do not recognise the PLO. No one has elected the PLO. They are in charge, but nobody elected them. The Palestinians have two faces now. They have no rights in the eyes of the world, and no rights in the eyes of their leaders.'

A family explains its decision to take up Lebanese citizenship: 'We feel it's the only answer. It's for the future of our children. We'll keep our Palestinian identity papers; we will not forget Palestine.'

Um Tawfiq in Bourj Al-Shemali, one of the two large recognised camps in the south, is fatalistic: 'During the 1970s we lived in Damour and Tel al-Za'atar. We were there during the massacre at both camps. The K'Taab (The Phalangists) took my husband on both occasions. The second time, he never came back. At Tel al-Za'atar they took my youngest son too. I moved here with my four daughters and remaining son. During the camps war, Amal took both my son and one of my daughters. In 1986, they took my daughter, she was 17, they left her body at the door of this house. They did exactly the same with the body of my son in 1987.

'I used to get money from the PLO as the widow of a martyr. Now nothing. In the last two years they gave us widows two months money out of 24. I can't class as a hardship case with UNRWA. I try to do as much house cleaning as I can, but I am getting old now and people prefer younger girls.

'There is nothing in this peace for us. They have forgotten us. All this, for nothing.'

'Abu Amar, he will never get Jerusalem. It is impossible. Israel will never allow it.'

'Countries outside have not helped the Palestinians, they have forgotten us.'

Ahmed from Sabra in Beirut: 'Rumours abound in the camps. They tell us the camps will close, that we will be moved out of the way to the north of Lebanon, to Europe. But if we move from here, we move further away from Palestine, further away from what is rightfully ours.

Um Ibrahim and sister: Shatila, Beirut

We know the Lebanese have put up with our presence for so long, but where is the answer for us?'

Um Ibrahim takes care of her elderly sister, too sick to move. Her son was shot dead at the massacre at Shatila. His sister shows his photograph: 'We make peace with them. We make peace with these people who were responsible for killing us.

'I would like to go to visit my home in Jaffa, but I am afraid. If they do this to us outside Israel, what would they do to us in Israel? My sister still has the key to her house in Jaffa. She had just had her bedroom decorated when we all had to leave. She didn't want it to be damaged while she was away.'

At the UNRWA school on the edge of Sabra camp, children speak of their hopes.

Fatima was six when her father was shot dead by the Amal. Her little brother saw it happen: 'My mother no longer gets money from the PLO. My brother who is 16 has to work to support the whole family, but he can only get casual work. We can't count on his money.'

Rola reads from her copy book: "'Acre is famous and beautiful. It is built by the sea and is renowned for its lemon trees and other fruits." I want to go back to Palestine, but how? If we ever could go back I know it would be difficult at first, but we'd get used to it.'

Hussein's little sister died of starvation during the camps siege of 1987: 'If I could have the chance, I would go back to Palestine. My family is from Cabri, they tell me about it.'

An old lady in one of the Beirut camps speaks for many: 'To forget the refugees from 1948 is to forget what really happened. We have lost our homes, we have lost members of our families, we have lost everything and yet we have struggled all this time in the hope that somewhere there was justice. Where is that justice?' ❏

## MAHMOUD DARWISH

# The speech of peace

In a world divided by its duality,
just East and West,
neutrality is in vain.
Who are we?
Are we East: There is no
livelihood in the East.
In the East, the party of iron
order,
In the East, the system grows
nothing in the market but plans.
Are we West? in the West our
enemies sow
ambiguity about the Arab ruler.
In the West: Rambo and Shambo,

Coca,
Jeans, Disco, Circus and
freedom for the cats.

Who are we? Is it true we are an
error?
Let us spend thirty years in war,
And the solution is in the West.
Are we really a mistake?

Can the locusts eat the elephant
and drink up the Nile?
There is place on the land for all
and in the land there is ample

place for happiness.
Here we stand steadfast over
five thousand years
of glory and love
no matter how the darkness
lapses.

Long Live Peace!!
I am the return of rationalism,
and no rationalism after me,
I knew resistance,
I knew opposition,
food will evade us.
Oh Nation, did you not fear your
destiny?
Food is Peace.
Oh people it is time to correct
our history
and compete with civilisations
in word and deed.
It is time to teach our enemy
peace — lesson and solution.
We will deprive them of all pre-
texts,
so that they will not be able to
escape Peace.
What do they want? What?
Do they want all of Palestine?
        *Ahlan Wasahlan* (Welcome).
Do They want the fringes of
Sinai?
        *Ahlan Wasahlan.*
Do they want the head of
the Sphinx, this deluder of
time?
        *Ahlan Wasahlan.*
Do they want the heights of
attack on Syria?

        *Ahlan Wasahlan.*
Do they want the river of
Lebanon?
        *Ahlan Wasahlan.*

Do they want to revise the
Quran of Othman?
        *Ahlan Wasahlan.*
Do they want Babylon in order
to exile Nabu's head?
        *Ahlan Wasahlan.*
I shall give them all they

'Tomorrow you will awaken...'

want of us
and all they do not want of us,
I will take the Peace because
Peace is firmer than the ground,
stronger and richer.
They are mean misers,
We are generous — generous.
Long Live Peace.

For the sake of Peace,
I return soldiers from the
barracks to the Capital
and will make them policemen
against the mobs, to defend
Security
against this growing sinful
opposition.
Peace with others, there is not
peace with the dissidents here
Here... no leftist factions will
exist.
We shall grind the meat of the
left,
and veil the daylight from the
angry.
In prison there is room for all
for the old and for the suckling
for the cleric and the unionist
and the maid.
Peace with others.
There was not a peace signed by
opposers here.
Here there is obedience and
harmony.
Long Live Peace!
God will reward and judge those
who died
defending our memories and our

illusions.
Let bygones be bygones,
Who died, died.

I shall annihilate memories,
I shall cancel Martyr's Day and
forget hatred,
I shall plow the sad graveyard of
the Martyrs,
And remove their bones and
bury them elsewhere
One by one.
In my state their gatherings are
illegal
For the living or the dead
may not agitate rot.
Death has no right to infringe
On bitter forgetfulness which is
in us.

I shall break all guns and let
pigeons roost in them,
I shall break the memory of War.
Sleep as you have not slept.
Tomorrow
You will awaken to bread and
prosperity... Sleep.
Tomorrow
You will awaken to my heaven...
Rest and Sleep.
Long Live Peace!
Long Live Order!
*Shalom... Salaam...!!!*

*Excerpted from* The Speech of
Peace, *reprinted from* Challenge
Magazine. *Translated by Samir
Habash* ❏

# Medical Aid for Palestinians

Registered Charity Number 263670

Medical Aid for Palestinians is a British-registered charity dedicated to the medical and humanitarian needs of the Palestinian people.

MAP in its present form was relaunched under a new Board of Management in 1984 in response to the massacres of Palestinians in the camps of Sabra and Shatila in Beirut and the destruction of most of the health structures in Lebanon.

Since the outbreak of the Intifada, MAP has increased its material and personnel support to health institutions in the West Bank and Gaza. MAP receives regular funding from the British Government's Overseas Development Agency, the Commission of the European Communities and from UK and international trusts.

MAP is best known for its volunteer-sending programmes. Since its first medical support team went into the camps of war-torn Beirut in July 1985, MAP has sent more than 300 volunteers to Lebanon and the Occupied Territories.

Ten years ago MAP sent six medical volunteers, led by Dr Swee Chai Ang, and half a ton of medical equipment into the besieged camp of Bourj al Barajneh to perform emergency surgery there in Haifa Hospital.

---

Today MAP is still in Lebanon and is funding the redevelopment of the medical services there.
In Haifa Hospital, MAP will:—
- complete essential building repairs and repainting work
- carry out urgent maintenance work on the sewage, water and electrical systems
- move the operating theatres back above ground
- upgrade the x-ray, pharmacy and laboratory departments
- plan training programmes to upgrade the skills of the medical staff

If you would like to support this appeal, or would like further information about our work, please contact Medical Aid for Palestinians, 33A Islington Park Street, London N1 1QB, tel 071 226 4114

---

# REVIEW

RONALD WRIGHT

# A swim with the tide

*A Fish in the Water: A Memoir.*
Mario Vargas Llosa, Faber, London
1994. £15.

I first saw Mario Vargas Llosa at a political meeting in Cusco, the old Inca capital high in the southern Andes of Peru. It was a cold August night in 1988, about a year since the novelist had been pricked into activism by a government plan to nationalise the banks. Austere pre-Conquest stonework lining the streets held messages for him: *Vargas, Champion Of The Bankers; Cusco Hates You*; and, subtler and perhaps more wounding, *Peru Is Not A Novel*. About 50 people — apparently all the faithful that could be raised — stood in a dark patio while chorus-girls sang *Mario! Mario! Mario!*

A few months later I saw him in different surroundings: at an elegant lunch on the twentieth floor of a bank tower in Toronto. Here he seemed more at home, smoothly reciting the message he repeats in this beguiling book — that a monetarist revolution was the only way to save Peru, and he was the man to lead it. He presented himself as a heroic intellectual, a Václav Havel forced by his country's need and his own idealism to dirty his hands in politics. His Democratic Front was, he said, the best hope for restoring true democracy to a country ravaged by demagogues.

This went down well in the business district of Toronto, as it did in most of the world outside Peru. It was easy to talk seamlessly about a place few of his listeners could imagine and fewer still had visited, easy to massage gringo prejudices by saying, as he does here, that politics in Peru 'had almost always been in dishonest and mediocre hands', an observation from which he exempts only himself, a few friends, and his Uncle José Luis who was president in the 1940s.

Inconvenient questions were so unexpected that like Lima's earth tremors they produced sudden cracks of rage in the novelist's grand façade. Why, for example, had he allied himself exclusively with parties of the traditional ruling class, the white *criollo* elite to which only a tenth of Peruvians belonged? 'Because in politics, sadly, one must be pragmatic.' In that case, how could he speak of reviving democratic ideals when some of these same allies had, during the most recent constituent assembly, tried to restore a shameful cornerstone of Peru's old 'democracy': the exclusion of illiterates from the vote? Literacy was defined as literacy in Spanish, and about half the country

San Pablo, Peru: the richness of a culture...

veau-riche'; poor people who fail to vote for him are 'lumpenproletariat'; a newspaperman he dislikes is 'an exquisite product [of] dung-collecting journalism'. Hernando de Soto, the influential economist and ally with whom Vargas fell out, is dismissed as 'a prima donna... an opportunist... a sly and sneaky enemy'. When he keeps this cheap vitriol in its bottle, the novelist can be more dangerous. His cleverest device is the disarming confession, used both to elicit sympathy for himself and to patronise opponents. With Olympian disappointment he claims to have 'invented' the faithless Soto, to have 'forged for him an image of an intellectual', to have trusted him 'with my characteristic naivete'.

He describes loyal members of his alliance, on the other hand, as gifted with 'impeccable democratic credentials', as solidly 'middle-class', determined to expose the 'Trojan Horse of Communism'. His supporters cannot be the rich, for there are not enough rich in the country 'to fill a theatre [or] even a living room'. One can argue about definitions of 'rich' and 'middle class', and the size of some people's living rooms, but his associates' names — Thorndike, Cooper, Grundy — reveal many to be from the Anglo-Saxon cream on

spoke Quechua, the Inca language, so this had amounted to an ingenious form of apartheid throughout most of Peru's existence as a state. His answer: 'That's not true.'

Half of *A Fish in the Water,* which combines an account of his political campaign with a memoir of early life, applies fresh plaster to such cracks. The tone is sometimes inconsistent with this aim: hyperbolic, petty, even coarse. He deplores snobbery yet calls opponents 'social climbers' and 'nouthe old Spanish elite.

Vargas Llosa's explanation for the failure of Peruvian politics in general and his own in particular sinuously avoids any responsible examination of social tensions, cultural incompatibilities, and unhealed historical wounds. He holds an archaic social-Darwinist view that Peru is not 'modern' enough, which is another way of saying that it is too Indian. 'Modernisation', he wrote more frankly in a 1990 *Harper's* essay, 'is possible only with the sacrifice of the Indian cultures.' This is of course the sacrifice that many white Peruvians have been eager to perform ever since the first of them leapt ashore with Pizarro.

The best part of *A Fish in the Water* is the memoir of Vargas Llosa's early years, from birth in 1936 to his departure in 1958 for a long voluntary exile. It is a charming if rather predictable account of a writer's formation: absent, then oppressive father; sudden uprootings; boarding school; a flirtation with Communism; an obsession with Europe consummated by escape to Paris and Spain. The revealing thing about this childhood is how little curiosity young Vargas has in anything Peruvian. He never seems to notice the ruined cities and pyramids around him, let alone the living Indians and the Inca language spoken by millions. Foreign nursery and adventure stories set the pattern of his life. Peru he defines as 'provincial', good for little except to be mined (as the world has always mined it) for raw material and local colour. To Vargas Llosa there is only one culture worth taking seriously:

European, especially French. In short, he falls prey to the old *criollo* inferiority complex, which found its purest expression in the building of jungle opera houses.

'My country', he writes in one of the book's most telling passages, 'manages to interest the rest of the world only because of its natural cataclysms, its record rates of inflation, the activities of its drug traffickers, its terrorist massacres, or the villainies of those who govern it.' He is unable to see that Peru might interest us because it is one of civilisation's half-dozen cradles around the world, a place of extraordinary historical depth, cultural achievement and diversity; a place where a wounded civilisation still lives and seeks a place in the modern world as something other than a deracinated labour pool. Vargas Llosa's blindness in this area speaks more loudly than his entire book about the main reason for Peru's modern decline: the white-settler mentality of its elite. The bloody Shining Path should not be mistaken for an Indian or even a nationalist movement, but it has thrived in Peru because the policies of ethnic denial and economic exploitation — the very policies Vargas Llosa advocates — have been forced on the Andes too many times, bringing misery and death to those who live there while profits fly to pale hands and foreign bank accounts. When Vargas mentions racism at all, it is usually to shift the blame onto the victims. He tells us, nonsensically, that 'the Quechuas' were racists in Pre-Columbian times, and charges President Velasco (1968-75) with exploiting 'racial prejudice and ethnic resentment' — a perverse caricature of well-intentioned reforms, such as official recognition of Quechua, aimed at ending ethnic repression by making room for indigenous culture in national life.

Other eminent Latin American writers — Asturias, Fuentes, Paz, Neruda, Galeano, and Peru's Arguedas — have felt a need to engage in various ways with the native civilisation around them, but not Vargas Llosa. 'I've never liked the Incas,' he once admitted in the *New York Times*, though by his own account he changed that tune while campaigning in Cusco. As an artist, of course, he has no obligation to like Incas; his material is up to him. But the leap from Vargas Llosa's pen to his politics is neither as great nor as recent as many imagine. Long before any overt campaigning, he had become a propagandist for a narrow vision of Peru that denigrates the history and experience of more than half its population. In a perennial essay on the Conquest, for instance, he contrived to blame the Incas for their own defeat, asserting that they allowed themselves to be butchered by the Spaniards because they were an 'anthill' society unable to recognise the value of freedom which, he added in an Orwellian twist, was the great gift of the conquistadores. This wasn't history — it flouted both the primary documents and the best modern research on the period. It was supremacist myth-making designed to justify the racial

and political order.

Even in fiction he has not been content to take his literary choices and leave others to take theirs. For many years he has tried, as he tries again here, to discredit Peru's other major novelist of this century, José María Arguedas (1911-1969). Arguedas, also a white Peruvian, grew up in the Andes, was bilingual and, in addition to producing the masterpiece *Deep Rivers,* became a noted ethnologist and translator of Quechua manuscripts. No other writer was so qualified to explore the Andean world and the Peruvian cultural dichotomy. In 1977 Vargas began damning Arguedas with sly praise: he was so good — the argument went — that he had us believing in his tales of racism and Dickensian injustice, when in fact the conditions he portrayed so brilliantly did not exist; his work, Vargas concluded, was 'a beautiful lie'. To get an idea of how this sort of thing plays in Peru, one has to picture, say, a conservative South African writer returning home to run for president in alliance with the old right wing of the National Party after a literary career in which apartheid has never been addressed except to claim that Alan Paton and Nadine Gordimer were liars.

So why *did* Mario Vargas Llosa, after so many years aloof, want to be Peru's Margaret Thatcher? Those hoping to find a straight answer in this book are likely to be disappointed, for while *A Fish in the Water* may be intended as an apologia, it is also an exercise in self-deception. Right

CARLOS REYES/ANDES PRESS AGENCY

El Monton rubbish dump, Lima: ...the poverty of the uprooted

to the last page the author keeps insisting that if he had won, things would be different — he would have brought stability, prosperity and honesty to Peru; he would have avoided the abuses of his cynical opponent, Alberto Fujimori. Yet throughout the book he reveals innumerable lapses from his own moral code. He abhors nepotism and patronage, yet tells, unabashed, how almost every job and sinecure he held as a young man was obtained through pull. He extols Uncle José Luis as a model politician, but we soon learn how nicely the family did with public appointments in those palmy days. More serious are Vargas Llosa's revelations about his own campaign, during which he failed to inspire or enforce elementary standards among his closest colleagues, his would-be cabinet.

If Vargas the politician has any saving grace, it is that Vargas the writer can't resist a good tale, even at his own expense. The best one — worthy of García Márquez — involves the venerated statue of Our Lord of Miracles, whose procession through the Lima streets is attended by a devout and supposedly impressionable multitude. In a meeting at their candidate's home, the high command of the Democratic Front — men hitherto described as upright realists poised to transform Peru — propose a masterstroke. At the frenzied height of the procession, the Lord of Miracles will be induced by electronic means to pronounce for Vargas Llosa! '"If the Christ Clad in Purple speaks, we win," Pipo Thorndike stammered excitedly.' ❏

# INGER FAHLANDER

Travelling between Tallinn and Stockholm, the *Estonia* sank in a storm on 28 September, carrying down more than 900 passengers. Among them was the translator and human rights activist Inger Fahlander. Inger, well known to a generation of Amnesty and *Index* staff in London, was a witty, generous and kind colleague. Her tenacity as a campaigner was particularly relished by *Index,* and by the Swedish Committee of *Index,* when, in 1992, she suggested that the Gothenburg Book Fair host a workshop on Freedom of Expression and invite *Index,* Article 19 and PEN to share a stand at the bookfair. She badgered the right people and saw the idea through to completion in September 1993, when she and her son Jon helped us run a most successful stand. ❑

# HUMAN RIGHTS

## CAROLINE MOOREHEAD

# A deadly legacy

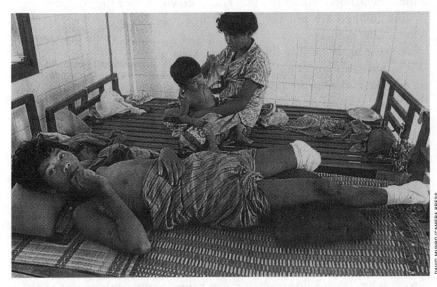

DAVID MUNRO/CAMERA PRESS

R ae McGrath, founder of a small organisation called the Mines
Advisory Group, returned not long ago from northern Iraq.
Surveying the vast tracts of land made uninhabitable by unexploded
mines, he was puzzled by one particular incident. A six-year-old boy,
playing in a meadow, had stepped on a mine and been killed. What made
it puzzling was that the boy, whose village lay in the heart of a heavily
mined area, knew all about mines and what they could do. So why had
he not taken greater care? Crouching down to look more closely at the

spot where the boy had died, Rae McGrath suddenly realised what had happened. The grass in the meadow had grown tall. From a six-year-old's line of vision, the mine would not have been visible. The boy died because he was too small.

Children constitute well over half the world's victims of exploding landmines. Amputees, now a familiar sight in many developing countries emerging from years of civil warfare, are for the most part boys and girls blown up while engaged in the rural tasks they have always performed — taking flocks to graze and collecting firewood and water. And, of course, playing; in the early days of the war in Afghanistan, before they knew better, children were attracted in their hundreds by the brightly painted mines, nicknamed 'butterfly', that rained down all over the country.

But children are not the only victims in what is now recognised as an appalling legacy of several decades of low intensity civil wars. While accurate figures are clearly impossible to calculate, the United Nations estimates that over 100 million unexploded mines, whether small and designed to maim, or 'bounding' to scatter steel fragments, are today lying throughout 60 countries, and that only an immense, co-ordinated, international effort involving vast sums of money could begin to touch the problem. Unexploded mines have other implications — for the economy, for health services and, increasingly, for returning refugees. Over half the health expenditure of Kurdistan is now said to go into caring for the victims of mines. The International Committee of the Red Cross, who are leading a major campaign against mines under their mandate covering weapons that are indiscriminate and cause excessive injury, have said it would take several thousand years to clear Afghanistan of its 10 million or so unexploded mines; and even then, given the mining and destruction of its former excellent irrigation system, the country's fragile economy can never fully recover. Afghanistan, always poor but previously self-sufficient in food, is destined never to be so again (*see Afghanistan, p46*).

**It would take several thousand years to clear Afghanistan of its 10 million unexploded mines... the country's fragile economy can never recover**

Landmines are not, of course, new. Designed as a response to the tank in World War I, they were used extensively in World War II, particularly in Poland and Russia. But these were large, very heavy objects, easily visible and used mainly against specific military targets. It was not until the 1960s, with technological advances making them smaller and lighter — the popular P4 MK2 weighs less than three ounces — that landmines began to be seen in a new light: a cheap and efficient way of controlling and terrorising populations, emptying the countryside and crippling the opposing forces. Who can forget the 12-year-old boys in the Iran-Iraq war, sent by the army ahead of the troops as human mine-sweepers?

Laos and Cambodia provided the first examples of large-scale, random dropping of mines. By 1979, when the USSR invaded Afghanistan, landmines had become a standard offensive weapon, delivered by plane or artillery. Since then their use has spread steadily. Figures suggest that Iraq's offensive against the Kurds has left three to five million unexploded landmines, and the fighting in the former Yugoslavia a further two million. In Cambodia, where there are already 30,000 amputees in a population of little more than eight million, the Khmer Rouge are once again laying mines around villages and in the rice paddies.

It is the nature of modern warfare, with entire countries rather than battlefields the theatre of war, that has made the landmine the perfect weapon. Angola, in a state of almost perpetual conflict for over 30 years, during which foreign powers have never stopped pouring weapons into the country, has seen famines spread through areas too heavily mined to be farmed. Where relief cannot reach, people have no option but to return to the countryside in search of food. Every day, hundreds are being blown to pieces. Even if the recent and much promised ceasefire were to hold, the thousands of refugees who have fled the fighting would now find it too dangerous to go home.

Landmines play a grisly part in the world's growing refugee crisis. In Mozambique in October 1992, the Frelimo government and Renamo rebels signed a peace agreement, and plans were made for the two million Mozambicans living in camps over its borders, or scattered throughout the country, to return to their own villages. But for over three decades all sides in the war had been laying mines, along roads, around villages, in ditches and meadows. As the number of amputees grows day by day, to add to the 10,000-15,000 already maimed, it has become clear that landmines may prove a far greater killer in times of peace than in times of war. Mozambique is bankrupt. Its railway lines have been destroyed, and its hydro-electric dam at Cahora Bassa lies idle, the pylons that carry its lines along 890 kilometres not only mined by government forces to protect them from the rebels, but also booby-trapped by the rebels to prevent them from being rebuilt. It is thought unlikely that the power supply will be resumed before 1996. In the game parks, once attracting foreign tourists and foreign earnings, the elephants that escaped death at the hands of soldiers in search of ivory and food are now being blown up by landmines.

There are few secrets about mines. Meticulous work by human rights and humanitarian organisations, worried by what they see as a growing crisis no-one will take seriously, has established the existence of some 50 different models, manufactured and exported by just under 100 companies in 48 different countries. Mines are big business. The USA currently leads the field in mine manufacturing with 37 varieties, closely followed by Italy with 36; Belgium, Germany, Egypt and, increasingly, developing countries like Singapore and Pakistan follow their lead. Landmines come cheap — not much more than US$6 for a small, plastic model — but they cost somewhere between US$300 and US$1,000 each to make safe. To be effective, mine clearance can be done only by hand, a highly dangerous and time-consuming activity, made all the more lethal because the people doing it have no map of where the mines have been laid, and no idea of which model they will come across. The Mines Advisory Group and the Halo Trust, both based in England, are part of a growing number of

Cambodia: grisly harvest

NIC DUNLOP/PANOS PICTURES

organisations providing assistance and training in countries devastated by prolonged civil war; but they have to be seen against a background of 100 million unexploded mines.

Mines are the subject of one of the UN's more feeble treaties, the Landmines Protocol of 1983 which attempted to regulate their use, but not production nor sale. The very properties that make mines so lethal — the fact that they can lie dormant for up to 20 or even 30 years and that they can be triggered at any time as easily by a child as an elderly woman or a pig — also make them exceedingly hard to control. Who, once hostilities cease, has the time, will, money or skills to search for the relics of a war everyone longs to forget?

In the last few years, pressure has been growing among non-governmental organisations, and even among a number of unions — in Italy, the workers at the Valsella weapons firm near Brescia came out in protest recently over making mines — to impose a total ban on the manufacture, stockpiling and transfer of all landmines. The Protocol has now been in force for 10 years, which technically means that it can come up for revision. In the USA, Senator Patrick Leahy, author of the Landmine Moratorium Act of 1992 that has been responsible for a ban on sales from the USA, has compared mines to chemical and biological weapons in their inability to differentiate between soldiers and civilians. World-wide revulsion was what finally made toxic weapons so 'repugnant to the conscience of mankind' that they were banned. Senator Leahy and others now argue that only a similar sense of world disgust at so much casual destruction, allied to a real understanding of the financial cost to the world community in terms of failing economies and high numbers of permanently crippled people, is likely to see the same ban extended to mines — and even that will do nothing for the vast existing stockpiles, or save the untold numbers of Afghans, Cambodians, Mozambicans and Angolans losing limbs and even their lives in the months and years to come. ❑

**Recent books:** *Landmines — Legacy of Conflict*, Rae McGrath (Oxfam Publications), *Landmines in Angola* (Africa Watch), *Landmines in Mozambique* (Arms Project, Human Rights Watch), *Violent Deeds Live On: Landmines in Somalia and Somaliland* (African Rights & Mines Advisory Group), *Landmines: a Deadly Legacy* (Arms Project & Physicians for Human Rights)

AMNESTY INTERNATIONAL

# Beware the ministries of truth

When Amnesty International was founded just over 30 years ago, the belief that ordinary citizens around the world could — through letter-writing and other means of popular protest — make a difference to the international protection and promotion of human rights was easily dismissed by governments as just so much do-gooding noise. Few perpetrators of human rights violations could have imagined then that the relatively simple idea which gave birth to AI would capture the imagination of such a wide public, and that this organisation would become such a formidable challenge to their authority and their impunity.

But three decades later, the language and tactics of human rights activism have become more than a little familiar to governments intent on violating or tolerating the violation of the rights of their citizens. AI's techniques of mass membership action, as well as a battery of new tactics, remain in most instances as valid and effective as ever in working to stop, investigate and prevent such violations. For the past three years, those strategies have been directed against human rights abuses perpetrated by armed opposition groups as well.

But it would be naive of AI and other human rights organisations to think that governments and armed opposition groups can be caught off guard quite so easily as in the past. For nearly every foreign ministry in today's world — and a good many leadership councils of armed opposition groups — has become fluent in the language of human rights to a degree which would have seemed unthinkable to the first generation of AI activists.

Indeed, in recent years we have seen a proliferation of what might be called 'human rights bureaucracies' in governments whose human rights records open them to scrutiny and criticism. The purpose of these bureaucracies is clear — to deflect or undermine such criticism by giving the appearance of official commitment to ending human rights violations. Often employing the most sophisticated public relations techniques, some governments will now set up a human rights ministry or an investigative commission whenever they feel that their allies or trading partners need a little extra convincing about the sincerity of their intent to improve a bad human rights record.

On some occasions, a genuine, if modest, effort is made to see that these new mechanisms actually have some clout. But all too often they merely amount to bureaucratic window-dressing — a nice letter-head on which to reply to letters of protest and another well-titled, well-heeled diplomat to introduce at international gatherings. The whole human rights lexicon trips easily off the tongue and the democratic credentials of the country concerned get a much-needed facelift.

Behind the cosmetic surgery there is often no real political will to tackle the sources of human rights violations nor to hold those responsible accountable for their crimes. This development of the 'human rights bureaucracy' — a kind of back-handed tribute to the effectiveness of human rights activism — presents activists with subtler challenges than perhaps we have faced before. For now it is not just the dictator or the despot we must name and confront, but the politician or the diplomat adept at speaking the human rights language.

The need to recognise and expose these sham agencies and commissions for the paper commitments that they are has been a crucial message of AI's campaigns this year. In an important report on Colombia, for example, AI expressed concern that the wide range of measures put in place in recent years, ostensibly to guarantee the human rights of Colombian citizens, have merely 'generated a smokescreen of human rights protection that has helped hide the fact that other measures and steps which the government has taken seriously threaten human rights'.

A case in point would be the official programme in 1991 set up by the Colombian Government to resolve cases of 'disappearance' by establishing a victim identification plan involving a national register of unidentified bodies and the names of the 'disappeared'. An admirable initiative to be sure — but AI has nevertheless concluded that 'although the Colombian authorities have given assurances that the programme is functioning, no detailed information has been provided on its progress.' What is more, an independent local organisation of families of the 'disappeared' reported in 1992 that in spite of having delivered information on over 40 individual cases to the programme, there had been no official response to its submission. Similarly in Indonesia, where the president's own National Human Rights Commission was established by decree in 1993 to investigate the complaints of individual appellants as well as organisations. While AI has noted some of the surprisingly forceful statements which the commission has issued, its mandate confers no real power to carry out investigations of any consequence, and the government is under no obligation to heed the advice it proffers. Only one representative sitting on the wholly state-subsidised commission comes from a non-governmental organisation, and it is notable that none of the country's

> **Behind the cosmetic surgery there is often no real political will to tackle the sources of human rights violations nor to hold those responsible accountable for their crimes**

principal human rights defenders have agreed to serve on what they regard as a highly compromised body.

Persuading governments that a Pinochet or a Saddam Hussein has a human rights record worthy of denunciation can be hard enough. But when ambassadors and ministers are wined and dined by slick human rights bureaucrats who know their UN Basic Principles on the Use of Force from their Inter-American Convention on 'Disappearances', getting them to consider an alternative assessment of a country's human rights record requires additional fervour. This is now the task before us all: to explore fresh and more incisive methods of exposing the smoke-screen of lies contained in press releases from phoney ministries of human rights and reports of bogus commissions on truth. ❏

**Brian Phillips**

THE INFORMAL SECTOR
SERVICE CENTRE, NEPAL

# A democracy stumbles

In Nepal in 1990 a broad-based political movement succeeded in replacing an undemocratic and dictatorial regime that had oppressed any political activity for 25 years by a multi-party democracy. One feature of the people's movement, as it came to be called, was the emergence of a number of local human rights organisations, which played a leading role in the overthrow of the system. Among these is The Informal Sector Service Centre (INSEC) in Kathmandu which, in April 1994, published the *Human Rights Year Book 1993*, a hefty 496-page survey of the human rights situation in Nepal.

The report paints a picture in considerable detail of a four-year spiral of decline and, while it struggles to remain politically impartial, is highly critical of the present government. Following an historical account that covers the period up to 1960, *Human Rights Year Book 1993* summarises the principal developments of last year. No one who is familiar with Nepal, or with south Asia more generally, will be surprised by the results. The most impressive, albeit depressing, section is a 227-page survey which documents human rights violations throughout the country, district by district. It documents over 1,000 violations during 1993, a threefold increase on the previous year. These include allegations that 24 people were shot to death by police, and 153 tortured in custody and jail, six of whom died as a result. Also described are incidences of rape, suicide, degrading treatment, and deaths in prison due to inadequate medical care. Twelve appendices discuss topics such as the status of 'untouchables', trades unions, school teachers, the rights of children, and the situation of displaced people and refugees, in particular the 86,000 Nepali-speaking refugees from nearby Bhutan.

The last few years have been turbulent as Nepal adjusts to a new political culture, and the leftist political parties that form the main opposition to the ruling Nepali Congress Party have organised strikes and street demonstrations against the government on numerous occasions. Three people were shot dead on 26 June 1993 in Lalitpur and six in Kathmandu during the most violent demonstrations to have occurred since 1990. The demonstrations were demanding an investigation into what became known as the Das Dhunga incident in which two leading left-wing politicians died in suspicious circumstances. Various reports on the Das Dhunga incident are also reproduced in the *Year Book*.

Despite the gloomy picture, there are signs of hope. One is that such a report has been compiled and published at all — it could not have appeared five years ago — and that such issues are out in the open at last. The less desirable features of a society that has been run for centuries on an almost feudal system of patronage and favour are now being discussed critically and without fear of censure; measures are being taken to increase police accountability and improve police training. One of the weaknesses of the report is its frequent assumption that police shootings are a part of government policy, rather than the result of poor discipline and

**Despite the gloomy picture, there are signs of hope... such a report could not have appeared five years ago**

panicky reactions on the ground.

In the meantime, the ruling party is riven with internal conflict, mid-term polls loom, and the prospect of yet more unrest is likely. Human rights violations inevitably increase in number as political tension grows. In a country at peace with itself such issues can be tackled with a long-term policy — as is the Nepali government's stated intention — rather than by engaging in perpetual crisis management. Nepal's new democracy is stumbling and the events of this year will determine whether it stands or falls. ❑
*Michael Hutt*

*Human Rights Year Book 1993* (The Informal Sector Service Centre (INSEC), April 1994, 496pp) Available from The Informal Sector Service Centre (INSEC), PO Box 2726, Kathmandu, Nepal, tel (977 1) 270 770

HUMAN RIGHTS
WATCH/AFRICA

# Out of the eye of the world

Straddling as it does both Africa and the Arab world, Sudan occupies an awkward space in the imagination. It is, perhaps, this, as well as the lack of immediate strategic value that the prolonged conflict in southern Sudan no longer attracts much attention from the world's media.

Since 1983 this conflict has claimed 1.3 million lives. Seen as a bewildering and complex series of internal disputes, the equation has often been simplified into a battle between the 'mainly Christian' south and the 'Muslim' north. *Civilian Devastation: Abuses by all parties in the war in southern Sudan*, Human Rights Watch/Africa's latest survey of the region, details the horrific road down which the country has descended over the last 11 years to the present day. Without immediate and effective measures to curb these crimes the population of southern Sudan is in real danger of being irreversibly damaged.

In 1983 an army battalion led by John Garang crossed the border into Ethiopia to establish the Sudan People's Liberation Army (SPLA). In the early days the SPLA drew support from a wide base in its call for a united, democratic Sudan. But, almost from the start, the movement was plagued by internal disputes. The

split in 1991 was the culmination of these problems. While it appeared on the surface to be a political divergence, with the SPLA-Nasir faction led by Riek Machar advocating an independent south, the ethnic differences between his and Garang's SPLA-Torit became increasingly obvious as factional infighting intensified.

The coup in 1989 displaced the civilian government of Sadiq ul Mahdi and brought the military-backed National Islamic Front to power. Khartoum upscaled its efforts to unite the country under an Islamic banner.

Compiled from a wide range of sources including a series of interviews conducted in Population Centres inside Sudan as well as refugee camps in Uganda and Kenya (permission to visit Khartoum was not granted), the report catalogues a disturbing list of human rights abuses by all sides involved.

In conflicts of this kind systems of semi-subsistence are seen as both targets and strategic points of defence. Four groups are identified as being responsible for the creation of famine in the region: the army; the government-aligned militias; the SPLA faction and the civilian traders exploiting military control of commodities. In desperate pursuit of supplies, the armed groups, most notably Garang's SPLA-Torit faction have turned their guns on the civilian population. Garang lost their main source of supply with the fall of the Mengistu regime in Ethiopia.

In 1991 the government in Khar-

Southern Sudan: SPLA figher

toum began to replace English in schools in southern Sudan with Arabic. The subsequent protests in Juba were met with a sustained campaign of detention and torture against students and the Catholic clergy. The renewed military offensive in 1992 included widespread bombing and a scorched earth campaign in which villages were targetted, looted and razed to the ground. The army destroyed fields and sowed them with mines to prevent them being worked.

1991-92 also marked the first clashes between the SPLA factions. Fear and distrust among the civilian population was actively encouraged, playing on old animosities between the Nuer and the Dinka. Numerous reports tell of village raids, rape, looting, the abuse of prisoners and sum-

mary executions.

With the occupation of Somalia in late 1992 by the US/UN forces, the government in Khartoum, possibly fearing a similar intervention, agreed to allow relief agencies into the area east of the Duk Ridge in the Upper Nile province. The World Food Programme and others described the situation they found there as a famine of catastrophic proportions. The world paid little attention and, for a brief time, relief aid reached the region. By July the government had resumed operations: air bombardment and a ground offensive combining troops and armoured vehicles. Seventy-five thousand people were displaced, their homes, property and food supplies destroyed. In 1993 alone it is estimated that some 200,000 people perished as a

**JASON GARNER**

result of this conflict, either directly or as a result of sickness and starvation. Around 700,000 people are now estimated to be internally displaced, which means that they do not qualify as refugees.

While the government in Khartoum is unrelenting in its efforts to dislodge or destroy all opposition, the SPLA factions share the blame for the abuse of the civilian population. The factional fighting, preying on non-military resources, and the forced relocation of displaced civilians to vulnerable front line positions, as well as the ethnic persecution, add up to a list of serious violations of the rules of war.

The report sets present events in a clear and concise historical perspective and is a powerful indictment of a conflict that has continued unchecked for too long. It calls for all sides to respect human rights law, to allow monitors into the region as well as the Red Cross who, like other humanitarian organisations, have either been refused permission or been fired on. These are short-term measures. The authors see no longer-term solution until pressure is applied to bring the leaders to the negotiating table with a genuine commitment to halting the conflict. ❏

*Jamal Mahjoub*

*Civilian Devastation: Abuses by all Parties in the War in Southern Sudan* (Human Rights Watch/Africa, June 1994, 279pp) Available from Human Rights Watch, 485 Fifth Avenue, New York, NY 10017

HUMAN RIGHTS
WATCH/AFRICA

# Fault-lines

The conflict in the Balkans has focused attention on the existence of historical 'fault-lines' along which two or more cultures collide and are seemingly unable to coexist peacefully. Recognition of this phenomenon has brought the belated realisation that the roots of conflicts previously explained in terms of East-West hostility during the Cold War have roots in much older tensions, often forcibly repressed, which erupt into violence when the restraints are removed.

One such fault-line is the border between the Arab world and black Africa. Tension in this region is generally presumed to result from religious antagonism between the Muslim north and the animist and Christian south, as exemplified by the civil war in Sudan waged by the south against the north. Mauritania, where both the black and Arab population are predominantly Muslim, gives the lie to such oversimplifications.

As revealed in Human Rights Watch/Africa's new report *Mauritania: Campaign of Terror (State-Sponsored Repression of Black Africans)* this has not prevented the Arab-dominated government from implementing policies aimed at the subjugation of its black population and their culture. These abuses are the result of the government's 'Arabisation' policy which permeates all sectors of society.

The Mauritanian population comprises three roughly equal main groups: the *beydanes* (literally 'white men') of Arab-Berber descent, the *haratines* (also known as black Moors) who are former slaves (slavery was abolished in 1980, though the practice still persists), and the indigenous black African population.

Since independence in 1960 the country has been governed by the *beydanes*. Throughout the 1980s, racist policies aimed at reducing the employment prospects and stature of the black population multiplied. Opposition from the black population only provoked further repression.

Human rights abuses against the black population peaked in April 1989 following a border dispute with Senegal. The dispute was used as an excuse for the mass expulsion of thousands of blacks, extrajudicial executions, torture, and the confiscation of property. Repression was worst around the Senegal River valley in the south of the country where security forces destroyed villages, raped women, confiscated and stole the inhabitants' belongings, and destroyed their identity cards.

This was followed between late 1990 and early 1991, by a purge of the army and the civil service resulted in the detention of over 3,000 blacks and the death of 500. This finally provoked international condemnation of the military government of President Maaouiya Ould Taya. His attempt to deflect criticism by introducing a measure of democracy was little more than an attempt to cover up the campaign of human rights abuses inflicted upon the country's black population. The 1992 second presidential elections, which returned Taya to power, were marred by serious irregularities and there were widespread allegations of fraud. Many of the black population were unable to vote.

Since the elections the level of human rights abuses has declined, but blacks continue to be subjected to discriminatory policies. Many have lost their land and property and tens of thousands are unable to return to the country. The easing of government repression may have more to do with the success of the long term Arabisation policies than a change of heart by the government. This apparent success could set a precedent which Human Rights Watch/Africa is determined shall not go unnoticed. There is, they conclude, 'abundant evidence directly linking high-ranking government officials to human rights abuses against the black ethnic groups... Human Rights Watch/Africa believes that those responsible for egregious human rights abuses in Mauritania must be held accountable for their crimes.' ❏

*Jason Garner*

*Mauritania : Campaign of Terror (State-Sponsored Repression of Black Africans)* Human Rights Watch/Africa, April 1994, 156pp) Available from Human Rights Watch, 485 Fifth Avenue, New York, NY 10017

# LEGAL: INTERVENTION

A legal column dedicated to the memory of Bernie Simons
(1941-1993), radical lawyer and defender of human rights

ROBERT MAHARAJH

# A law fit for intervention

*Sovereign states or individual human rights? Which does the law favour?*

In response to the extraordinary shifts in the balance of world power following the collapse of the Soviet Union, the rules ostensibly governing the rights of states to use force within one another's boundaries have changed dramatically in recent years. Though the letter of the law remains the same, states have put forward new justifications based on radical re-interpretations of the existing law.

At the heart of the changes is a concept unique to the latter half of our century: the universality of human rights. The UN Charter is explicit in its commitment to upholding human rights standards around the world, and treaties such as the Universal Declaration of Human Rights and the Convention on Genocide are expressions of that commitment. This imperative has resulted in the confrontation of two competing concepts: state sovereignty, as enshrined in Article 2(7) of the UN Charter, and the defence of the fundamental rights of individuals as a justification for its violation.

The theory of 'humanitarian intervention' has a long history. First formulated in the early Middle Ages, it was the justification for European forays into the Middle East in defence of Christians suffering under Muslim rule. It was elaborated by Grotius in the seventeenth century, and later became the foundation of European claims that occupation of Africa was essentially a philanthropic, 'civilising' mission. In the first half of the current century, the Italian invasion of Ethiopia in 1935 was founded on much the same claim, and the suffering of the Sudeten Germans in Czechoslovakia was the justification put forward by the Nazis for their intervention in 1938. Ultimately, and perhaps inevitably, it became the means by which the naked exercise of force was clothed in legitimacy.

The UN Charter, drafted in 1945, sought via Articles 2(4) and 51 to impose a universal restriction on the use of force by individual states except for the purpose of self-

Signing the Charter 1945: a moment of vision in a bleak world

defence: collective security actions could be undertaken under the auspices of the Security Council whenever necessary. 'It spells', said Eleanor Roosevelt at the time, 'the end of the system of unilateral action, exclusive alliances, and spheres of influence, and balances of power.' Article 39 states that should the Security Council determine any 'threat to the peace, breach of the peace, or act of aggression', it may take action under Chapter VII, Articles 41 and 42. Article 41 empowers non-military sanctions, such as trade boycotts, arms embargoes or embargoes on international air flights; Article 42 adds the use of armed force such 'as may be necessary to maintain or restore international peace and security'. Article 43, a vital element in the original document, requires that standing forces be set up and placed directly under the Council's command before any action under Article 42.

The post-World War II vision of the founding fathers was quickly replaced by the antagonisms of the Cold War. Individual governments discovered that ad hoc responses allowed them to circumvent Article 43 requirements and thereby retain control over UN actions; the two superpowers deadlocked the process by the use of their Security Council vetoes. Interventions that did take place were unilateral, undertaken by individual states or groups of states. Their action was not 'collective' in the sense understood by the Charter, but in their own interests and in violation of its terms. The use of force had, therefore, to be legitimised by reference to earlier law, mostly evolved before 1945 out of treaty and customary rules. While the present tendency is for these to converge more closely with the terms of the Charter, they have never been superseded and continue to run in parallel with its provisions.

The most significant of these have been:

- *collective self-defence*: the right of one state to come to the defence of another under attack. This was the basis of the NATO agreement and the Warsaw Pact; the West's initial response to the invasion of Kuwait was justified on this ground
- *invitation*: the right of a government to request intervention by another state. The problem of distinguishing insurrection against a legitimate government from full-fledged civil war, has given intervening states a great deal of latitude. The US invasion of Grenada and the Soviet invasion of Afghanistan were both 'invited' by a government or individual of dubious legitimacy
- *protection of nationals abroad*: one of the justifications advanced for US actions in Grenada in 1983 and Panama in 1989
- *humanitarian purposes*: the re-emergence of this principle as a justification capable of overriding state sovereignty came in 1991. In the wake of the Gulf War, the US and the UK claimed the right to set up 'safe havens' to protect Kurds within Iraq. The Security Council, just emerging from its Cold War impasse, passed the historic Resolution 688. This sanctioned the states' action and for the first time in the Charter's history, brought 'humanitarian intervention' within its mandate.

From the Charter's inception until Resolution 688, member states had been averse to the invocation of the humanitarian principle on the grounds that it infringed sovereignty. India did not invoke it for its intervention in East Pakistan in 1971; nor did Tanzania for its 1979 excursion into Uganda. Vietnam's claim that its intervention in Cambodia in 1978 was justified on humanitarian grounds was rejected by the Security Council — despite widespread knowledge of the horrific excesses of the Pol Pot regime.

Resolution 688 itself passed with a majority of only one and, even then, a degree of contrivance was required on the part of the USA and UK: although the text makes no mention of Chapter VII measures, they determined, on the basis of what was a broad interpretation of its terms, that the 'mandatory language' employed must be of sufficient force to permit the use of force.

Since 1991, the collective security principle has come into its own: the use of force, it seems, must now be sanctioned by the supra-national 'world parliament', and 'humanitarian intervention under UN auspices' has become the favoured collective security method for dealing with the growing number of intra-state conflicts. It has been used in Bosnia, Rwanda, Somalia and Haiti. But in practise, the uneven balance of world power in which the actions of more powerful states appear at times to reduce the 'collective' nature of UN initiatives to post hoc status, has raised disturbing questions.

'We have probably reached a stage in the ethical and psychological evolution of Western civilisation in which the massive and deliberate violation of human rights will no longer be tolerated,' said Jávier Pérez de Cuellar, secretary general in 1991. But the collective UN vision has always been in conflict with the practical self-interest of individual states, a dualism that has been strongly criticised even within the organisation.

In Haiti a US-brokered agreement short-circuited the programme for the implementation of democratic constitutional structures. Dante Caputo, the chief UN envoy to Haiti, resigned complaining of 'the total absence of consultation, even of information on the part of the US government.' Washington, he said, had decided 'to act unilaterally in the Haitian situation.'

In Bosnia, the UN forces commander, Lt-General Francis Briquemont, resigned after complaining of the 'fantastic gap' that existed between Council resolutions on the 'safe areas' for Bosnians, and the will to implement them.

In Somalia, the US ignored UN warnings that all warlords must be disarmed and adopted a military strategy that targetted selected factions. The consequences are still apparent. While Victor Gbeho, leader of the UNOSOM II operation, talks of 'a better promise for peace than ever before', a more realistic view was expressed by one of his aides: 'What we are really trying to do is to install the sort of *junta* that America is trying to get rid of in Haiti, and then run like hell.'

The doctrine of state sovereignty, the legal foundation of modern state practice, has been diminished. As a result, weaker states fear the consequences of realpolitik: most recently, the 14 Latin American states that make up the 'Rio Group' refused to endorse the planned invasion of Haiti. It is clear that the UN is, nominally, at the heart of the process. It is time for reassessment. The catalogue of failures amassed since 1991 exposes the limitations of states' commitment to 'ethical concern', when weighed in the balance against their individual interests.

If the UN cannot overcome what Conor Cruise O'Brien has called its 'problems of delusion', and exchange its tactics of bureaucratic delay for a more rapid and effective approach to humanitarian intervention; if it cannot define more precisely its terms and conditions, its aims, intentions and the duration of intervention, the law will be again what it has so often been in the past: a veil to hide the motives of the powerful, thin sometimes to the point of transparency. ❏

# 1995 LOUIS M. LYONS AWARD

The Nieman Foundation for journalism at Harvard University invites nominations for the 1995 Louis M. Lyons Award for conscience and integrity in journalism.

The winner of the 1995 award, which carries a $1,000 honorarium, is to be selected by the 26 journalists in the Nieman Fellows Class of 1995. The award, created by the Nieman Class of 1964, is named in honor of the late Louis M. Lyons, curator of the Nieman Foundation for 25 years.

Past winners include Edward R. Murrow of CBS Television News; Tom Renner, reporter with *Newsday*, for his coverage of organized crime; Max du Preez of South Africa, editor of the *Vrye Weekblad*, and Gitobu Imanyara of Kenya, editor of the *Nairobi Law Monthly*, for their efforts to gain democratic freedoms for their countries; Jean Mario Paul of Haiti, correspondent with Radio Antilles Internationale, for his courage in the face of government intimidation; the journalists of *Oslobodjenje* for their commitment to serving the people of Sarajevo; and, in 1994, Abdelhamid Benzine, director of *Alger Républicain*, for his valiant and persistent struggle to save his newspaper despite insurmountable obstacles.

*Eligibility*: Any full-time print or broadcast journalist, domestic or foreign, for work done in 1994.

*Nominations*: Must be made by third parties, whether individuals or organizations. News organizations may nominate one of their own employees. Applications must contain the following:

- official letter of nomination
- one-page biography of the nominee
- two letters of recommendation
- three samples of the nominee's work.

*Deadline*: Entries must be postmarked by March 1, 1995. Material will not be returned. Applications must be submitted in one packet to:

Lyons Award Committee
Nieman Foundation
Harvard University
One Francis Avenue
Cambridge, MA 02138 USA
Telephone 617/495-2237
Fax 617/495-8976

ADEWALE MAJA-PEARCE

# The press
# in Nigeria

*This report was funded by the Swedish International Development Authority (SIDA) and the Norwegian Agency for Development Co-operation (NORAD). The full report will be available from* Index *in January 1995.*

Lagos street vendor: no chains on our press

In June last year the military government of General Ibrahim Babangida, after eight years in power, presided over the country's first general elections in more than a decade. The elections themselves had already been postponed on two previous occasions, and many were sceptical that they would ever take place, but few were prepared for Babangida's subsequent action when, without warning, he annulled the results even before the counting was over in what was assumed to be a last, desperate attempt to cling to power. In the event, he was forced to quit on 27 August, the date he had himself set for his departure, but rather than hand over to the presumed winner of the elections, Chief

Moshood Abiola, he enacted a decree — Decree 61 of 1993 — creating what he was pleased to call an Interim National Government (ING) headed by Chief Ernest Shonekan, a lacklustre businessman with little political experience. The ING survived less than three months in office before it was overthrown on 17 November by General Sani Abacha, the ING's Minister of Defence and, coincidentally, Babangida's former right-hand man.

There are those who would argue, with more than enough justification, that General Babangida's annulment of the June elections had less to do with his own desire to perpetuate himself in office than with the previously hidden political ambitions of General Abacha, and the hubris of a military which is no longer capable of divorcing itself from the nation's political destiny. Nigeria has been an independent country for 34 years; the military has been in power for all but nine of them. For most of that time there was little popular opposition to military rule per se. This was in part due to the shockingly corrupt behaviour of the so-called political class, which reached its apotheosis in the Second Republic (1979-83); but Babangida's own tenure, which quickly proved itself more corrupt than anything that had gone before, also happened to coincide with profound changes in the global political landscape, the most important of which, from the Nigerian perspective, was the end of apartheid in the former pariah state.

South Africa is free and Nigeria is in chains: this is the stark reality that faces a populace which, having gone to the polls to vote in an election deemed free and fair by the international community, is still waiting to be told why the candidate they voted in as President of Africa's most populous country has not only been denied his mandate but is currently in detention on a four-count charge of treason. To be sure, Chief Abiola hardly helped his own cause by appearing at first to acquiesce in the new-style coup and only re-discovering his mandate exactly one year after the annulment when, at a rally in Lagos, the commercial capital, he declared himself Head of State and Commander-in-Chief of the Armed Forces and was promptly taken into custody; but the crisis of legitimacy that continues to bedevil General Abacha has gone beyond the person of Abiola, who is merely a symbol of what has come to be regarded — à la South Africa — as 'the struggle'. Abacha knows this well enough, which is why he would have the disenfranchised believe — à la Lewis Carroll — that, 'What I tell you three times is true'.

General Abacha, who is not given to public speaking; who, indeed, has difficulty reading even one sentence without tripping over himself; and who, consequently, prefers to lurk in silence behind dark glasses on the grounds — presumably — that the less he says the quicker the problem will go away, has been forced to address the nation on no less than three separate occasions in his relatively short tenure. The last of these was on 17 August, when he steadfastly refused to explain why he was unable to de-annul the annulment and install the winner of the elections, and chose instead to brand his 'callous' detractors as 'opportunists':

'Recent developments in our country have clearly exposed the shameless tactics and insincerity of certain groups and individuals whose evil motives against our nation have been perpetrated under the guise of advocating for the de-annulment of the 12 June, 1993 presidential election. In their elusive search for relevance, these self-anointed saviours have deliberately ignored the obvious and widely acknowledged facts about the 12 June election — namely, that the said presidential elections were inconclusive and no results were declared, that the elections were aborted by a previous government which was replaced by another government before this administration came into being, and that 12 June was the culminating point of several anti-democratic injustices.'

Among the 'groups' with 'evil motives' were the two oil workers' unions — the National Union of Petroleum and Natural Gas Workers (NUPENG), and the Petroleum and Natural Gas Senior Staff Association of Nigeria (PENGASSAN) — which between them effectively control 90 per cent of the country's official export earnings, and whose respective leaderships he promptly proscribed in the course of his broadcast. But he also had in mind the independent press, which has been unrelenting in its opposition to military rule:

'The Nigerian press is one of the freest in the world. But such freedom should be matched with adequate responsibility. There is a great deal of misinformation being freely passed to the public. It is worrisome that some sections of our press have by their actions threatened our national unity and security and have ridiculed our

Chief Moshood Abiola

national pride as a people. The embarrassment of our citizens in the outside world are [sic] often predicated on false and damaging impressions which some sections of our press have unpatriotically championed.

'This administration remains committed to maintaining its track record of not muzzling the press or impairing its ability to perform its duties. Government would not shirk her responsibility to protect the rights of her citizens against the unsavoury acts of junk journalism. The press should remain steadfast to its cardinal objectives of educating, informing and entertaining and not constitute itself into paid agents of incitement and confusion. Our quest for a peaceful transition to civil democratic rule must not be jeopardised by a reckless press.'

There are more lies contained in these two paragraphs — not excepting the words 'and' and 'but' — than can be fruitfully unravelled in the space of this essay, and more, certainly, than is contained in any single issue of even the most junk-ridden publications, of which the country can boast a fair number; but if, at this late hour, no useful purpose is served by engaging in wearisome debates about the nature of patriotism, much less attempting to refute charges of treason, however veiled, one can hardly pass over in silence the insult contained in the blatant untruth that the Abacha administration has somehow resisted the seductive path of its predecessors.

On 2 January, less than two months after Abacha's ascendancy, security forces seized all 50,000 copies of *Tell*, the (admittedly abrasive) weekly magazine which had suffered in similar fashion on a number of occasions during Babangida's final year. The cause this time was its cover story, 'Return of tyranny: Abacha bares his fangs', which, in the words of Nosa Igiebor, the editor-in-chief, 'is just an analysis of the 10 new decrees

Who the cap fits: the Guardian: Friday, 8 July 1994

recently promulgated by the administration'.[1] Within hours, Dr Olu Onagoruwa, the Minister of Justice, distanced the government from what he claimed was the handiwork of 'over-zealous young operatives who have been appropriately advised not to do it again'[2] and proffered his apologies. But the management of the magazine remained unconvinced, and took the government to court for compensation for lost sales and advertising revenue, calculated at N11.5 million (US$1 = N50).

The Minister's apology, unprecedented in the history of military-press relations, was generally dismissed by media observers on the grounds that 'it is not possible for those ['over-zealous young operatives'] to act on their own when they know it is going to embarrass the federal government,'[3] although more hopeful (or more naive) Nigerians were prepared to give the government the benefit of the doubt, and not without reason. Dr Onagoruwa, in his previous incarnation, had made his name as a human rights lawyer with an enviable track record in defending the freedom of the press dating back to the early 1970s; and in an interview published as late as September last year, only two months before he accepted his current post, he reiterated his apparently uncompromising hostility to military rule — 'the Nigerian rulers, especially the military, have been particularly vicious' — in the course of explaining why the pressure group he belonged to, the Movement for National Reformation (MNR), had launched a Media Staff Relief Fund for embattled journalists:

> 'We discovered there was a need to reform the social structure, to introduce more equity into the system. Because of this, there was a lot of conflict with the government. Babangida closed down media houses...and to the chagrin of the MNR, we saw that newspapers, very courageous (publications) like the *News, Tell* magazine, *The Punch*...were being harassed, their news- papers were being closed and they became more inventive, ingenious... So [it was] suggested in one of our meetings that there must be a way that the MNR, being a movement that is dedicated to the restoration of liberty and federal equity, should help these journalists.' [4]

Why Dr Onagoruwa subsequently chose to dine with the devil can only remain a matter of speculation, especially when the devil, after a brief lull, proceeded to bare his fangs in time-honoured fashion. The first intimation came in early April with the arrest of three members of the editorial staff of *Newswatch* magazine, who were charged with sedition and criminal intent to cause fear, alarm and disaffection among the military and the public following the publication of an interview with a retired Brigadier-General who claimed that General Abacha was planning to remain in power for five years, and that the Constitutional Conference which he had convened as proof of his democratic credentials (Abacha: 'I must stress the unflinching commitment of this administration to an early return to civil democratic rule') was merely a ruse for his own personal ambitions. All three journalists were subsequently freed by presidential pardon after they had spent a week in prison, but worse was soon to follow.

In the early hours of Saturday 11 June, 18 armed anti-riot policemen and 20 agents from the notorious State Security Service (SSS) stormed the premises of Punch Nigeria Ltd, arrested *The Punch* editor, Bola Bolawale, and sealed up the offices. At about the same time, another detachment of treason-busting patriots carried out a similar operation at the offices of Concord Press Nigeria Ltd and its sister publication, *African Concord Magazine*. Bearing in mind that the publications of the Punch group — *The Punch* (daily), *Sunday Punch* and *Toplife* (both weeklies) — have consistently remained amongst the most outspoken newspapers in the country since they were founded in 1973; and that the Concord group — *National Concord* (daily), *Sunday Concord, Business Concord, Idoka, Isokan, Weekend Concord* and the *African Concord* (all weeklies) — is owned by Chief Abiola, the timing of their closures was hardly fortuitous, coming as they did on the eve of Abiola's 'treasonable' declaration. The following day, Abacha made his second address to the nation, in the course of which he promised to deal with 'those elements in our society engaged in acts of confrontation, sabotage, rumour-mongering, false alarm and distortion of the facts'.

In the subsequent court hearings, the police claimed to have received information through an undisclosed source that both publishing houses were being used to store arms and other offensive weapons, although they didn't care to explain why, having found none, they didn't immediately withdraw. Following a series of adjournments, the Federal High Court in Lagos finally ruled in favour of the Punch publications on 29 July. In his 22-page judgment, Justice Tajudeen Odunowo, who declared the closure 'illegal and unconstitutional', ordered the security forces to vacate the premises and awarded the newspaper N25 million in damages. Bola Bolawale, who had been held in custody for three days following the raid, was awarded N100,000 for his unlawful detention. The papers were forced to wait another 10 days before the security forces finally complied with the court order; but the group's victory, such as it was, as well as the on-going case involving the Concord group, which was subject to even more adjournments, were both rendered meaningless when, on 6 September, the government finally dispensed with its bogus pretence of legalism (Abacha: 'We believe that the judiciary is the vital custodian of our individual liberties') and simply proscribed them by decree.

Also proscribed on the same day were all five titles of Guardian Newspapers Ltd — *The Guardian* (daily), *Guardian Express* (afternoon daily), *Financial Guardian*, *Lagos Life*, and *African Guardian* (all weeklies) — following a similar occupation of its premises by an estimated 150 armed policemen in the early hours of 15 August. At the time, the government didn't even bother with the absurd fiction that Nigerian journalists had now taken to gun-running, but the closure may have had something to do with the lead story in the previous day's edition of *The Guardian*. 'Inside Aso Rock: the raging battle to rule Nigeria' claimed that there was a split in the 11-man (no women!) Provisional Ruling Council, the country's highest law-making body, between the hawks and the doves, and that this split reflected the wider division within society between the northern conservatives and the southern progressives.

To understand why such an article might have ruffled a few feathers, one has to understand three things: first, that Nigeria, whether under the civilians or the military, has effectively been ruled since independence in 1960 by a self-appointed, Islamic-oriented northern clique — variously referred to as the Kaduna Mafia, the Sokoto Caliphate, and the Hausa/Fulani Oligarchy — who are prepared to drag the country into another civil war rather than share power on a more equitable basis; second, that the economy of Nigeria, including its vast reserves of oil and natural gas, is almost exclusively generated in the largely Christian (and better educated) South; and third, that in so far as either or both of the aforementioned are a simplification of the facts, they are held to be true by a press which is itself almost exclusively centred in the South.

**South Africa is free;**

**Nigeria is in chains**

The southern dominance of the Nigerian press along the so-called Lagos–Ibadan axis, estimated at about 80 per cent of all publications, is a problem that exercises the hearts and minds of the northern power-brokers to a degree that seems almost comical given their privileged position in the political life of the society. Witness, for instance, the intemperate outburst of Umaru Dikko, the most notorious of the Second Republic politicians and currently the most vocal spokesperson of the

Nigeria 1993: an aborted appeal

ruling elite, in the course of a recent magazine interview:

'You people think you can go on persecuting people. But we will prove to you that we are equal as citizens of this country, whether we own newspapers or we don't. You go and write nonsense and bastardise our country in the eyes of the world. If you want politics, come into politics. We are tired of persecution. You people have been rude to all our leaders. This time around, you are joking... We are not going to take it. You people are rude, very rude. You have all the time caused trouble in this country. Nobody is good but you.'[5]

Amid all this bile, of which the above is only a sampler, Umaru Dikko conspicuously failed to mention that the North has been trying to develop its own indigenous press for the last 30 years and more, beginning with the establishment of the *Morning Post* in 1961 (now defunct) and the *New Nigerian* in 1965, precisely in order to correct the perceived imbalance. Since then, a multiplicity of publications have come and gone (and continue to do so), but none has ever posed a serious challenge to the predominance of southern press, and for one simple reason: their seeming inability to challenge the prevailing mores of their section of the society lest they undermine the very basis of their power. So, for instance, no northern-based publication will ever suggest that a northern politician is corrupt, which is absurd; or, as happened only recently, allow an article alleging that the son of an Emir (traditional ruler) is known to deal in drugs. In the words of one southern editor with personal experience of the northern press:

'...the main trouble with the northern press is that the publishers and editors find it difficult to expose traits that are odd, bizarre, unusual, weird, incredible, shocking about the elite, the people, places and events. Maybe its anathema in the North to expose the evils some local leaders and Emirs do...

'What I am saying, in effect, is that instead of vilifying the Lagos press boys, the Northern press boys should emulate them. Please hold your anger. What this means is that the Lagos newspaper business thrives because there are no sacred cows. To the Lagos press boys, news is news as long as it can sell and promote their products.'[6]

To the extent that there is a conspiracy, in other words, it is largely of the North's own making, although one would have a hard time trying to explain this to the likes of Umaru Dikko, who nevertheless appears to have few problems getting his voice heard in the pages of a press he otherwise affects to despise.

The degree of self-censorship which operates in the northern press obviously works to its disadvantage by making its products unattractive to a sophisticated readership with limited spending power and plenty of choice. At the national level alone, there are 21 daily newspapers, 22 weekly newspapers and 19 weekly newsmagazines. The vast majority of them are privately-owned business concerns whose success is inseparable from their ability (and determination) to operate in an atmosphere of maximum freedom consonant with military rule. *The Guardian* is a case in point, hence the article which ostensibly led to the closure of the entire group even though its publisher and chairman, Alex Ibru, was at the time the Minister for Internal Affairs.

Consider, for example, Alex Ibru's response to his previous travails under the Babangida regime. In May 1991, the then governor of Lagos State, Colonel Raji Rasaki, ordered the closure of the Guardian group following a story in the *Guardian Express* on a riot at the local polytechnic in which two students were shot dead. The paper's editor and three reporters were subsequently charged to court for publishing 'false news with intent to cause fear and alarm to the public', and the publisher was 'ordered' (but this is the military) to apologise to the government for the embarrassment caused. Ibru flatly refused to comply, saying that he would only do so if the report was proved to be false. This was despite his own reckoning that the closure, which lasted nearly a month, was costing him N1.2 million daily.

The loss of revenue occasioned by the closures of newspapers and magazines is, of course, part and parcel of the government's strategy for bringing them into line — or driving them out of business. For Alex Ibru, a millionaire businessman with many other concerns, the matter is not as serious as it is for the proprietors of, say, the Punch group; but the real victims in all such cases are the employees, who might have to forego their salaries for the duration, and this in a country without even the most basic welfare system. Not that they are well paid to begin with. An experienced journalist can expect to earn in the region of N50,000 per annum. Accommodation in a city like Lagos would easily swallow half of that, leaving N480.76 a week for all other expenses. Out of this, transport to and from work will account for N100, perhaps more. A daily meal, which is all that most journalists can afford, will account for another N350, calculated conservatively at N50 per day. The balance, N30.76, is the price of a bottle of beer. Following the closure of the Punch group, the management was able to pay all 142 journalists their full salary for the month of June only; in July, this was cut by half. According to the chairperson of *The Punch* chapel of the Nigerian Union of Journalists, Nseobong Okon-Ekong, the attendant hardship led to 'the loss of two staff of *The Punch* whose deaths could be...linked to the closure'; and added: 'There are reports of several of our colleagues on their sick bed.'[7]

The disincentive to practice the kind of confrontational journalism that has been the hallmark of the Punch group since it was founded in 1973 is immense, and why any statement concerning the freedom of the press in Nigeria is necessarily circumscribed by the arbitrary nature of military rule. This freedom is further undermined when the proprietor also happens to be nursing presidential ambitions of his own. The fact that both *The Punch* and *Concord* were closed on the same day might lead one to suppose that there was fruitful comparison to be made between them, but this would be erroneous. Where *The Punch* is genuinely independent, in the sense of holding 'these truths to be self-evident',

April 1994: Newswatch in the dock

*Concord*'s commitment to the fundamental freedoms has always been hostage to Chief Abiola's political agenda ever since he founded the group in 1980. At the time of the closure of Guardian Newspapers in 1991, for instance, Abiola publicly urged the proprietor to apologise to the government rather than 'stick to ludicrous principles at [sic] the interest of journalists who were (on remand)'.[8] One year later, he did just that when the government closed the Concord offices following the publication in *African Concord* magazine of an exclusive interview with General Babangida in which the erstwhile dictator inadvertently recommended that the people take to the streets in protest against spiralling inflation. The government, for its part, magnanimously accepted the Chief's apology as proof that the Concord group had 'rejected [the] path of undermining national interest and security'.[9]

The pity of it is that Abiola, who is possibly even wealthier than Alex Ibru, let slip the chance to make a lasting contribution to Nigerian journalism; Ibru, by contrast, who founded his own group in 1983, oversees an empire which, in *The Guardian*, publishes the best newspaper in the country by far, and one of the best in the continent. This is said without prejudice to *The Punch*, which has always been hampered by its lack of resources; conversely, Ibru's ability to sink enough money into his newspaper at its inception meant that *The Guardian* was quickly able to establish an unrivalled authority in the market-place, a position it has maintained ever since. The paper was selling in excess of a quarter of a million at the time of its closure. This was more than half that of its nearest rival, the government-owned *Daily Times*, the flagship of Daily Times of Nigeria Ltd, itself the biggest newspaper publishing group in the continent.

The hallmark of *The Guardian* (motto: 'Conscience Nurtured By Truth'), is the depth and range of its coverage of important national issues, coupled with an ability to separate news from comment. The latter would seem to be the proper job of any newspaper worthy of the name, except that no other Nigerian newspaper, whether government or private, is able or willing to do this on a consistent basis. The sole exception was the *Daily Times* for a brief period in the late 1980s and early 1990s, but this eventually proved too much for the government, which sacked the innovative managing editor and plunged the group back into debt, now running at N15.4 million annually. From the point of view of tyranny, after all, accurate reporting of the facts is necessarily subversive, since tyranny can only work, to the extent that it can be said to work, by hoodwinking the populace into believing the exact opposite of what it knows.

**The Lagos newspaper business thrives because there are no sacred cows... news is news as long as it can sell and promote their products**

The fact about Abiola's detention, for instance, was that it exacerbated the on-going political crisis in the country. The government itself appeared to recognise this when, on 5 August, it offered to release him on bail on condition that he renounce his mandate, an offer which Abiola rejected out of hand. Consider, then, the successive headlines in *The Guardian* (6-10 August): 'Abiola granted bail, rejects conditions'; 'How Abiola's Rejected Bail Was Contrived'; 'Why Labour backed bail for Abiola, by Bafyau'; 'NLC [Nigerian Labour Congress] insists on Abiola's total freedom'; 'Govt may stop Abiola's trial, says Bafyau'. *The Daily Times*, in contrast, limited itself to one headline on 6 August, 'MKO gets bail, with conditions', and nothing thereafter. *The Guardian's* headlines, in other words, were true both to the facts — Abiola was granted bail but rejected the conditions — and to the mood of the country — that Abiola's rejection of the conditions had ramifications beyond the immediate event.

It's perfectly true, of course, that *The Guardian* has always had an 'attitude' about what Wole Soyinka, the Nobel laureate, once termed 'this denigration of the popular will',[10] as witness the editorial following the government's bungled attempt to release Abiola, which said in part:

> 'We are convinced... that an overly legalistic response... would not be enough. The trial of Chief Abiola is, as is well-known, a political trial. Chief Abiola is not a criminal. What the administration ought to have done all along — and what it must still do if there will be peace in Nigeria — is sort the entire matter out politically.
>
> 'The Federal Attorney-General ought to be asked to discontinue the court proceedings and the nation saved this charade. The political crisis can only be settled by genuine dialogue not the unrestrained and impolitic use of the coercive instrument of state power...
>
> 'We find extremely short-sighted a use of state power which tunnels unwittingly at the very root, plinth and sustenance of civil order in the country so recklessly. For, if the faith of the citizenry (and, hence, in civil order) continues to be subverted, are the authorities enamoured of the destination of the continuing slide to anarchy in Nigeria?'[11]

Measured in terms of the more extremist publications in the country, *The Guardian*'s editorial is hardly abrasive, although its very reasonableness, verging on a rather endearing pomposity, might for that reason be even more maddening to a regime which could only have been threatened by the newspaper's professionalism in the first place, and which it obviously attempted to defuse in advance by co-opting its proprietor into its ranks. This isn't as daft as it sounds. Such crude reasoning would be entirely in keeping with an administration that is necessarily programmed to operate according to the mentality of the barracks, and which, on the evidence of its own behaviour, obviously believes that power for its own sake is the ultimate in the human condition. It would also explain why Alex Ibru, having signally failed to do what was expected of him, was unceremoniously dumped by General Abacha in a cabinet reshuffle on 27 September, which also saw the end of Dr Olu Onagoruwa's brief and unhappy adventure in politics. But Ibru, who has never been known to voice a political opinion, at least managed to escape with his reputation intact; Onagoruwa, who has been known to voice many political opinions, was co-opted only because of his reputation, a fact which he only began to perceive (and dimly at that) when it was already too late, and which left him without cover when his masters had no further use for him.

In a country where pretensions to probity are viciously dealt with, preferably with the collusion of the culprits themselves, there have been few sorrier sights than the minister of justice calling a press conference in order to deny all knowledge of the decrees which banned the three newspaper houses: 'In fact the Federal Ministry of Justice has not seen a copy of these laws,' he protested. 'We disown responsibility for these laws. Neither can we vouch for their authenticity.' The only explanation he could then offer the incredulous journalists was the one he evidently believed himself, which was the existence of hidden enemies — 'certain bureaucratic and political forces', as he put it — who were attempting to undermine the credibility of the government for their own selfish ends. As one political observer remarked, in what was perhaps the only possible response to such levels of self-delusion: 'He should disappear for a year. We hope he will keep quiet and go to sleep because any talk by him will annoy Nigerians.'

The decrees banning the newspaper groups — Decree 6 (Concord), Decree 7 (Punch) and Decree 8 (Guardian) — are to remain in effect for a period of six months, with provision to extend them for a further six months by 'the appropriate authority'. The fact that the closures of both *The Concord* and *The Guardian* preceded the enactment of the respective decrees was also provided for, as follows:

'Any person who on the direction of the appropriate authority had at any time before the commencement of this decree dealt with or acted in compliance with this decree or thereafter deals with any copy of the newspapers or weekly magazine proscribed or prohibited from circulation pursuant to this decree should stand indemnified in respect thereof and no suit or any other proceedings whatsoever shall lie at the instance of any person aggrieved in respect of an act, matter or thing done in respect of such direction or in compliance and whether any such suit or other proceeding has been or is instituted in any court shall abate and be of no effect whatsoever.'

Kanu, Northern Nigeria: 'news is news', even when it comes from
the South

To make absolutely certain that its back was fully covered, the government enacted another decree on the same day, 'The Military Government (Supremacy and Enforcement of Powers) Decree 12 of 1994', which divested the courts of all authority to question the actions of the government. Additionally, Decree 12 gave the chief of general staff and the inspector-general of police the power to detain any person for up to three months without charge or trial, with provision to renew the three-month detention indefinitely. Finally, yet another decree, 'The Constitution (Suspension and Modification) Amendment Decree 5 of 1994', empowered the Federal Government to try all cases of treasonable felony, which neatly (or brutally) circumvented the problem of how best to proceed with Abiola's trial without risking tiresome arguments about the separation of powers. The military can arrest him, the military can try him, and the military can pass whatever sentence it likes on him. Period.

In a very real sense, of course, the enactment of these decrees was a final admission of failure — even desperation — by a government which, only the previous month, made great play of its commitment to 'maintaining its track record of not muzzling the press or impairing its ability to perform its duties' as part of its wider claim to legitimacy. But the scale of that failure, already apparent in the closures of *The Punch* and *Concord*, was further underscored the same month by the sudden appearance in Lagos and Port Harcourt (easily the two most important urban centres in the South) of counterfeit copies of the four most outspoken weekly news magazines: the *News*, *Tempo*, *Tell* and *TSM*. The authentic 18 June issue of *Tempo*, for instance, with the cover, 'Zero Hour: Expect civilian coup', became, in the counterfeit issue, 'Zero Hour: Abiola makes U-Turn'. Similarly, *TSM*'s cover of 19 June, 'June 12: Abacha Must Go — Nigerians in a TSM National Opinion Poll', was changed to, 'Public Opinion Poll: Only Abacha Can Save Nigeria, Special edition on June 12', but erroneously dated 18 June.

This was not the first time that counterfeit editions of awkward publications had found their way into the market, although only *Tell* — once in August last year and once again in April this year — had previously received what might be regarded as a back-handed compliment. As on both previous occasions, the government denied all responsibility for what could only be regarded as a bizarre attempt to garner support, claiming instead that they were got up by the magazines themselves in order to generate public sympathy, as if the magazines (unlike the government) possessed unlimited amounts of money to throw around, and this at a time when they were facing a financial squeeze. Only a month later, all four magazines were forced to raise their cover price by 25 per cent because, according to the *TSM*, 'the costs of newsprint and art paper are on the upward surge. It has been so bad that paper costs alone add up to 98.3 per cent of the N30 cover price.' But what disturbed most people wasn't so much the existence of the counterfeits, which were easy enough to spot for what they were (poor production, different type faces and sloppy grammar, to say nothing of such an unlikely about-turn), so much as the realisation, chilling enough under the circumstances, that the mixture of ineptitude and cynicism which fuelled the entire exercise revealed everything one needed to know about the collection of criminals that seeks to control the destiny of a 100 million souls.

Just how long publications like the *News*, *Tempo*, *Tell* and *TSM* will continue to survive under the current dispensation is anybody's guess, although even the most optimistic must by now be cured of the delusion that anything good can possibly come out of this regime. As General Sani Abacha prepares to enter his second year in office, it is also clear that the military and the narrow political interests which it serves have temporarily prevailed, which in turn means that their overthrow will be bloodier than anybody ever wanted. This, apparently, is the price of democracy in Nigeria more than three decades after the country 'won' its independence from the colonial denigration of the popular will, but which in reality looks very much like more of the same. When that time comes, as it must, General Abacha will wish he had listened to the voices which have been trying to warn him, but which he insisted on regarding as irresponsible, unpatriotic, divisive and reckless. So much the worse for him; so much the worse, alas, for Nigeria. ❏

● *On 5 November, Bayo Onanuga, founding editor of the* News *(now banned),* Tempo *and* PM News *was awarded the Commonwealth Press Union 1994 Astor award 'for his outstanding contribution to Commonwealth press freedom'.*

**Notes**
1. Quoted in: 'Critics suspect govt apology over *Tell* seizure', *The Guardian*, 17 January, 1994.
2. Ibid.
3. Ibid.
4. 'Press freedom fighter', *Media Review*, Vol 3, No 8, September, 1993.
5. 'We are ready for war', *The African Guardian*, 8 August, 1994.
6. Martins Oloja: 'The trouble with the northern press', *The Guardian on Sunday*, 14 August, 1994.
7. '*Concord, Punch...* 51 days under the hammer', *The Guardian*, 1 August, 1994.
8. 'Making the press see red', *Media Review*, Vol 2, No 5, May, 1992.
9. Ibid.
10. 'Power and creative strategies', *Index on Censorship*, Vol 17, No 7, August 1988.
11. 'Curiouser and curiouser', *The Guardian*, 12 August, 1994.

# INDEX INDEX

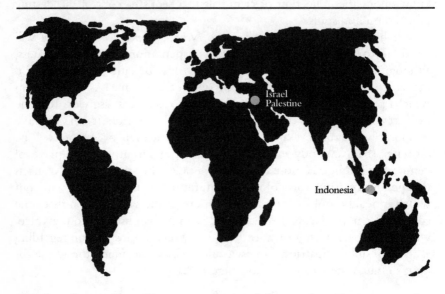

## Voiceless in Gaza, speechless in Java

It wasn't the most auspicious beginning for the would-be state of Palestine. After years spent struggling to win a measure of autonomy over the Israeli-occupied territories, the Palestinian National Authority promptly used its new power to censor, to limit that hard-won freedom, by banning the paper *An-Nahar* for 'harming Palestinian interests'.

The *An-Nahar* ban was lifted in September but, in all other respects, the state of press freedom in both Israel and PNA territory has worsened. We shouldn't forget, of course, that the peace process there is still just that, a process. Agreements may have been signed but it looks increasingly as if the political manoeuvrings of the main players in the drama — Israel, and the rival Palestinian groups Islamic Jihad, Hamas and the PLO — are little more than the continuation of war by other means; and, sometimes, by the same means.

The murder of Hani Abed, of the pro-Islamic Jihad weekly *al-Istiqlal*, in Gaza sharpens the dilemma journalists in the region now face: how to report — and express opinions on — the highly charged political situation without being seen to favour not only the aims of terrorist organisations but also their methods, thus making themselves a target for terrorist reprisals from the other side.

No-one knows for sure who blew up Abed's car on 2 November. Mossad and Hamas are the likeliest suspects. No-one knows either how far Abed had crossed the hazy line between reporting the story and participating in it. Some say he was the head of Islamic Jihad's military wing in Gaza; Reuter refers to him merely as an 'activist'. It is clear, though, that when the space for free discussion and dissent becomes too narrow, writers and journalists have to start dodging bullets.

Such constriction is also choking dissent in Indonesia. After a brief flirtation with greater openness, the Suharto regime has now apparently decided that enough is enough. One year after the information minister warned the press to 'avoid the trappings of liberal and Communist ways of thinking', three of the country's leading independent publications (*DeTik*, *Editor* and *Tempo*) are banned, NGOs are prevented from organising, and all discussion about legitimate topics of interest — a recent banking scandal, the Asia-Pacific Economic Co-operation summit, not to mention the horrors of East Timor — is extremely circumscribed.

The worst effect so far of the recent clampdown is endemic self-censorship. Journalists remember the violence unleashed by the regime in the 1960s on those suspected of Communist subversion: a possible return to such a policy is the threat veiled behind official 'guidance' to editors on how to avoid 'endangering national interests and stability'. Which is why the formation of the new Alliance of Independent Journalists (AJI) to loosen the state's stranglehold on the press is an act of tremendous bravery that merits greater international support than it has so far received.

The Suharto regime clearly means to be the sole arbiter of the Indonesian national interest, just as the PLO wants to dictate the interests of all Palestinians — even though one might think the Palestinian interest lay, at least in part, in having an unfettered press. If they insist on this course, the PNA could squander the chance for democracy, and the 'new dawn' of Palestinian freedom, heralded on the White House lawn just over a year ago, could turn out to be a false dawn. ❏

**Adam Newey**

*A censorship chronicle incorporating information from Agence France-Presse (AFP), the American Association for the Advancement of Science Human Rights Action Network (AAASHRAN), Amnesty International (AI), the BBC Monitoring Service Summary of World Broadcasts (SWB), the Central American Centre for the Protection of Freedom of Expression (CEPEX), the Committee to Protect Journalists (CPJ), the Canadian Committee to Protect Journalists (CCPJ), the Inter-American Press Association (IAPA), the International Federation of Journalists (IFJ/FIP), the International Federation of Newspaper Publishers (FIEJ), Human Rights Watch (HRW), the Media Institute of Southern Africa (MISA), International PEN (PEN), Radio Free Europe/Radio Liberty (RFE/RL), Reporters Sans Frontières (RSF), the West African Journalists' Association (UJAO) and other sources.*

## ALBANIA

Several Greek and Cypriot journalists and media technicians were reportedly arrested and deported while covering the trial of five leaders of the ethnic Greek organisation Omonia (*Index* 3/1994, 4&5/1994). Agni Vavoritou of Star Channel and technicians Kostas Papadopoulous, Tassos Dimopoulos and Kosta Iliopoulos were deported on 7 September. Kosta Markellos of Sky Channel and technician Kostas Pantazis were deported on 8 September. On 11 September Andreas Panagopoulos of Channel ET-1 was expelled and declared 'undesirable' for five years for 'anti-Albanian activity and co-operation with the Greek Secret Service'. (PEN)

Prison sentences of between six and eight years, imposed on the five Omonia leaders after their convictions for espionage and possession of weapons in September were reduced by between one and two years in October. US observers report that the trial failed to meet the requirements of Albanian law and of the International Covenant on Civil and Political Rights, which Albania has ratified. (Minnesota Advocates for Human Rights, Reuter)

On 3 November, three Constitutional Court judges Ylvi Myrtja, Natasha Sheshi and Thimjo Kondi resigned, accusing the other six judges of deliberately delaying hearings on an opposition challenge to the legality of the referendum on the new Constitution. The referendum, held on 6 November, overwhelmingly rejected the Constitution, described by opposition parties as 'authoritarian'. (RFE/RL, Reuter)

## ALGERIA

The murder of journalists continues: the body of Mouloud Barroudi, a cameraman for the National Agency of Film News (ANAF), was found near his home on 24 September; Smail Shaghdi, a journalist with the official Algerian Press Service (APS), was killed in Algiers on 25 September; Tayeb Bouterfis, of the government's Berber-language radio station, was assassinated in Baraki, south of Algiers, on 16 October; Farah Ziane, editor of the weekly *Révolution Africaine*, was killed near his home in Blida on 19 October; and APS reporter Mohamed Salah Benachour was shot dead on 27 October in Boufarik. Eight papers withheld publication for three days from 19 October in commemoration of murdered journalists. (CPJ, RSF, PEN)

Nadir Boulegroune, director of the weekly *El Moudjahid*, has disappeared following his court appearance in Algiers on 28 September. (RSF)

Cheb Hasni, a popular singer of rai music, was shot dead in Oran on 29 September. His murder follows the kidnap of Lounes Matoub, a musician known for his advocacy of Berber rights, on 25 September near Tizi-Ouzou in the Berber region of Kabylie. (*Telegraph, Guardian*)

Kadour Bouselham, journalist with the government daily *Horizons*, was kidnapped on 20 October in Hassine by a group of armed men. (RSF)

It was reported in November that a secret government decree was issued in June, requiring all media to limit reporting of political violence and security matters to the communiques issued by the interior ministry. The decree itself 'shall not be published and any person...concerned with it shall be notified of its provisions by excerpts.' (Article 19)

The interior ministry suspended the papers *El Ouma* and *al-Wajh al-Akhar* for one month from 7 November for publishing 'subversive information and apologising for crime'. (CPJ)

Recent publication: *Secret Decree: New Attack on the Media in Algeria* (Article 19, November 1994, 14pp)

## ANGOLA

Antonio Gouveia, a member of the independent Angolan Journalists' Union (SJA), received death threats in early September following publication of his reports in an August edition of *Correio da Semana* about South African mercenaries fighting in Angola's civil war. (MISA)

State security agents detained *Imparcial Fax* journalist Mariano Costa on 20 September and questioned him about his sources for reports he had published in September about the UNITA movement. After his release, the phone lines at his office were cut, and he was warned not to publicise his detention, which has gone completely unreported in the Angolan press. (MISA)

## ARGENTINA

Human rights lawyer Elena Mendoza has been receiving death threats since early September in connection with her work for the *Abuelas de Plaza de Mayo*, pressing for compensation for a girl who disappeared during the years of military rule, and who was later found alive. The threats come from a caller who says he is a member of a 'task force' that is no longer operational but that 'could be reactivated'. (AI)

Lawyer Federico Alfredo Hubert received several threats in mid-October over his work for the family of Diego Rodríguez Laguens, allegedly beaten to death by police in San Pedro, Jujuy, in February. On 14 October three cars kept Hubert's house under surveillance. Hubert also received a telephone call the same day in which he was warned 'not to make so much noise'. Laguens's mother and the independent forensic expert investigating his death have also been threatened. (AI)

## AUSTRALIA

State MP John Newman was shot dead outside his Sydney home on 6 September. Newman, a well-known campaigner for the deportation of Asian criminals, had received death threats, which he believed came from the Chinese Triads. (*Guardian*)

The federal government is to introduce legislation to override Tasmanian state laws prohibiting homosexuality. Canberrra says it is obliged to act because Tasmanian law conflicts with Australia's international legal obligations. At present, consensual gay sex is punishable in Tasmania by up to 21 years' imprisonment. (Reuter)

A federal government task force investigating pornography on computer bulletin boards has concluded that it would be too expensive and difficult to regulate them through legislation. The Attorney-General has asked bulletin board users to adopt self-censorship to protect children from obscene or offensive material. (*Sydney Morning Herald, Australian Financial Review*)

The High Court re-interpreted the country's libel laws on 12 October when it ruled that the Constitutional definition of representative government implies that discussing politicians' public conduct and political opinions does not constitute defamation. The ruling bars two pending libel cases brought by state and federal legislators against newspapers. (*Sydney Morning Herald*)

The government introduced a Racial Hatred Bill on 1 November to crack down on racist statements in public. The bill would also enable people to seek redress for racially offensive public behaviour. Civil libertarians condemn the proposals as a threat to free speech. The Attorney-General, however, argues that exceptions to free speech are justified to help people who are 'put under threat on the basis of their race'. (Reuter)

## AUSTRIA

Wolfgang Purtscheller, a correspondent for *Der Standard* who specialises in coverage of right-wing political groups, was severely beaten by police and detained for 10 hours on 22 September after questioning the arrest of a person of African origin. The police also confiscated his notebook. (RSF)

Lojze Wieser, a Slovene-language publisher in Klagenfurt, received a hand-written death threat on 31 October. The letter began with the Nazi salute 'Sieg Heil' and was marked with swastikas. Earlier in October police intercepted a letter-bomb intended for Wieser. (*International Herald Tribune*)

### BANGLADESH

On 10 September, during a demonstration organised by opposition parties in Dhaka, Shahadat Hossain, a photographer for the daily *Milliet*, was badly hurt by gunfire. It is not known who shot him. (RSF)

Finance minister M Saifur Rahman announced on 22 September that the Government would soon take a decision on lifting the embargo on the import of newsprint. Newsprint distribution is a state monopoly and on 1 October the country's only newsprint factory closed for maintenance, causing a shortage of paper and provoking accusations that the government is operating an indirect form of censorship. (*Daily Star, Asiaweek*)

At the beginning of October Taslima Nasrin (*Index* 10/1993, 3/1994, 4&5/1994) cancelled a visit to France because the authorities would only grant her a 24-hour visa.

"TROP DE LIBERTE TUE LA LIBERTE" *

\* ADAGE CAMBODGIEN

'Too much freedom kills freedom' (A Cambodian saying)

On 27 October the European Parliament passed a resolution condemning the French decision and deploring the refusal of all EU members to grant Nasrin asylum. Her trial for insulting religious sensibilities is due to begin in Dacca on 10 December. (*Guardian*, Reuter)

Recent publication: *Fundamental Rights of Women Violated with Virtual Impunity* (Amnesty, October 1994, 23pp)

### BELARUS

On 21 October the Belarusian Central Commission on Elections and Referenda was approached by a group seeking a referendum on making Russian an official language, alongside Belarusian; and another denouncing the

Belavezha agreement of 1991, which dissolved the USSR and created the CIS. (SWB)

### BOLIVIA

A letter-bomb was sent to Carlos Mesa of Canal 7 television on 29 October. The device, which contained a letter signed 'Commando Dignity', was defused safely. The home of Canal 2's owner, Luis Soruco Barba, was damaged by gunfire on 30 October. Both men are well-known critics of ex-dictator Luis García Meza, who is soon to be extradited from Brazil to face trial for crimes committed during his regime. (RSF)

### BOSNIA-HERCEGOVINA

On 30 August Mohammed Husein Navab of the Tehran

daily *Kayhan* was shot dead in western Mostar, an area controlled by HVO (Croatian) forces. A witness said a member of a Croatian police special unit had ordered Navab to accompany him. (FIEJ)

In September the bullet-ridden body of Risto Djogo, head of Bosnian Serb television was found in Lake Zvornic. Djogo, a Karadzic loyalist, had denounced Serbia's President Milosevic on TV. (*Guardian, Sunday Times*)

The Sarajevo edition of *Vecernje Novine* reported in late September that Radio Foca journalist Enes Hrnjicic had been freed from Foca prison. He was imprisoned on 15 April 1992. (PEN)

Boro Maric, Banja Luka bureau chief for the Belgrade daily *Vecernje Novosti*, was arrested with 40 members of the 'illegal' Tajfun Information Centre on 2 October. He was released on 4 October but re-arrested next day. (RSF)

## BRAZIL

César Gomes Gama, José Antonio Moura Bonfim, Marcos Cardoso and Elenaldo dos Santos Santana, journalists with the paper CINFORM in Sergipe state, have all received death threats following the paper's ongoing investigation into a death squad known as A Missão (The Mission). On 15 September the journalists were told anonymously that they 'would not last the weekend'. The threats intensi-

fied in October. (AI)

## BULGARIA

In September the Constitutional Court ruled that a Parliamentary decision to replace several members of the Supreme Judicial Council is unconstitutional because it violates a previous ruling that all SJC members are appointed for five years, regardless of Parliament or the recently adopted law on the judiciary (*Index* 4&5/1994). (RFE/RL)

Nadia Dunkin, a key witness in the murder trial of three former guards at a labour camp near Lovetch, was found dead, apparently murdered, in September. Dunkin had been a prisoner at the camp where opponents of the Communist regime were held from 1959 to 1962. (RFE/RL)

Recent publication: *Turning a Blind Eye to Racism* (Amnesty, September 1994, 11pp)

## BURMA

Khin Zaw Win (*Index* 4&5/1994) was sentenced to 15 years in prison on 6 October. Writer San San Nwe, her daughter Mo Mo Tun, and opposition NLD MPs-elect Khin Maung Swe and U Sein Hla Oo (*Index* 4&5/1994) were also sentenced to seven years. All five were charged with 'spreading information injurious to the state'. San San Nwe recieved a further three years for 'currency violations'. (PEN)

Opposition leader Aung San

Suu Kyi (*Index* 10/1993, 4&5/1994) held talks with members of the ruling State Law and Order Restoration Council (SLORC) in September and October. No details were released but the meeting was given prominent coverage by the state media which described the discussions as 'frank and cordial'. (*Daily Telegraph, Independent*)

Recent publication: *Paradise Lost? The Suppression of Environmental Rights and Freedom of Expression in Burma* (Article 19, September 1994, 36pp)

## BURUNDI

Alexis Bandyatuyaga, a journalist with National Radio and Television of Burundi, was killed by the Burundian army on 15 September, one of 13 men executed after several hundred people were rounded up by the security forces. (AI)

## CAMBODIA

On 8 September newspaper editor Nuon Chan, an outspoken government critic, was shot dead by gunmen on motorbikes. (*Far Eastern Economic Review*)

Alain Lebas and Romain Franklin, reporters for the French daily *Libération*, were barred from entering the country on 30 October, apparently in reprisal for an article they wrote about French aid to the Cambodian military. (RSF)

A draft press law being debated by the National Assembly in early November would impose criminal penalties for various activities including publication of material that 'may cause turmoil to public security'; that 'humiliates or degrades national organs or public authorities'; or impugns the 'inviolability' of the King. (HRW)

## CHILE

In late September a Chilean judge ordered the closure of the German-run group Colonia Dignidad, whose operators have for more than 10 years been accused of neo-Nazi violence, child pornography, keeping other Germans in the compound against their will and of collaborating with the dictatorship of General Pinochet (1973-1990). (*Latinamerica Press*)

## CHINA

It was reported in October that the latest work of Liang Xiaosheng, well-known author of *Snow City* and *A Red Guard's Own Words*, has been banned for criticising China's economic and political reforms and suggesting the system is failing to bring about the aims of socialism. (*Central Daily News*)

On 3 October the Communist Party's propaganda department appointed a large team of full time 'newspaper readers' to vet the national press. The censors will look for any deviation from reporting 'only positive and patriotic news'. (*South China Morning Post*)

Wei Jinsheng (*Index* 7/1992, 1/1994), held incommunicado without charge at an undisclosed location since April 1; and Ren Wanding, pro-democracy activist and Tiananmen Square veteran, are to share the prestigious Robert F Kennedy human rights award for 1994. Ren Wanding wrote and circulated articles on freedom of expression, the rule of law and human rights at the time of the Tiananmen Square massacre. He is currently serving a seven-year prison term in Beijing and is seriously ill. (Reuter, RFK memorial program)

Yang Zhou (*Index* 1/1994) was found guilty on 11 October of 'publishing reactionary material and stirring up public unrest' and was sentenced without trial to three years of 're-education through labour'. Observers say this form of punishment is being used increasingly to silence dissidents without attracting the attention of a formal trial. (PEN)

On 12 October it was reported that the 'ultra-leftist' Beijing journal *Zhenli De Zhuiqiu* (Pursuit of Truth) has been purged for its anti-reform stance. (SWB)

The family of Gao Yu (*Index* 10/1993, 4&5/1994), former deputy editor of *Economics Weekly*, was informed on 11 November that she has been sentenced to six years in prison for 'leaking state secrets', following a closed trial in which she was not legally represented, her second

trial for substantially the same offence. A court official told her lawyers that they were not notified of the trial because the court had been 'unable to find them'. (PEN, CPJ)

Recent publications: *Organ Procurement and Judicial Execution in China* (HRW/Asia, August 1994, 42pp); *Use of Criminal Charges Against Political Dissidents* (HRW/Asia, October 1994, 22pp)

## COLOMBIA

Martín Eduardo Muñera, an announcer for Radio Reloj, was murdered in Medellín on 3 September. The motive for his murder is unclear. (IAPA)

On 19 September Liberal Party congressman Arlén Uribe Márquez was shot dead in the northeastern city of Medellín, where he was a university professor. At the murder scene, his killers left the banner of the Camilist Union (UC), a faction of the National Liberation Army (ELN) guerrillas. (*Latinamerica Press*)

Five armed men who claimed to be officials from the Attorney-General's office forced their way into the office of the United Workers' Federation of Antioquia (FUTRAN) in Medellín on 26 September. When told that the union's president was not in the office, they opened fire on two other officials, Hugo Zapata, who was killed, and Carlos Posada, who was seriously injured. Several FUTRAN officials have been murdered by the paramilitary group COLSINGUE or have received death threats in recent months. (AI)

Prominent human rights activist Jairo Barahona was violently abducted from his home in Bosque on 29 September by four armed men who claimed to be members of the elite Anti-Extortion and Kidnapping Unit (UNASE). He has not been seen since. The men threatened to kill Barahona's wife if she made the abduction public. (AI)

Orlando Villar Jímenez, a press aide to several members of Congress and a former journalist with Radio Super, was shot dead in Bogotá on 7 October. The murder of Jímenez, who had worked as press relations officer during the successful presidential campaign of Ernesto Samper, is believed to be connected to his political activities. (CPJ, Reuter)

On 10 October Hernando Cuadros, leader of the Tibú branch of the oil worker's trade union USO, was abducted from his home and murdered. Unsuccessful attempts were also made to kidnap USO activists Edgar Riaño, Dario Lotero, Luis Hernández and Monerge Sánchez. All the incidents are believed to be the work of paramilitary groups acting in collaboration with the armed forces. (AI)

### COSTA RICA

On 26 August the Journalists'

Association declared its support for the compulsory licencing of journalists. Opponents of licencing argue that it would contravene article 14 of the American Convention on Human Rights. (CEPEX)

On 14 October it was reported that a constitutional hearings court had annulled the law preventing foreign investment in the media and advertising agencies. The hearing was initiated by a Canadian company seeking to purchase a 51 per cent share of the daily *La República*. (CEPEX)

### COTE D'IVOIRE

Emmanuel Kore, editor with the independent daily *Soir Info*, was arrested on 18 September after he had been working on a report on the future of the presidential guard stationed at Yamoussoukro. Unconfirmed reports say he was released on 27 September. (UJAO)

### CROATIA

Zagreb police reportedly detained demonstrators trying to prevent the eviction of a family from a former-Yugoslav army flat on 27 September. (AI)

Antonija Rajkovi of Radio Vukovar and freelance photojournalist Steve Gaunt were freed on 29 September after a month's detention on spying charges in Serb-held Krajina. The charges were dropped but the two were barred from entering the territory for two years. (Reuter, IFJ, FIEJ)

### CUBA

Former journalist and writer Norberto Fuentes was allowed to leave the island for Mexico on 26 August. He was accompanied by Colombian Nobel laureate Gabriel García Márquez, who had interceded on his behalf. Fuentes, acclaimed for his book *Hemingway in Cuba*, began a hunger strike on 3 August in protest at being prevented from attending a PEN conference in the USA. (IAPA, PEN)

Lázaro Cuesta, a senior member of the National Commission of Independent Unions (CONSI), was beaten by four unidentified assailants on 30 August. CONSI president Lázaro Corp was allowed to leave the country in late August and arrived in Miami on 21 September. He had earlier been detained and interrogated about his contacts with Belgian and German diplomatic staff. (HRW)

René del Pozo Pozo, a member of the unofficial Cuban Commission for Human Rights and National Reconciliation (CCDHRN), was detained by police on 12 October in Havana. Del Pozo has previously been detained several times and forced to sign a statement denouncing his own anti-government broadcasts on the US-funded station Radio Martí. The police have also warned him to avoid any further contact with foreigners. (HRW)

On 28 October the official

Prensa Latina agency suspended transmissions to Latin America and the Caribbean without explanation. (SWB)

Recent publication: *Repression, the Exodus of August 1994 and the US Response* (HRW/Americas, October 1994, 19pp)

REPORTERS SANS FRONTIÈRES

### ○ CYPRUS

Several Jehovah's Witnesses were tried in late October and early November for refusing to perform military service. Dimosthhenos Demetraki Loizou, Theodoros Antoni Charalambous, Georgios and Alvertos Karamanos and Georgios Costa Antoniou face up to a year in prison if found guilty. Panayiotis Dimitris Talia was sentenced to six months' imprisonment on 26 September. (AI)

### CZECH REPUBLIC

Josef Tomas, editor of the anti-Semitic journal *Politika*, closed down by the authorities in 1992, was given a seven-month suspended sentence on 22 September for disseminating racist material and defaming the Czech nation. (RFE/RL)

### DENMARK

On 23 September the European Court overturned the conviction of Jens Olaf Jersild for 'abetting dissemination of hate speech'. Jersild had broadcast an interview with a youth gang of racist skinheads on 21 July 1985. (HRW)

### EGYPT

Mohamad Labib, a cameraman for Egyptian television, was one of five people killed on 17 September when Islamic militants opened fire on a convoy of UNICEF personnel and police near Luxor. (EOHR, CPJ)

Mustafa Bakri, editor-in-chief of *al-Ahrar*, the Liberal Party newspaper, was detained by State Security (SSI) on 18 September and questioned about articles published in the paper. The interrogation apparently revealed that Bakri's telephone had been tapped since he took over as editor in April. (EOHR, CPJ, RSF)

Montasser al-Zayyat, a member of the Egyptian Organisation of Human Rights and one of 37 lawyers arrested during a protest march in May (*Index* 4&5/1994), is still in detention on charges of involvement with a clandestine organisation, spreading false information and contact with terrorists. The evidence appears to be based solely on recorded telephone conversations between Montasser al-Zayyat and human rights organisations in Egypt and abroad. (EOHR, Lawyers Committee for Human Rights)

Naguib Mahfouz, Nobel Prize-winning author and columnist for the daily *al-Ahram*, survived an assassination attempt in Cairo on 14 October when he was stabbed in the neck. (CPJ, PEN)

Journalist Abd al-Mun'im Gamal al-Din, arrested in February 1993, remains in prison in Tora despite being acquitted by a Cairo military court in October 1993 (*Index* 4/1993). (PEN)

Recent publication: *The Condition of Human Rights in Egypt: The Annual Report of the Egyptian Organisation for Human Rights* (Arabic and English editions) (Egyptian Organisation for Human Rights, 1994, 131pp)

### EL SALVADOR

The daily *El Latino* won its appeal against a conviction for defamation in early October. The paper had published accusations made by the former head of the People's Revolutionary Army, Joaquín

Villalobos, that businessman Orlando de Sola had financed death squads. The court's original ruling had been criticised by both de Sola and *El Latino* for setting a precedent whereby liability in such cases might fall automatically on the publication carrying the allegations rather than on the individual making them. (CEPEX)

## EQUATORIAL GUINEA

On 6 and 7 October, in the run up to the municipal elections, opposition activists Indalecio Abuy, Indalecio Eko, Tomás Nzo, Amancio Gabriel Nze and Plácido Micó of the Convergence for Social Democracy (CPDS) were arrested along with Victorino Bolekia Banay of the Popular Democratic Alliance (ADP) and José Mecheba Ikaka of the National Democratic Union (UDENA). The government has already reneged on agreements allowing opposition parties to participate in a pre-election census. (AI)

## ETHIOPIA

Berhane Mewa and Melaskatchew Amha, both journalists with *Dewol* (*Index* 3/1994) were released on bail in late August after being detained for six months without access to lawyers. (AI)

About 500 people were arrested on 20 September outside the court where the leader of the All-Amhara People's Organisation (AAPO), Professor Asrat Woldeyes, was on trial for inciting violence. 257 of those

arrested have been charged for holding an illegal demonstration. In October the editor of *Tobia*, Goshu Mogues, was sentenced to six months in prison for publishing a letter from Asrat Woldeyes, in which he said that he 'has no hope of a fair trial'. (RSF, AI)

Keleme Bogala and Tewedros Kebede, journalists at *Zog*, were arrested on 10 October and are being held without charge. Kumsa Burayu and Tolera Tessema, editor and deputy editor of an Oromo-language magazine, were detained on 4 October. It is believed that they are being held for publishing a military communique from the armed Oromo Liberation Front (OLF). (AI)

Tesfaye Tadesse, legal advisor to *Lubar* magazine (not, as stated in *Index* 4&5/1994, its publisher) and chair of the Ethiopian Human Rights Council's legal committee is still detained without charge. (AI)

It was announced on 1 November that the trial of members of the deposed Dergue regime will begin on 13 December. A total of 1,315 officials and military commanders of the former government of Mengistu Haile Mariam are to be brought to trial for charges of aggravated homicide, genocide and crimes against humanity. Mengistu fled to Zimbabwe after being ousted in 1991 and Zimbabwe's president Robert Mugabe has opposed his extradition. He is charged for the killing of

Emperor Haile Selassie, who died in detention after the 1974 coup, the death by starvation of an estimated one million people due to forced collectivisation, and the killing of hundreds of thousands in civil war and political violence during the 'Red Terror' against rival Marxists in the 1970s. (*Times*, *Sunday Telegraph*, SWB, Reuter)

## EUROPEAN UNION

On 21 September the European Commission said it was abandoning any effort to set EU-wide limits on media ownership, going against a non-binding resolution passed by the European Parliament in January, that called on the Commission to propose legislation on the subject. On 27 October the Parliament voted to demand the Commission set a precise timetable for introducing legislation to limit ownership. (*International Herald Tribune*, *Guardian*)

Recent publication: *Media and Democracy in the Single Market* (European Parliament Green Group, 1994, 63pp. Rue Belliard 97-113, 1047 Brussels, Belgium)

## FRANCE

On 20 September education minister François Bayrou issued a directive banning the wearing of prominent religious symbols, such as the Muslim head scarf, in public schools. However, more 'discrete' symbols such as the Catholic crucifix or Jewish skullcap may still be worn. On 4 October police in Lille prevented 20 Muslim girls wearing head scarves from entering a school. In Mantes-la-Joile, Paris, on 5 October two schoolgirls and one policeman were hurt when police tried to disperse a group of 30 people protesting the ban. On 24 October a girl known as Hadja was expelled from her school for wearing a head scarf. (*International Herald Tribune, Telegraph*)

Recent publication: *France: Shootings, Killings, and Alleged Ill-Treatment by Law Enforcement Officers* (Amnesty International, October 1994, 35pp)

## GAMBIA

On July 29, a week after the military coup, the new Armed Forces and Provisional Ruling Council (AFPC) ordered that 'all political parties shall cease to exist and no person shall assemble or associate for the purpose of forming a political party or engaging in any political activities.' On 3 August the AFPC issued the Political Activities (Suspension) Decree which gives the government far-reaching powers of censorship and states that 'no person shall engage in any political propaganda by means of a newspaper publication'. (Article 19)

On October 12 Halifa Sallah and Seedia Jatta, journalists with *Foroyaa*, the organ of the opposition People's Democratic Organisation for Independence and Socialism (PDOIS), were fined 1,000 dalasis for contravening the Political Activities

(Suspension) Decree. They were also ordered to 'refrain from any political activities until the Decree is lifted'. They face three years in prison if they fail to comply with the order. (RSF, Gambian *Daily Observer*)

Kenneth Best, managing editor of the *Daily Observer*, was deported to Liberia on 30 October. Best, a Liberian refugee, was accused of illegally employing Liberian workers in the Gambia though observers believe his expulsion is related to calls by the *Observer* for the government to set a timetable for a return to civilian rule. (RSF, Journalists' Safety Service, Article 19)

In early November Alie Badara Sheriff of the *Daily Observer* and an unnamed Senegalese reporter with *Diplomatic Magazine* were badly beaten by security forces, apparently because they were both mistaken for Rodney Sieh, a journalist with the *Observer* and the BBC. Sieh was himself later beaten by police. On 6 November another *Observer* reporter, Abdullah Savage, was attacked by soldiers while on his way to interview several former government ministers. (Article 19, RSF)

## GEORGIA

Zurab Grdzelishvili of the news agency *Tshakinform* was shot dead as he returned home late at night on 26 October. (ITAR-TASS)

Recent publication: *Torture*

*and Gross Violations of Due Process in Georgia* (HRW/Helsinki, August 1994, 20pp)

## GERMANY

On 21 September the Bundestag passed a bill making it an offence punishable by up to five years' imprisonment to deny that the Holocaust happened (*Index* 1&2/1994). The bill gives expanded powers to the domestic intelligence service and extends the ban on Nazi symbols to cover anything reminiscent of Nazi emblems or slogans. (*International Herald Tribune, Daily Telegraph* )

Authorities refused permission for a planned march by Kurdish women's groups from Mannheim to the European Council in Strasbourg to highlight discrimination against Kurdish women in Turkey at the end of September. French authorities, having previously banned the march on grounds of public order, finally allowed it to go ahead on 3 October. Germany had earlier banned a festival of Kurdish culture, planned for 24 September in Hanover. The bans were imposed because of alleged involvement of the banned Kurdish Workers Party (PKK). (Reuter, Kurdistan Information Centre)

On 12 October the federal prosecutor's office announced that it was investigating claims that members of the banned Kurdish Workers Party (PKK) are 'punishing' Kurds found reading or distributing a book critical of PKK leader Abdullah Oclan. The prosecutor's office is also investigating several people for attempted murder following attacks in Bremen and Hamburg on Kurds who had renounced PKK membership. (Reuter)

## GREECE

On 21 October it was announced that Parliament has passed a law banning toy advertisements on television between 7am and 10pm, in order to protect parents from demands by their children. The conservative opposition New Democracy Party, which opposed the ban said that no similar law existed in other EU member countries. (Reuter)

Lawyers acting for 312 jailed religious conscientious objectors say that prison governors at Kassandra and Kassavetia prisons and at the Sindos Military Prison are refusing to free conscientious objectors who are eligible for release under Law 2207/94. They also allege that objectors already released have been told that they must report for military service.

## GUATEMALA

Edwin Miguel Quezada (*Index* 4&5/1994), formerly with *Prensa Libre*, went into exile on 19 August, after receiving death threats at the end of July. (CCPJ)

A street child, Sergio Miguel Chávez, nicknamed *El Chupado*, was shot dead at point blank range, apparently by a member of the municipal police, on 7 September in Guatemala City. (AI)

Víctor Hugo López Escóbar, director of the news programme *Nuevo Diario del Aire* on Radio Progreso, was shot dead by unidentified assailants on 12 September. He is the third journalist to be killed in the past 11 months. (IAPA)

Representatives of COPMAGUA, an organisation of Mayan communities, criticised the government and the URNG guerrillas for excluding them from the peace talks in mid-October. They reiterate the importance of including Mayan organisations in the negotiations. (*Latinamerica Press*)

Recent publications: *Institutional Violence: Civil Patrols in Guatemala* (Robert F Kennedy Memorial Center for Human Rights, August 1994, 81pp); *Massacres in the Jungle: Ixcán, Guatemala, 1975-82* (Ricardo Falla, 1994); *Trade Unionists Against Terror: Guatemala City 1954-1985* (Deborah Levenson-Estrada, 1994, 288pp)

## HAITI

The influential Creole-language weekly *Libète* again ceased publication on 5 September, owing to the intensification of death threats and harassment against staff (*Index* 4&5/1994). (CPJ)

Jean-Michel Caroit, correspondent for *Le Monde* and Radio France Internationale, was prevented from entering

the country on 12 September. Under the state of emergency, reporters were required to obtain a visa from the Ministry of Information and the Army High Command before entering by land across the border with the Dominican Republic. (CPJ)

US invasion troops occupied state radio and television headquarters on 30 September. American officials in Haiti accused the stations of inciting violence and criticising the US government's support for President Aristide. (CPJ)

Reuters photographer Lee Celano, John Bowner of Associated Press, CBS News cameraman Mario Delatour, and NBC News cameraman Maurice Roper were wounded by supporters of the military during a pro-democracy march on 30 September. An unidentified Haitian driver for a US television crew was shot dead the same day. (CPJ)

Well-known artist Stevenson Magloire was found dead on 8 October in Port-au-Prince, brutally beaten to death by a gang believed to be closely connected to the military. His death came a few days before the return of President Aristide, of whom he was a strong supporter. (*Independent, Times*)

## HONG KONG

Steve Vines, editor of *Eastern Express* which was well known for its anti-Beijing stance under his editorship, was sacked by his publishers on 11 September. Vines says he will sue for unfair dismissal. (*Guardian*)

The government decided to drop the long-standing 'good relations' clause from the Film Censorship Ordinance on 5 November. The clause allows censors to cut or ban a film if 'there is a likelihood that the exhibition of the film would seriously damage good relations with other territories'. Beijing has objected to the proposed change. (*South China Morning Post*)

Ghulam Muhammad Lone, an Indian contributor to the Urdu-language press in Srinagar, Kashmir and to the English-language *Greater Kashmir*, was murdered together with his son on 29 August. Local police blame Kashmiri militants, but Lone had reported receiving threats from an Indian security officer for having reported troop movements in the area. (CPJ)

On 7 October the Karnataka regional service of the national television monopoly Doordarshan inaugurated a news broadcast in Urdu, interrupting prime-time broadcasting in Kannada, the official language of Karnataka, and sparking riots in Bangalore in which at least 26 people were killed. The Urdu language is closely associated with India's 160 million Muslims and Bangalore is the centre of Karnataka's Muslim minority. The broadcasts were seen by some as an attempt by the ruling Congress Party to

attract Muslim votes in the state assembly elections, starting on 29 November. On 13 October the Election Commission banned further broadcasts until after the elections, calling them a 'violation of the model code of conduct'. (Reuter, SWB)

At the beginning of October the central government ordered the release of Syed Ali Shah Gilani and Abdul Ghani Lone, leaders of Kashmir's pro-independence All Party People's Conference (APPC), detained without trial since October 1993. On 14 October Shabir Ahmed Shah, the influential moderate Kashmiri leader, was also released. His release is seen as an effort by the Indian administration to prepare for elections in the state of Jammu and Kashmir next spring. The APPC refuses to participate in any Indian elections, however, and demands instead a referendum on Kashmiri independence. (*Far Eastern Economic Review, Times*)

Recent publications: *Continuing Repression in Kashmir: Abuses Rise as International Pressure on India Eases* (HRW/Asia, August 1994, 23pp); *Arms and Abuses in Indian Punjab and Kashmir* (HRW/Arms Project, September 1994, 59pp)

Attempts by non-governmental organisations to mobilise against a draft decree imposing strict registration procedures on them were hampered by the government crackdown

on dissent in the run-up to the Asia Pacific Economic Co-operation (APEC) summit on 15 November. On 22 September, soldiers broke up an NGO meeting in Yogyakarta because the organisers had failed to obtain a permit. A rescheduled meeting on 27 September was also broken up. (Legal Aid Institute)

In order to enforce a ban on the US film *True Lies*, the government ordered the seizure of all laser discs in the country in early October. The film, banned after pressure from Muslim groups, was reported to be circulating on laser disc. All discs are now banned until a method of regulating their use is found. (Reuter)

The information minister said on 21 September that the existence of the unofficial Alliance of Independent Journalists (AJI) (*Index* 4&5/1994) was 'unjustified'. On 8 October, at a meeting with all leading editors, the official Association of Indonesian Journalists (PWI) demanded the 're-education' of AJI members. The editor of the *Jakarta Post* reportedly said that he would take 'firm measures' against AJI members on his staff. AJI members were subsequently dropped from the *Jakarta Post* team covering the APEC summit. (*Far Eastern Economic Review*)

Staff at the banned magazines *DeTik* and *Tempo* (*Index* 4&5/1994) tried unsuccessfully to resurrect their publications under new titles in early

October. *Simponi*, a defunct tabloid relaunched by the owners of *DeTik*, closed on 5 October after only one issue. The PWI withdrew its endorsement from *Simponi*'s editor, Syamsu Hadi, for hiring non-PWI staff, thus invalidating the paper's licence. Former *Tempo* staff produced one issue of *Berita* on 8 October. Editor Puta Sedia said he was awaiting 'guidance' from the Information Ministry as to whether he could continue publishing. (*Asiaweek*)

A warrant for the arrest of George Aditjondro, a prominent academic at Satya Wacana University, central Java, was issued on 5 October after he took part in a panel discussion on the presidential succession at the Islamic University of Indonesia. Aditjondro believes the charges are part of the campaign to stifle dissent prior to the APEC summit. (Reuter, AI)

*Jakarta Round-Up*, a live radio talk show on Trijana FM renowned for its coverage of sensitive political issues, was abruptly cancelled on 6 October after an edition on the country's political system and recent media bans. Programme host Nooripud Binarto accused the network, which is owned by one of President Suharto's sons, of self-censorship but Trijana FM's chief executive, Azhar Nasoba, denied that the show was pulled due to government pressure. (*Jakarta Post*, Reuter)

Muchatar Pakpakan, leader of

the independent Indonesia Welfare Labour Union (SBSI), was sentenced to three years on 7 November for inciting worker violence. Strikes in Medan, northern Sumatra, in April resulted in rioting in which one person died. Most senior SBSI members are now in prison, along with many other labour activists. (Reuter)

Recent publications: *The Limits of Openness: Human Rights in Indonesia and East Timor* (HRW/Asia, September 1994, 83pp); *Power and Impunity: Human Rights Under the New Order* (Amnesty, September 1994, 126pp); *Tightening up in Indonesia Before the APEC Summit* (HRW/Asia, October 1994, 21pp); *The Press Under Siege: Censorship in Indonesia* (Article 19, November 1994, 31pp); *Censorship, Silence and Shadowplay: Freedom of Expression in Indonesia, 1994* (PEN American Center, November 1994, 65pp)

## IRAN

During a state visit to France in August President Hashemi Rafsanjani reiterated the irreversible nature of the *fatwa* against Salman Rushdie (*Index* 4&5/1994). (*Guardian*)

134 Iranian writers signed an open letter to the Ministry of Culture and Islamic Guidance on 15 October, announcing the formation of an independent and professional association of writers inside Iran (see page 63). On 30 October the *Tehran Times* responded by calling for legal action against

the signatories, saying that Iran 'does not pretend to have a government that tolerates unlimited freedom of the press'. (PEN)

## IRAQ

A group of 35 Iraqi and foreign journalists from Reuters, Cable News Network and Agence France-Presse were attacked and robbed by five gunmen while travelling on an Information Ministry bus near Basra on 10 October. (*International Herald Tribune*)

## IRELAND

On 26 September journalist Susan O'Keeffe (*Index* 4/1993) flew to Dublin to answer a charge of contempt of court resulting from her refusal to name her sources for a Granada TV documentary that alleged widespread corruption in the Irish beef industry. She will be tried at the Circuit Court on 26 January, and faces a fine of up to £10,000 or a two-year prison sentence. (National Union of Journalists)

On 27 October Ireland's film censor banned Oliver Stone's *Natural Born Killers*. No reason was given. In Britain the Board of Film Classification has postponed the film's release for 'at least a year'. (Reuter)

## ISRAEL AND OCCUPIED TERRITORIES

Jamal al-Barghouth, a correspondent for the daily *al-Quds*, was arrested on 26 August at Ben-Gurion Airport as he was returning from holiday. He is believed to be under a four-month administrative detention order in the Negev prison. (RSF)

Three journalists have been assaulted by Israeli security forces on the West Bank: on 20 August, Khaled Az-Zighari, a Reuters photographer, was shot and wounded while covering a clash between Palestinian youth and Israeli soldiers in Ramallah; on 9 September another Reuters photographer, Mazen Daa'na, was beaten up and had his film seized in Hebron; and on 12 September Nasser Hussein al-Shoyokhi, an AP correspondent, was severely beaten at a roadblock when he attempted to photograph soldiers stopping a UN vehicle. (RSF)

The Palestinian Broadcasting Corporation (PBC), which began transmission in Gaza in September, has been banned by Israeli authorities from opening an office in Hebron. PBC's director, Salim Abu Salah, was told that the PBC could establish offices in autonomous areas only. (Reuter, SWB)

Mordechai Vanunu (*Index* 1/1987) began his ninth year in solitary confinement on 1 October. (Campaign to Free Vanunu)

Munis Abu Shilbayeh, a Reuters Television cameraman, was arrested at his home in Jerusalem on 12 October. No reason for his arrest has been given by Israeli authorities. (RSF)

Travel restrictions imposed after the Tel Aviv bus bombing on 19 October have prevented journalists from the West Bank and Gaza reaching their press offices in East Jerusalem. However, the travel ban was lifted to allow reporters to cover the Israel-Jordan peace treaty signing in Eilat on 26 October. (IFJ)

Recent publications: *The Human Rights of Persons with Disabilities* by Angela Gaff (Al-Haq/ICJ, 1994, 140pp); *The Applicability of Human Rights Law to Occupied Territories* (Al-Haq/ICJ, 1994, 98pp)

## ITALY

On 18 October a list was circulated among Northern League parliamentarians in Rome, naming 11 journalists who 'must be definitively excluded from all channels of information for having deliberately falsified declarations which went against the League', and saying that 'as such, interviews will not be granted to them'. The journalists are from the main dailies across the political spectrum, such as *Corriere della Sera, La Stampa, La Repubblica* and *Il Giornale*. (RSF)

## JORDAN

Nidal Mansour, editor of the Arabic-language weekly *al-Bilad*, was arrested on 18 September after publishing an article about the military. The press code prohibits publication of anything deemed detrimental to the army's image. Mansour, who also faces trial for an earlier article,

was released on 20 September after protests from fellow journalists. (AFP, RSF, Reuter)

## KENYA

David Makal and Bedan Mbugua of *The People* were released in September after being jailed in June for criticising a court ruling as politically inspired (*Index* 3/1994). (PEN)

Article 19's legal observer at the trial of Koigi wa Wamwere (*Index* 3/1994) was arrested on 27 September. Ten other people were also arrested at the trial for wearing T-shirts of the organisation Release Political Prisoners. Four are believed to be still in custody. (Article 19)

An Australian man working in the resort of Lamu was deported for being a homosexual, it was announced on 2 November. The man was reported by a Nairobi paper to be organising an international conference on gay issues. In October President Daniel arap Moi made several speeches in which he warned of the 'dangers' from homosexuality, multiparty democracy, cults and human rights organisations, especially Amnesty International. (SWB, Reuter)

A Kenyan MP said on 3 November that 16 supporters of the opposition FORD-Kenya party were killed after the party retained its seat in a by-election in the slums of Mathare, Nairobi's largest constituency. The ruling

KANU party said the violence was tribally-motivated and blamed supporters of the winning candidate. (SWB, Reuter)

Recent publication: *Human Rights Violations in Kenya: The Case of Koigi wa Wamwere et al* (Robert F Kennedy Memorial Center for Human Rights, August 1994, 10pp)

## LATVIA

On 28 October state prosecutor Olgerts Sabanskis was assaulted and told that he would be killed if he continued with the prosecution of former Communist Party leaders Alfreds Rubiks and Ojars Potreki, currently on trial on charges related to attempts to foment a coup in August 1991. (RFE/RL)

## LEBANON

Parliament passed a law in October to licence private television and radio stations. The new law also prohibits slander of heads of state and religious leaders, stirring up of sectarian tensions and the promotion of Lebanese-Israeli relations. The ban on news broadcasts by privately-owned media, however, (*Index* 4&5/1994) has been permanently lifted. (Reuter)

## LITHUANIA

Bomb threats were received by the independent radio stations M-1 and Radiocentras on 12 October. Police say the threats might be connected with the murder a year ago of *Respublika* journalist Vitas

Lingys (*Index* 10/1994), who was killed while investigating organised crime. (SWB)

Opposition politicians accused the ruling Lithuanian Democratic Labour Party of pressuring the state television network to drop programmes such as 'Parliament Studio' and 'News and Opinions'. An LDLP spokesman said the government played no part in cancelling the programmes, but that it reserves the right to be 'dissatisfied' with the network's output. (SWB)

## MALAWI

David Nthengwe (*Index* 3/1994), editor of the weekly *Independent*, was beaten up and detained without charge on 3 September. This is the latest in a spate of incidents of police brutality against journalists. (MISA)

## MALI

On 26 September Issa Doumbin, a journalist for the weekly *Le Republicain*, and Yero Dabo from Radio Kledu were harassed by security guards at the annual congress of the ruling party, the Alliance for Democracy in Mali (Adema). On 24 September Ramata Dia and Opa Kane of the weekly *La Cigale Muselée*, were thrown out of the congress along with the entire Radio Liberté team. (RSF)

On 13 October the independent station Radio Kayira's transmitter was sabotaged, reducing the signal range from 50km to 400 metres. (RSF)

Thursday 20 October. Imprisoned journalists' day. 'Here's a scoop for you... 20 more years in prison!'

## MAURITANIA

Seven independent newspapers suspended publication on 1 September in protest at the government's increasing harassment of publications such as *al-Bayane*, *Le Calame*, *L'Eveil Hebá*, and *La Verité*, all of which have had editions seized (*Index* 3/1994, 4&5/1994). (UJAO)

## MEXICO

On 1 and 2 November Mexico City's Newspaper Vendors' Union threatened to close down newsstands if they continued to sell the paper *Reforma*. (IAPA)

Gunther Dietz, the German representative of the Mexico-based International Indigenous Press Agency (AIPIN), was detained in Morella, Michoacan province, on 29

September and subsequently expelled from the country. (AIPIN)

Recent publications: *Mexico at the Crossroads: Political Rights and the 1994 Presidential and Congressional Elections* (HRW/Americas, August 1994, 24pp); *Killings of Gay Men in Chiapas: the Impunity Continues* (Amnesty, October 1994, 13pp)

## MOLDOVA

On 29 October Parliament passed a press law which, it is claimed, imposes no restrictions on the activities of journalists. However, legal experts from the Conference on Security and Co-operation in Europe argue that certain provisions, such as that allowing for fines for 'libelling the state', are more appropriate 'to fascist and dictatorial regimes than democratic ones'. (SWB)

Authorities in the pro-Russian breakaway region of Trans-Dnistria forbade the use of Latin script in schools at the end of October, despite protests from parents and pupils. A campaign to re-introduce Latin script in Moldova began in 1988 and has been a central concern of the movement for Moldovan independence. (SWB)

## NAMIBIA

It was reported in September that the Ministry of Fisheries and Marine Resources is seeking to prosecute those responsible for leaking a confidential government report. The report, which advised against allowing seal culling, was not implemented by the government. It is not known who leaked the document to news media, but a member of staff at the Namibian Broadcasting Corporation informed the Ministry of the leak. (MISA)

In the run-up to national elections in December — the first since independence in 1990 — the Namibia Women Action for Equality Party (NAWAFEP) has complained of harassment by security forces and members of the ruling party. NAWAFEP members have received menacing phone calls and relatives of presidential candidate Ilenikelao Latvio have also been threatened. (MISA)

## NETHERLANDS

On 5 September Bas Ten Hout, journalist with the television network RTL-4, was harassed and threatened by Erwin Karselius, a member of the right-wing party Centrumdemocraten (CD) in the corridors of the Parliament building. Karselius recognised Ten Hout as the undercover journalist who infiltrated the CD earlier this year. (Journalists' Safety Service)

On 20 October the television station Veronica broadcast the documentary 'Illegal Police Methods' after the Justice Ministry withdrew charges against the station, allowing the programme to be shown. On 13 October police had raided the station's news desk and the home of journalist F Salverda, where they seized confidential reports alleging irregular police activity. Despite allowing the broadcast, the Ministry has left open the possibility of prosecuting Veronica for broadcasting conversations held by the head of the criminal research team and recorded by criminal groups. (Journalists' Safety Service)

## NICARAGUA

Despite a presidential decree of 25 March, abolishing the two per cent duty on newspaper sales, municipal authorities in Managua continue to levy the tax. In a letter to the mayor of Managua on 6 September, the editors of *La Prensa, Barricada, El Nuevo Diario, La Tribuna,* and the weekly *El Semanario* argue that the tax infringes freedom of expression. (CEPEX)

The Nicaraguan Association of Radio Broadcasting (ANIR) and the Nicaraguan Chamber of Radio Broadcasting (CANIRA) are concerned that the proposed Telecommunications and Postal Law, which was introduced into the National Assembly in late September, could be used to impose financial penalties on radio broadcasters. Officials say the law will not apply to radio stations but broadcasters are requesting clarification of the law. (CEPEX)

On 28 October at least 100 journalists and students demonstrated outside the Sandinista Party (FSLN) offices to protest the dismissal of Carlos Fernando

Chamorro, editor of the FSLN's daily paper *Barricada*. Two other journalists have also been dismissed by a party-owned radio station. Chamorro, the son of President Chamorro and a member of the moderate faction within the FSLN, was fired for not representing the party's official views in the newspaper. In early November the paper's financial editor Roberto Larios was also dismissed. (IAPA, CEPEX, FIP)

### NIGERIA

On August 23 Nobel laureate Wole Soyinka's passport was confiscated at Lagos airport as he tried to board a plane to Stockholm. In October the UN cultural organisation UNESCO appointed Soyinka a consultant, making him eligible for a UN passport. On 3 November, however, his UN passport was also confiscated as he tried to board a plane for Europe at Lagos airport. (*International Herald Tribune*, Article 19)

At least 14 publications, including the dailies *Concord, Punch* and the *Guardian*, and the weeklies *African Concord* and *Guardian Magazine* (*Index* 4&5/1994), were formally banned by decree on 7 September, despite a high court ruling of 19 August ordering the State Security police to vacate the *Concord* offices and allow the paper to publish. Since the decrees were issued a number of prominent members of pro-democracy and human rights organisations have been detained by security forces. (CPJ, RSF)

Bayo Onanuga, editor-in-chief of *Tempo* and *The News*, was arrested on 26 September and charged with slander against the minister of justice and the secretary-general of the Government. He was released on bail two days later. (CPJ, RSF)

Writer Ken Saro-Wiwa, imprisoned since 22 May, has gone on hunger strike to protest his continued detention without charge or trial (*Index* 3/1994). (PEN)

Recent publication: *The Dawn of a New Dark Age: Human Rights Abuses Rampant as Nigerian Military Declares Absolute Power* (HRW/Africa, October 1994, 19pp)

### PAKISTAN

On 10 October, the day before a general strike intended to force new elections, hundreds of supporters of opposition leader Nawaz Sharif were detained. Official sources say 713 people were detained in all, but a government spokesman in Karachi admitted that 1,100 had been jailed in that city alone. Opposition leaders claim a further 3,000 were detained in Sindh, Prime Minister Benazir Bhutto's home province. (*International Herald Tribune, Independent, Telegraph*)

Aftab Ali Beg, a photographer with the Urdu daily *Jang*, was beaten and arrested by soldiers in Karachi on 25 October. He had been photographing a military operation to recover illegally held weapons in the Liaquatabad quarter of the city. He was released after protests from fellow journalists. (RSF)

On 3 November Islamic activists shot dead Mr Badiuzzaman, a member of the Northwest Frontier Province Assembly in Mingora, Swat district. They also beseiged the house of provincial sports minister Habibur Rehman and prevented him from addressing a by-election rally. The activists are agitating for the enforcement of *sharia* law. (Reuter)

### PALESTINE (GAZA-JERICHO)

Muhammed al-Ejla, a journalism student at Gaza's Islamic University and correspondent for the East Jerusalem-based newspaper *An-Nahar*, was arrested on 6 September and held for two days at Gaza Central Prison. The ban on *An-Nahar* imposed in July (*Index* 4&5/1994) was lifted on 5 September, reportedly after the departure of managing editor Osman al-Anani, who was known to be sympathetic to Jordan (see page 53). (CPJ, RSF, Reuter)

The Palestinian National Authority issued licences in September for three new Arabic-language publicatons. Imad Falouji, a former Hamas leader, has launched a daily, *al-Watan*; and Alaa al-Saftawi will publish *al-Istiqlal*. *Filastin*, a tabloid weekly published by Taher Shriteh (see below) began publication on 23

Let me know when Jimmy Carter gets here!

September. (Reuter, *Jerusalem Times*)

Seven journalists were arrested by Palestinian police on 12 October following the kidnapping of an Israeli soldier. Mustafa al-Sawaf, a correspondent with *An-Nahar*, and Ahmed al-Khatib, a photographer, were briefly detained. A Reuters Television crew — reporter Taher Shriteh, cameraman Shams Oudeh, sound technician Sawah Abu Seif and photographer Ahmed Jadallah — were twice arrested and released after being questioned about videos of the kidnapped soldier. Taher Shriteh was arrested again on 26 October, with his brother Amer, and released without charge on 4 November. (Reuter, CPJ)

Journalist Hani Abed from the weekly *al-Istiqlal* was murdered on 2 November when a bomb exploded in his car in Khan Younis, Gaza. (RSF)

Recent publications: *The Transfer of Health Services to a Palestinian Authority: Annual Report 1993* (Physicians for Human Rights, August 1994, 44pp); *Media and the Challenge of Change in Palestine* (IFJ, Arab Journalists' Association, General Union of Palestine Writers and Journalists, June 1994, 44pp)

## PAPUA NEW GUINEA

Bill Errington, an Australian freelance photographer, was shot during a battle between government forces and secessionist rebels on Bougainville island. The uncertainty over the photographer's condition highlights the paucity of information about the conflict. The government tries to prevent journalists from visiting Bougainville. (RSF)

## PERU

Augusto Esteban Chacón Quispe of Radio Wilmacayo, detained without trial for 15 months on charges of abetting a group of terrorists who escaped from Qencoro prison, was finally acquitted by a tribunal of 'faceless judges' on 26 October. (FIP)

On 31 October it was reported that the public prosecutor has ratified radio journalist Alfonso Castiglione Mendoza's 20-year prison sentence for collaborating with terrorists. The Supreme Court will now consider the sentence. At least two other journalists have spent over a year in prison without trial on similar charges: Pedro Váldez Bernales and Juan de Mata Jara Berrospi are accused of links to the Shining Path because of their work with the paper *El Diario* prior to its banning in 1988. (FIP, Instituto Prensa y Sociedad)

Recent publication: *Finding Their Voice: Peruvian Women's Testimonies of War* by Kristen Herzog (Trinity Press International, 1994)

## PHILIPPINES

Radio reporter Lidya Macas was killed by an explosion in her home on 19 August, bringing to 12 the number of media workers killed in the Philippines since July 1992. (Philippine Movement for Press Freedom)

## POLAND

On 29 August the public prosecutor closed down six of the 12 unlicenced television stations belonging to the Polonia 1 chain. The National Audiovisual Council (CNRT) is also charging Polonia 1's Italian founder, Nicola Grauso, under a law that limits foreign ownership of broadcast media. The six stations were reportedly using frequencies normally reserved for the army. Polonia 1's six other stations also face closure. (RSF)

On 23 September a new bill governing state secrets was passed by the Sejm. A weaker version of the bill that included an amendment to allow journalists to reveal state secrets in the 'interests of society' was unexpectedly rejected by the Senate on 7 October, which could mean that the Sejm's original bill will come into force. (SWB)

The former president, General Jaruzelski, was attacked by an elderly man wielding a large stone while signing copies of his book *Martial Law: Why?* in Warsaw on 11 October. (SWB)

## ROMANIA

Parliament passed an amendment to the Penal Code on 18 October prohibiting 'propaganda promoting the setting up of a totalitarian state', with a maximum penalty of five years in prison. An amendment to prohibit fascist and communist propaganda was defeated. (RFE/RL)

On 25 October the Chamber of Deputies voted to maintain the present law prohibiting homosexual acts, rejecting a Senate proposal that only homosexual acts which 'cause public scandal' should be illegal. The matter will now go before a committee of members of both houses. (RFE/RL)

Television Free Trade Union leader Dumitru Iuga alleged in November that President Iliescu is routinely informed in advance of the contents of the 7.30 evening news bulletin by Dumitru Popa, Romanian Television Society Chairman. (*Free Romanian*)

Staff at the presidential press office were instructed not to give any information to journalists from the daily *ZIUA* in early November. In the weeks prior to this, several *ZIUA* reporters — Florin Gongu, Vlad Pufu, Bianca Afrem, Marius Gherghe and Silviu Marculescu — were beaten or harassed by police. *ZIUA* has recently broken a story about safety standards at a heavy water factory, claiming that an accident at the plant in June, in which 17 people died, was hushed up by the power company Renel. (IFJ, SWB)

## RUSSIAN FEDERATION

*Russia:* Vladislav Nechayev, head of current affairs at St Petersburg television, was badly beaten by two assailants on 8 October, possibly in connection with large-scale redundancies at the station. Bella Kukova, station director and chair of the redundancies committee, was also severely injured in a similar attack in September. (SWB)

On 18 October Dmitri Kholodov, of the popular pro-reform daily *Moskovsky Komsomolets*, was killed when he opened a booby-trapped briefcase in his Moscow office. The murder is thought to be linked to Kholodov's ongoing investigation into corruption in the former Soviet army in Germany. Several other journalists working on the same story have also received death threats. (*Guardian*, Channel 4)

Yuri Korolev, photography editor for the monthly *Delovye Mir*, was found dead on 9 November, on the road between Moscow and his home in Peredelkino, some 10 kilometres from his burned-out car. Police say his murder is unrelated to his work, but Korolev's colleagues dispute this. (RSF)

President Yeltsin vetoed a new set of amendments to the media law on 10 November, saying that they would limit access to information, restrict the participation in Russia's social and political life, and exclude state bodies from founding new publications. (SWB)

*Chechnia:* Grozny television was unable to broadcast on 15 September, after a bomb attack destroyed its transmitter. The station is now using low-powered transmitters to broadcast to the capital, but the rest of the country is without any service. (SWB)

## RWANDA

A total of 37 journalists, mostly Rwandan, have been killed in Rwanda since the massacres began in April. It is not clear whether any local journalists are still alive (see page 55). (RSF)

Recent publications: *Rwanda: Death, Despair and Defiance* (African Rights, September 1994, 442pp)

## SAUDI ARABIA

Leading cleric Sheikh Abdullah bin Abdel-Rahman al-Jibrin issued a *fatwa* on 2 October against publishers of statements by the Committee for the Defence of Legitimate Rights (CDLR), a London-based opposition group. Muhsin al-Awaji, an agriculture professor and co-founder of the CDLR, has been held in incommunicado detention since 8 September. (Reuter, *Independent*, AI, AAASHRAN)

## SENEGAL

On the night of 18 September the headquarters of the UJAO were broken into and vandalised. The manuscript of a report on press freedom in West Africa was stolen. (UJAO)

A fire at the private station Sud FM Sen Radio on 5

October caused serious damage to electrical wiring that links the station to its transmitter. There are signs that the fire was started deliberately. (UJAO)

## SERBIA-MONTENEGRO

*Serbia:* In late September the Culture Ministry announced measures to tax recordings of 'turbo folk' (a popular blend of folk and rock music with a nationalist message) as part of the government's war on 'all forms of cultural kitsch'. (*Independent*)

On 3 October Serbian authorities imposed a five-year ban on Dick Verkijk, Belgrade-based correspondent for Dutch public radio, on the grounds that his work is 'counter to the interests of the State'. (RSF)

On 4 October the IFJ protested to the Belgrade government over action by the authorities against a range of independent press and broadcasting media in Serbia. The IFJ said the measures taken, including attempts to renationalise independent media such as the newspaper *Borba*, 'contrast sharply with the government's declared commitment to the resolution of conflict in the region'. (IFJ)

*Kosovo:* On 16 September Amnesty named 14 ethnic Albanians who were beaten by police at Decani police station. They were among some 50 ethnic Albanians arrested at a concert two days previously. Amnesty warns that the incidence of such abuse is 'esca-

lating dangerously'. (AI)

Ganimet Podvorica, an ethnic Albanian, was arrested on charges of 'terrorism' on 17 September and is currently being held in Prishtina. Because of the seriousness of the accusation there are fears that Podvorica may be tortured. (AI)

Recent publication: *Police Violence in Kosovo Province — The Victims* (Amnesty, September 1994, 27pp)

## SINGAPORE

Christopher Lingle, an American academic at the National University of Singapore (NUS), was questioned by police on 17 October about an opinion piece he wrote for the *International Herald Tribune* which disputed statements made by a Singaporean foreign affairs offical, referred to unidentified 'intolerant regimes in the region', and criticised the judiciary in certain states. Lingle, who could be charged with contempt of court and criminal defamation, has since resigned from the NUS and left Singapore. (*Independent on Sunday*, Reuter)

## SOMALIA

Swiss journalist Pierre Anceaux was killed on 1 September by unknown gunmen. (Journalists' Safety Service)

## SOUTH AFRICA

It was reported in September

that the Department of Home Affairs has set up a task force to review censorship laws in the Republic. (*Southern African Report*)

Home affairs minister Mangosuthu Buthelezi, started a scuffle with a participant in a live television interview on 26 September, after taking issue with what was being said. The minister subsequently issued an unconditional apology for his behaviour. (*International Herald Tribune*)

At a conference of the Organisation of African Unity (OAU) in October, deputy president Thabo Mbeki announced that open governance legislation within a Feedom of Information Act would be adopted by Parliament next year. (*Southern African Report*)

On 20 October the South African Broadcasting Corporation released its draft language policy (*Index* 4&5/1994), which envisages removing Afrikaans programming from TV-1. Afrikaner leaders say such a move is unconstitutional. (SWB)

## SPAIN

Pepe Rei, an investigative journalist with the controversial Basque daily *Egin*, was imprisoned without bail on 24 August after a court heard pre-trial evidence on his alleged collaboration with the banned separatist guerrilla group ETA. A public prosecutor testified that Rei's handwriting had been discovered on documents found in Paris

last year when ETA member Carlos Almorza Arrieta was arrested. Rei admits that the writing is his, but denies giving the documents to anyone from ETA. Rei is well known in Spain for his investigations into political corruption and drug trafficking. (Reuter)

## SRI LANKA

On International Journalists' Day, 8 September, the minister of information, aviation and tourism announced that the era of press suppression by open and covert threats ended with the election in August of the People's Alliance Party government of Chandrika Kumaratunga. The new government will examine laws restricting journalistic freedom, he said. (*Island*)

On 24 October a bomb exploded at a public meeting held by the United National Party, killing presidential candidate Gamini Dissanayake and more than 50 of his supporters. The Tamil separatist group, the Liberation Tigers of Tamil Eelam (LTTE), was thought to be responsible, though it denies this. The government subsequently reimposed the emergency measures, which had been lifted in August, including a nationwide curfew. The measures were briefly revoked in early November to allow the presidential election to take place. (*Asiaweek, Telegraph*, Reuter)

Recent publication: *An Agenda for Change: the Right to Freedom of Expression in Sri Lanka* (Article 19, October 1994, 55pp)

## SUDAN

Over 30,000 street children were rounded up in Khartoum and taken to Islamic re-education camps in July and August. The children were reportedly whipped and threatened with execution if they did not adopt Islam, and forcible mass circumcisions in preparation for conversion to Islam have also been reported. (*Sudan Human Rights Voice*)

Osman Idris Abu-Ras, former administrator of the banned publication *Al-Hadaf*, is reported to have been abducted by security forces in Khartoum on 4 August. He is thought to be detained in the 'ghost houses' used for the torture of political detainees. (*Sudan Human Rights Voice*)

On 11 September security forces closed down the offices of the daily paper *al-Khartoum*, which is banned in Sudan and published in Egypt. *Al-Khartoum* journalist Mohamed Abd al-Seed (*Index* 4&5/1994) was released on 10 October after four months in detention. (RSF, CPJ)

Recent publication: *Secret Detention and Torture in Northern Sudan* (Amnesty, September 1994, 6pp)

## SWITZERLAND

A referendum held on 25 September approved a new law that makes racial discrimination, racist propaganda and denial of the Holocaust illegal. (*International Herald Tribune, Guardian*)

## SYRIA

It was reported in October that a number of writers and journalists remain in prison: Nizar Nayyuf, Jadi Nawfal and Salama George Kila, charged with membership of the banned Committee for the Defence of Democratic Freedoms and Human Rights (CDF); Khalil Brayez, arrested in Beirut in 1970; writer Tadrus Trad, Abdallah Muqdad of the Syrian Arab News Agency, and Rida Haddad, journalist at the Ba'ath Party paper *Tishrin*, all arrested in 1980; Ahmad Swaidan, journalist for *al-Kifah al-Ummal* and Isma'il al-Hajje, arrested in 1982; Faysal Allush, journalist, arrested in 1985; Samir al-Hassan, Palestinian editor of *Fatah al-Intifada*, and Anwar Bader, a radio and television reporter, arrested in 1986; and Faraj Beraqdar, a poet, arrested in March 1987. Trials of some of these detainees began in 1993 and are continuing. (PEN, RSF)

## TAIWAN

Hsu Jung-chi, owner and director of the banned pirate radio station Voice of Taiwan (*Index* 4&5/1994), was arrested on 13 September during a press conference held to protest a recent court decision that bars him from leaving the country. (RSF)

## TAJIKISTAN

A report released by the Committee to Protect Journalists on 26 October puts the number of journalists murdered in Tajikistan since 1992 at 26. (CPJ)

Recent publication: *Human Rights in Tajikistan on the Eve of Presidential Elections* (HRW/Helsinki, October 1994, 13pp); *Political Prisoners in Tajikistan* (HRW/Helsinki, October 1994, 10pp)

## TUNISIA

Mohammed Najib Hosni, a human rights lawyer who was arrested on 15 June, remains detained without trial in El Kef prison. He is well known for his work in civil liberties cases and has represented Moncef Marzouki, ex-president of the Tunisian League for Human Rights (LTDH) (*Index* 3/1994, 4&5/1994). (AI, Lawyers Committee for Human Rights)

## TURKEY

Three *Özgür Ülke* journalists — Nezahat Özen, Gürsel Sahin and Metin Dag — were detained in a police raid on the paper's Diyarbakir office on 20 September. Gürsel Sahin and Metin Dag were released in October but claimed they had been tortured in prison. Nezahat Özen was formally arrested and remains in detention. The Diyarbakir office manager, Kadriye Özcanli, was also charged under the Anti-Terrorist Law on 30 September. (RSF, AI)

Vehbiye Tüzün, *Özgür Ülke's* Urfa correspondent, was arrested at the bus station in Diyarbakir on 2 October. Police confiscated identity cards of witnesses, threatening them with reprisals if they reported the arrest. After being released Vehbiye Tüzün alleged that she had been tortured and made to testify against *Özgür Ülke*. (AI)

Two *Özgür Ülke* journalists, Serpil Korkmaz and Selda Surmeli, were arrested in Tunceli on 7 October while reporting on a meeting held to protest abuses by the army. (Reuter)

On 26 October journalist Oral Calilslar was sentenced to two years in prison for 'separatist propaganda' under the Anti-Terrorist Law after publishing a book containing interviews with Abdullah Ocalan, head of the Kurdistan Workers' Party (PKK) and Kemal Burkay, head of the Socialist Workers' Party of Kurdistan and Turkey (TKSIP). (RSF, Reuter)

Recent publications: *File of Torture: Deaths in Detention Places or Prisons (1980-1994)* (Human Rights Foundation of Turkey, September 1994, 56pp); *Forced Displacement of Ethnic Kurds from Southeastern Turkey* (HRW/Helsinki, October 1994, 27pp); *Censorship and the Rule of Law in Turkey: Violations of Press Freedom and Attacks on* Özgür Gündem (Article 19 & Kurdistan Human Rights Project (UK)/Medico (Germany), 1994, 54pp)

## TURKMENISTAN

Murad Esenov, political correspondent for the radio sta-

**Radio Mille Collines: alias 'Radio death'**

tion Svoboda and editor of the opposition newspaper *Turkmen Ili*, was attacked by at least four assailants armed with iron bars on 4 October near his home in the Otradnoye district of Moscow. Before the attack Esenov had received threats from Turkmen government officials. (*Komsomolskaya Pravda, Nezavisimaya Gazeta*)

### UGANDA

*The Citizen,* which has close links with the opposition Democratic Party (DP), closed in September because of rising costs and a split within the DP. It is the fourth Ugandan publication to close in the last five months. (*The Monitor*)

*The Monitor*'s editor, Wafula Oguttu, was arrested in early October after publishing a story about President Museveni reprimanding three

of his ministers. He was later released and charges of defamation were dropped. (*The Monitor*)

A government-sponsored bill to give the state greater control over the media was rejected by Parliament on 2 November. (Reuter)

Recent publication: *Uganda: Recommendations for Safeguarding Human Rights in the New Constitution* (Amnesty International, August 1994, 10pp)

### UKRAINE

The Crimean television centre was seized by security forces loyal to Crimea's Premier Meshkov on 11 September. Two MPs later managed to break into the station, where they switched off the Russian radio channels and broadcast an appeal to the security

forces to defy Meshkov. (SWB)

On 19 October the Ukrainian Presidium of the Supreme Council voted 13 to 3 in favour of lifting the ban on the Communist Party of Ukraine. (SWB)

### UNITED KINGDOM

On 17 September the prime minister, John Major, announced that the six-year-old broadcasting ban on the voices of spokesmen for 'terrorist organisations' would be lifted immediately. (*Guardian*)

Kani Yilmaz, spokesman in Europe for the Kurdish Workers' Party (PKK) was arrested on 26 October on his way to address members of Parliament. Although his entry into the country on 23 October was deemed lawful, the Home Office now says that his presence poses a threat to national security. On 10 November, Yilmaz was re-arrested following an extradition demand by the German authorities. (Kurdistan Information Centre, *Times*)

On 31 October the House of Commons defeated a motion ordering the Privileges Committee inquiry into corruption to be held in public. (*Times*)

As the Criminal Justice and Public Order Bill received the Royal Assent and become law on 3 November, many lawyers and civil liberties activists expressed grave concern about its potential effects. Among its 171 provisions are a reduction in an accused person's right of silence; the creation of a new criminal offence of aggravated trespass; and expanded police powers to stop and search vehicles and passengers. (Liberty)

Recent publications: *Prisoners Without a Voice: Asylum-Seekers Detained in the United Kingdom* (Amnesty, October 1994, 69pp); *Censored: Freedom of Expression and Human Rights* (National Council for Civil Liberties Report 8, 1994, 75pp, £3)

## UNITED NATIONS

Taiwanese news media were once again denied UN accreditation in early November (*Index* 4&5/1994), when a Taiwanese application to attend the 7 November meeting of the UN Convention on International Trade in Endangered Species (CITES) was rejected. (Freedom House)

## USA

In May Maryland became the first jurisdiction in the country to make it a crime to steal free newspapers when the intent is to prevent others from reading them. The law came in response to a series of thefts, primarily of student newspapers. In the 1993-94 academic year 35 student newspapers across the country were stolen in protest over their contents. (Student Press Law Center)

A new sexual harassment policy was instituted in Los Angeles County in September after a court decided that the

First Amendment protects a firefighter's right to read sexually-explicit magazines while at work, as long as he refrains from commenting on them. (Associated Press)

According to a report compiled by the Center for Media and Public Affairs in September, Latinos are generally ignored or portrayed negatively on television. Latinos accounted for only one per cent of all characters on television programmes in 1992, and 16 per cent of those characters committed crimes. Latinos make up nine per cent of the US population. (Associated Press)

In September the Department of Housing and Urban Development (HUD) issued new guidelines to protect the speech of protesters in fair-housing complaints. Constitutionally protected activities, such as leafletting or holding meetings, will no longer be investigated. The policy comes in response to a case this summer in Berkeley, CA, in which three people who objected to a low-income housing project in their neighbourhood were threatened by HUD with substantial fines. (*New York Times*, Associated Press)

A planned exhibition at the government's Smithsonian Institution is to be altered following criticism from Congress and veterans groups in September. The National Air and Space Museum planned to display the Enola Gay, the aeroplane that dropped the atomic bomb on

Hiroshima, for the 50th anniversary of the bombing next May. Some found the portrayal of the Japanese in the aftermath too sympathetic. (*Washington Post*)

On 16 September former San Francisco police chief Richard Hongisto and two police officers were found guilty of civil rights violations for the 1992 seizure of 2,000 copies of *The Bay Times*, a gay newspaper that had parodied Hongisto (*Index* 8/1992). (*New York Times*)

Despite concerns of civil libertarians about privacy issues, Congress passed legislation on 7 October to ensure that phone companies switching to digital technology will keep their networks accessible to wiretapping by law enforcement agencies. (*New York Times*)

On 17 October, Energy Secretary Hazel O'Leary announced a new policy aimed at giving greater protection to whistle-blowers within the Energy Department. Hailed as unprecedented, even by government critics, the policy is meant to encourage employees to voice concerns without fear of reprisal. (*New York Times*)

The Smith/Helms Amendment to the Education Bill, which would have prohibited any positive mention of homosexuality in schools receiving federal funds, was out-manoeuvred and replaced by a provision banning the encouragement of sexual activity of any kind. The bill became law in October (*Index* 4&5/1994). (PEN, Associated Press)

The US Court of Appeals for the District of Columbia held a rare full-member hearing on 19 October to review the constitutionality of federal regulations restricting 'indecent' programming on the airwaves to between midnight and 6am. Courts have consistently struck down the regulations because they are over-broad. The most recent ruling came in November 1993 (*Index* 1&2/1994). (*Boston Globe*)

At the end of October, the Massachusetts Court of Appeals agreed to consider *Bowman v the Department of Public Welfare*, a case pitting free speech against sexual harassment concerns. The case, which could have national implications, involves charges by Sylvia Bowman that David Heller, her co-worker at a state agency, sexually harassed her when he pasted a photo of her face atop pictures of nudes in sexual poses and showed them around their office. At the time, Bowman was running for president of her local union. Heller, who opposed her candidacy, claims the pictures were political satire, as protected by the 1988 Supreme Court ruling in *Falwell v Hustler*. Bowman claims that the pictures created a 'hostile' work atmosphere, an argument given credence by the Supreme Court last year. (*Boston Globe*, legal briefs)

Recent Publications: *Beyond the Burning Cross: The First Amendment and the Landmark RAV Case*, by Edward J Cleary (Random House, 1994); *Winning Through Reason, Not Fear: Meeting the Challenge of the Religious Right* (People for the American Way, 1994); *Dictatorship of Virtue: Multiculturalism and the Battle for America's Future*, by Richard Bernstein (Knopf, 1994)

## UZBEKISTAN

The arrest of Dadakhan Hasan, singer-songwriter and prominent member of the opposition Erk Democratic Party, was reported on 12 October. The Ministry of Internal Affairs alleges that Hasan was in possession of several rounds of ammunition, a charge frequently brought against Erk members. (RFE/RL)

It was reported on 25 October that Steve Levine, Central Asia Correspondent for *Newsweek*, has been expelled from the country. (RSF)

## VENEZUELA

Human rights activists have called on the government to stop indiscriminate army and police searches on shanty-towns in the southwest of Caracas. In the largest such raid, in the 23 de Enero neighbourhood on 9 September, some 8,200 homes were searched. The raids are intended to curb violence in the capital, where currently up to 30 people are murdered

each weekend. (*Latinamerica Press*)

In September two dozen national security police agents searched the home of Aníbal Romero, a well-known academic, newspaper columnist and critic of President Caldera. The police say they were looking for evidence of a plot to overthrow the government, but Romero believes they were trying to intimidate him. In late July six central constitutional guarantees were suspended, allowing security forces to seize property, conduct searches and make arrests without the usual legal safeguards. (*Latinamerica Press*)

## ZAIRE

The press and information minister announced a new tax on newspaper publishing on 10 September. He also asked editors to 'observe professional ethics' in their work and spoke of the use of 'emergency procedures', which some in the press have taken as a veiled threat of closure against papers of which the government disapproves. (SWB)

***

*Compiled by: Daniel Brett, Laura Bruni, Robin Jones, Robert Maharajh, Vera Rich (Europe/CIS); Philippa Nugent (Middle East); Anna Feldman, Jason Garner, Oren Gruenbaum (Africa); Colin Isham (Central Asia); Nan Levinson, Lesley McCave, Nathalie Vartanpour-Naalbandian (Americas); Nicholas McAuley, Atanu Roy, Jason Stephens (Asia)* ❏

**MAHMOUD DARWISH**, the pre-eminent Palestinian poet, has lived most of his life in Lebanon and Palestine. The author of 14 volumes of poetry and numerous prose works, he now lives in Paris. His most recent book, *Memory for Forgetfulness*, a prose poem, will be available in English translation in January 1995 from Harvard University Press.

**HERVÉ DEGUINE** is Africa specialist with Reporters Sans Frontières.

**ALEX DE WAAL** is co-director of African Rights, London.

**ALEX DICK-READ** is a freelance writer on Caribbean affairs, based in the British Virgin Islands.

**BASSEM EÏD** is a Palestinian journalist and field work co-ordinator for B'Tselem, the Israeli Information Center for Human Rights in the Occupied Territories.

**ZORAN FILIPOVIC** was born in Bosnia and has written widely about the Balkan war. His photographs have appeared in *Life* magazine, *Die Zeit, Le Figaro* and the *Times*. He currently lives in Zagreb.

**JULIE FLINT** is a freelance journalist writing on Middle Eastern Africa.

**TIMOTHY GARTON ASH** visited, wrote about and supported the dissident intellectuals of central Europe throughout the 1980s. His works include *The Uses of Adversity* (1989, Granta) and *We the People* (1990, Granta).

**SABINE GOODWIN** visited the camps in Lebanon this autumn. She wishes to thank Medical Aid for Palestine for all their help.

**GENEVIÈVE HESSE** is a journalist with Reporters Sans Frontières.

**MICHAEL HUTT** is lecturer in Nepali at the School of Oriental and African Studies in the University of London.

**ANTHONY HYMAN** is a journalist and academic specialising in Afghanistan and central Asia.

**RYSZARD KAPUSCINSKI** is a Polish journalist and writer. His most recent book, *Imperium* (Granta, 1994), covers the former territories of the Soviet Union.

**IVAN KLÍMA** was born in Prague in 1931. He edited the journal of the Czech Writers' Union during the Prague Spring. In 1969 he was visiting professor at the University of Michigan, but returned to Czechoslovakia the following year. His latest novel, *The Spirit of Prague*, and a collection of essays, *Waiting for the Dark, Waiting for the Light*, are published by Granta, UK in November.

**CRISTINA L'HOMME** is a journalist with Reporters Sans Frontières.

**JAMAL MAHJOUB** has published two novels on Sudan: *Navigation of a Rainmaker* (1989) and *Wings of Dust* (1994), both published by Heinemann. In 1993 he won the *Guardian* African Short Story Prize with 'The Cartographer's Angel'. He currently lives in Denmark.

**ROBERT MÉNARD** is the founding director of Reporters Sans Frontières.

**ADAM MICHNIK**, Polish former dissident, is now editor-in-chief of *Gazeta*

*Wyborcza.*

**DAVID MILLER** is lecturer in Media Studies at Stirling University and a member of the Stirling Media Research Institute. His book *Don't Mention the War: Northern Ireland, Propaganda and the Media*, was published by Pluto Press, London, in November.

**CAROLINE MOOREHEAD** is a writer and film-maker specialising in human rights. Her most recent book is *Bertrand Russell: a Life* (Sinclair Stevenson, 1992).

**BRIAN PHILLIPS** is a campaign co-ordinator at the International Secretariat of Amnesty International.

**MILEN RADEV** is a Bulgarian cartoonist, illustrator and graphic designer working in Berlin. He regularly reports for the BBC World Service on east German issues.

**JANE REGAN** is a freelance writer who reports frequently from Port-au-Prince. Her most recent collaboration was with James Ridgeway on *The Haiti Files: Decoding the Crisis* (Essential Books, Washington, DC, 1994).

**WOLE SOYINKA** is Nigeria's foremost novelist, playwright, poet and critic, as well as being an outspoken campaigner for democracy. In 1986 he became the first African writer to win the Nobel Prize for Literature.

**STEPHEN SPENDER**, poet, author and critic, was a founder of *Index.*

**ACIL TABBARA** is a journalist with *Libération,* Morocco.

**DAVRELL TIEN** is a freelance journalist based in Sweden, with a particular interest in the former Soviet Union.

**LUIS ROJAS VELARDE** is a journalist with Reporters Sans Frontières.

**W L WEBB** was formerly literary editor and assistant editor at the *Guardian*, London and *Guardian* Research Fellow at Nuffield College, Oxford.

**RONALD WRIGHT** is the author of *Cut Stones and Crossroads: A Journey in Peru* (1984, Penguin USA) and *Stolen Continents* (1992, Pimlico Press).

**POLAND**

**JACEK FEDOROWICZ** is a satirist, cartoonist, and TV personality.

**KRYSTYNA KOFTA** is a writer and dramatist living in Warsaw. Her first novel, *Vizier* was published in 1978. Her next book *Wiory* (1980) — a child's view of the 1958 revolution in Poznan — was passed by the censor, but because of its political content, created delays in the publication of her following work, *The Pavilion of Small Predators,* which did not appear until 1988. 'In thought, word and deed' was written in 1981 and published in the journal *Odra* in 1989.

**BARBARA STANOSZ** is Professor of Logic in the Philosophy department at Warsaw University, and editor of the journal *Bez Dogmatu* (Without Dogma).

**DAWID WARSZAWSKI** is the pen name of Konstanty Gebert, a former underground activist and journalist involved in Jewish cultural life.

**INDEX** wishes to thank:

**Charity Know How** for their generous support for the Polish country file

the **European Commission** for its funding for translations from *La Lettre* of Reporters Sans Frontières

the **Arts Council of England** for their continuing support for translations from literature worldwide

the **Swedish International Development Authority** (SIDA) and the **Norwegian Agency for Development Co-operation** (NORAD) for funding the report on THE PRESS IN NIGERIA, a short version of which appears in this issue. Full report available from **INDEX** in January 1995

Forthcoming:

**COUNTRY FILE** Turkey
**RADIO IN AFRICA** Adewale Maja-Pearce and Richard Carver
**GAY LIFE AND LITERATURE** The post-Communist outing in Russia and Eastern Europe
**ON DEATH ROW** Capital punishment in the USA, the Caribbean and China
**REPORTERS SANS FRONTIÈRES** A survey of the year as seen by *La Lettre*
**COUNTRY FILE** United Kingdom: the secret state
**REWRITING HISTORY** History in the post-War worlds
**PAKISTAN** Blasphemy: the uses and abuses of religion
**LATIN AMERICA** New writers new readers